An OPUS book

WHY HUMANS HAVE CULTURES

Why Humans Have Cultures

EXPLAINING ANTHROPOLOGY AND
SOCIAL DIVERSITY

MICHAEL CARRITHERS

Oxford · New York
OXFORD UNIVERSITY PRESS
1992

Oxford University Press, Walton Street, Oxford OX2 6DP

Oxford New York Toronto
Delhi Bombay Calcutta Madras Karachi
Petaling Jaya Singapore Hong Kong Tokyo
Nairobi Dar es Salaam Cape Town
Melbourne Auckland

and associated companies in
Berlin Ibadan

Oxford is a trade mark of Oxford University Press

British Library Cataloguing in Publication Data
Data available

Library of Congress Cataloging in Publication Data
Carrithers, Michael.
Why humans have cultures: explaining anthropology and social
diversity/Michael Carrithers.
p.   cm.
"An OPUS book"—Half-title.
Includes bibliographical references and index.
1. Anthropology.   2. Culture.   3. Social evolution.   I. Title.
GN25.C37 1992 306—dc20 92–5476
ISBN 0–19–219227–2
ISBN 0–19–289211–8 Pbk

Typeset by Best-set Typesetter Ltd.
Printed in Great Britain by Biddles Ltd.
Guildford and King's Lynn

In memoriam
The Ven. Tambugala Anandasiri

Preface

THIS book is the fruit of two projects. The first project was to write an introductory book, an invitation, making anthropology available to the curious and the needful. That project was to show anthropology as an activity which helps us to understand, and deal with, human social and cultural diversity. The second project also concerned such diversity, but I meant it as an invitation to colleagues in anthropology and cognate disciplines. It began from the question, Why do humans have such diverse cultures and ways of life? This is a question about the very foundations of diversity. So one project was for those on the threshold of anthropology, and the other for those at its centre.

Can two such different purposes and two such different readerships be combined? In the course of events I came to think not only that they could be, but that they should be, and I hope that this book shows one way of doing it. For one thing, the skills of anthropology are still relatively close to the skills of ordinary readers and doers in today's complex world. One does not have to acquire intricate new ways of thought, like those of mathematics, to gain entry. Indeed some of the attitudes of anthropology have now begun to blend unremarked with everyday common sense. To be sure, there are some endeavours, such as medicine, where the methods and results need not be widely intelligible for them to be effective. As long as it works, who cares if everyone knows how it is done? But anthropology is quite specifically an affair of understanding, the understanding by those of one society or culture of those of another society or culture. If anthropology offers a remedy for ills, or at least the beginnings of one, then that remedy is understanding itself.

M. C.

Department of Anthropology
University of Durham

Acknowledgements

THE creation of even so individual a thing as a book by a single author is really a social matter, though only the author takes the blame and gets the credit. These are some people who are not marked in the bibliography, but who have made a great contribution to this book, by argument, by advice, by example, or by support: Sandra Bell, Alex Carrithers, Amy Carrithers, Rob Foley, Esther Goody, Keith Hart, Signe Howell, Desmond McNeill, Bob Layton, P. Lee, Liz Oughton, Caroline Ross, Vilas Sangave, Malcolm Smith. And to these I must add S. J. Tambiah, whose spirited opposition through a number of publications has made me think very hard about some matters.

I also owe a debt to the Anthropology Department of Durham University, which has provided an encouraging environment for so interdisciplinary an enterprise, and to the British Academy, which gave me research leave at a vital time.

Parts of Chapters 3 and 4 appeared in 'Why Humans Have Cultures', *Man* NS, 25 (1990), 189–206. Much of Chapter 5 appeared in 'Narrativity: Mind-reading and Making Society', in Andrew Whiten (ed.) *Natural Theories of Mind: Evolution, Development and Simulation of Everyday Mind-reading*, Oxford: Basil Blackwell, 1991. And much of Chapter 8 appeared in 'Is Anthropology Art or Science?', *Current Anthropology*, 31 (1990), 263–82.

Contents

I

The Question

THE ancient Greek philosopher Socrates asked a question which has echoed ever after: how should one live? The question calls for deep and transforming reflection on ourselves as individuals. Anthropologists ask a related question: how do we live together? This seems to set out a different array of problems. Not 'Who am I?', but 'Who are we?'. Not 'What should I do in general?', but 'How do we associate with each other?'. Not 'What ought to be done?', but 'What is done?'.

Yet the anthropologist's question is no less consequential. Socrates urged that we reflect on ourselves (he said, 'the unexamined life is not worth living'); anthropologists would insist that such reflection must include our mutual, shared life as well. And here the 'we' means we human beings. As a species we display great intensity of mutual concern and tremendous dependency on each other. The fact that we are social animals is not just an adventitious, accidental feature of our nature, but lies at the very core of what it is to be human. We simply could not live, could not continue our existence as humans, without our sociality. As Maurice Godelier wrote, 'human beings, in contrast to other social animals, do not just live in society, they produce society in order to live'.[1] So in an anthropologist's perspective, no enquiry which regards humans merely as individuals could be complete. We cannot know ourselves except by knowing ourselves in relation to others.

But to stress the relatedness of people to each other does not yet fully capture what is peculiar about humans or what particularly concerns anthropologists in studying human sociality. For our sociality has a further and, in comparison with other species, a particularly surprising dimension, namely its tremendous variability. Human beings do not just produce society, but society in forms which are incalculably various, constantly mutable, and labyrinthine in their elaborateness. No other species exhibits such intricacy and fecundity of forms of common life. It is as if we have needed, in our vast collective history, to change society almost as much as we have needed it in the first place. It is as if we have needed to render our common arrangements more and more entangled and Byzantine. We have devised what Ruth Benedict called a 'great arc' of different ways to work, to speak, to conduct domestic life, to dominate and control each other, and to engage with unseen realities. If each discipline can be said to have a central problem, then the central problem of anthropology is the diversity of human social life.

So the question, 'How do we associate with each other?' brings with it an overwhelming richness of detail and complexity. It is commonly said among anthropologists that the island of New Guinea alone has 700 languages, and correspondingly 700 differing forms of culture and society. How many more different forms of life might there be in the human world as a whole? Think of Asia, of Africa, and of Europe, or even of North America, which, though it is often thought of as homogeneous, nevertheless displays many languages and many variations of culture and social arrangements. So on the one hand there is the sheer variety of human cultures, and on the other, there is the sheer complexity and comprehensiveness of any one way of life, which comprehends the linguistic, domestic, economic, political, and religious dimensions of experience. What would it take to document—let alone to interpret or understand—any one such culture? What would it take to document your culture? What would it take to document them all?

So anthropology is faced with a luxuriating abundance of material. But it is also faced with a serious perplexity over how to treat that material. Consider the following. Every anthropologist stems from a specific variant in the great field of human social and cultural diversity. Indeed anthropology itself arose in a certain milieu, in a certain culture, in the not very distant past. Nevertheless, a fundamental rule of thumb for anthropologists is to overcome, where possible, their own assumptions, their own received wisdom, their own culturally conditioned viewpoint, in order to understand as clearly as possible the viewpoint of those they study. It only stands to reason: if we read into others our own motives and understandings, how can we understand theirs? But how can anthropologists transcend their own culture? It is in our nature to have a viewpoint and a position in relation to others, and that viewpoint must be influenced by one's natal way of life. Yet if each anthropologist, like anthropology itself, is bound to some one form of life, what warrant can he or she possess to gauge another form of life? How can he or she reliably compare forms of life? Is there a more general standard, beyond one peculiar heritage, that we can use? If so, what is it?

And this last question, of a general standard valid for the description and understanding of all forms of life, points forward to another: is there in fact a fundamental, shared human nature? In one perspective, there must be, for the very perception of diversity depends on it being a diversity of something. To be a species suggests that there are traits that we all share. But what, amongst all our diversity, could those traits be? And, again, how are we to discern them from the narrow ledge of one person's, or one society's, experience?

It would be hard to exaggerate the difficulty of these and related questions. They form not just a problem, but a dense and tangled knot of puzzles right at the heart of anthropology. Each strand of the knot leads to the others. If we could settle on just what social and cultural diversity does exist, we might then be able to settle on what unites the diversity. And if we could do that, then we might establish consensus on how to describe that diversity. But, of course, without settling on how to describe the diversity, we can hardly settle on what diversity exists, and so it goes. On a gloomy view, we could never escape this circle of doubt.

But on the more optimistic view I take here, there is something we can do about it. We can, gently and tentatively, pick up one strand and see where it leads, and then follow that strand on to the next and beyond, and, in the process, begin to loosen the whole knot. I cannot, of course, pretend that I have untied the whole knot here. This is merely a continuation of anthropologists' collective work on the puzzle. But I do follow each of the three questions I have raised: What unity underlies the cultural diversity of humanity? How does the diversity come about? And how can we come to understand that diversity reliably?

One strand

I start by asking the following question:

> Given the diversity of human forms of life, what must be true of humans in general?

I phrase the question in this slightly awkward way for two reasons. First, I want to emphasize that it involves a specific premiss, something I want to regard as agreed, basic, and unquestioned: the archive of different human possibilities. This is where I pick up the knot and begin to follow the strands. Even the small teaching library here in my university department has a thousand or more titles, and those few books refer to many more than a thousand of the (still many more) distinguishable forms of life that now exist or have existed. There is no reason to regard this archive as infallible, or to think that forms of life are the sort of thing that could actually be counted. (Is there one American Way of Life, or are there many? and what of Chinese, British, or Indian ways of life?) But the archive does bear reliable witness to one thing at least: the magnitude of differences across forms of life. Such differences may encompass language, means of livelihood, political organization, domestic arrangements, religious institutions, psychological ideas, cosmological persuasions, dress, and so forth. I will question what is meant by diversity, but its sheer scale will not be doubted. You must start somewhere, and I start from the tremendous variability of human social and cultural life.

Second, the question demands an account of human nature that shows how socio-cultural variability is possible. This is the sense of the phrase 'in general': we want to know not about each individual variant of human life, but about the ground on which all the variants are built. Perhaps the best way to phrase this is to say that the question concerns variability, not variation. Actual variation—as for example between hunter-gatherers in South-West Africa and in Australia, or between Buddhism in Britain today and in ancient India—is explicable in specific historical, social, political, cultural, and economic terms. We can, to the extent that information is available, account for such cases without raising explicitly the question of human nature.

An explanation of variability, on the other hand, must account for the very possibility of those different forms of life. It must show what all humans must share in order to be able to create diversity, and therefore it concerns human nature explicitly. To ask about hunter-gatherers and Buddhists—or about anthropologists—is to ask about socio-cultural variation. To ask about humans and human nature is, in this context, to ask about what makes that, or any, variation possible. My concern here will therefore be with only one set of the universals that unify our species, namely that set of capacities that allows us to create cultural diversity. There might be many other universals in our social and mental life that are part of anthropology's knot, but I will not consider them here.

What sort of response might we find to the question of diversity thus phrased? I have already begun to use notions drawn from biology. Is the response to be biological? Or is there something more, something specifically human that runs beyond biology and demands a different style of explanation? This is a sensitive and explosive question, and some of the most forcefully expressed and contentious beliefs of the nineteenth and twentieth centuries have been brought to bear on it.

Let me first clarify some terms. The biological anthropologist Geoffrey Harrison has recently complained of my using 'anthropology' to mean social and cultural anthropology alone. He said that this usage improperly ignored the existence of biological anthropology, which is well respected among the sciences.[2] I agree with him, and I apologize. So let me here give notice that when I write 'anthropology', I shall in fact mean social and cultural anthropology, unless I state otherwise. It is a matter of convenience only, not an assertion of policy.

In my understanding, the problem that faces both biological and social anthropological thought is summarized in these words of Daniel Bullock:

Though human history appears somehow discontinuous from prior natural history our sense of theoretical order creates a need to comprehend it as another chapter of natural history. The difficulty has been to find a way to so comprehend it that does not reduce the themes of our chapter of natural history to those used in prior chapters. There is to be something genuinely new in our chapter, just as there was something genuinely new in each prior chapter.[3]

This subtle, balanced statement opens the possibility that I want to exploit in about a third of this book, namely that we can show how the capacities which underpin cultural diversity came into being. We can show, that is, the evolutionary history of the potential for diversity.

These remarks may be met with scepticism or a lack of interest among some of my colleagues in social and cultural anthropology. For most of the twentieth century the diversity of social life has been taken by them as irrefutable empirical evidence that evolutionary explanations have little purchase in human social life. The argument has gone something like this: we have documented a previously unimagined variety of cultures. This variety reveals the plasticity of humankind. Such plasticity, the capacity to be formed by the life of the society into which one is born, is the single most important human universal, the decisive trait that separates human from animal. It presupposes a quality of mind, an ability to learn, and other capacities such as speech, which have no clear counterpart among other species. So the sheer fact of cultural diversity comprises in itself a sufficient proof for human uniqueness. We social and cultural anthropologists need have little to do with evolutionary thought.

One reason for accepting this argument has lain in the

unreliable nature of attempts to explain our species, or differences within our species, from a biological or evolutionary point of view. From the last century right up to the present, many writers have clothed some doubtful social or political opinion in evolutionary garb, and the persistent tendency has been, in Bullock's words, to 'reduce the themes of our chapter of natural history to those used in prior chapters'. Perhaps the most egregious example has been the use of notions of relative nearness to, or distance from, our animal forebears to justify racist political arrangements. These have left a bad taste in the mouth and a deep distrust of biology and of Darwinism among social and cultural anthropologists.

Yet if we see these matters aright, there is no need to sever ourselves as a species from the larger book of natural history. It is true that, in many ways, we are very like our near cousins, the social primates. It is also true that we differ from them. The similarity makes the comparison relevant; the differences make it illuminating. And in recent years the illumination has grown stronger as the researches of primate ethologists, child psychologists, linguists, and philosophers have uncovered a new, more powerful, and subtler capacity for diversity than had so far been imagined.

A second strand

I will not describe this capacity here, except to say that it constitutes an active and creative ability. We are, all of us, quite as effective at producing cultural diversity as we are at preserving continuity. And this harmonizes with the argument of a second third of the book, that there is greater changeability and flexibility in culture and society than anthropologists have until recently recognized. This opinion, one which regards cultures as essentially mutable and labile, has been growing among anthropologists, and I now describe briefly how I came to it through some of my own research.

For some time I have been concerned with Jains, a minority religious group of India, among whom I have done fieldwork. Jainism is more than 2,400 years old, and the question which has engaged me is that of continuity and change. On the one hand, Jains appear to have preserved their religion for a very long time, a striking success for tradition and the weight of conventionality. On the other hand, a close view of Jainism in medieval times, as well as in the late nineteenth and twentieth centuries, shows continual change and innovation. Nor is there any reason to believe that the case has been any different from the beginning. On this view, Jainism has always been changing. How are we to reconcile these perspectives, of the long and the short term?

I have been pursuing the question in two directions. One enquiry, reflected only briefly in this book, is into Jainism itself. The other is into the way we think about cultures, societies, and history. I have come increasingly to believe that anthropologists, myself included, have not yet managed to think very clearly about these issues. Anthropologists are used to representing cultures in the present tense: 'Jains do this and Jains assert that'. It seems perfectly reasonable to mean by this no more than 'Jains nowadays, hereabouts, generally do this and assert that'. To write in that way is defensible, even necessary, as a basic practical introduction for those un-acquainted with Jainism and as a way of inserting Jains into the archive of scholarship.

But it sometimes seems that the present tense means something more, that for many anthropologists the society in question was in fact unchanging and traditional, as though 'Jains do this' meant 'Jains have always done this'. This second kind of present tense is far more suspect, and many anthropologists have come to question it. At the very least such an assertion makes assumptions about the past which often turn out to be false. Still, for many anthropologists such a contrast between traditional and modern, between ahistorical and historical societies, remains a basic operating assumption. On this view the events and changes that have occurred in a traditional society are merely accidental, epiphenomenal, mere ruffles on the great sea of tradition, stability, and cultural conservatism.

Some parts of this book answer in passing to that mis-apprehension, but as I thought more about the problem I became convinced that the central difficulty lay in an even more profound inadequacy. To write of other societies in this history-less way leaves the impression that there just are these societies, these cultures, which sprang into being spontaneously. Along these lines there is no way to account for any substantial cultural change in the distant past or, *a fortiori*, in the recent past and present, because change is not what is really happening. Anthropology, on this view, is just about cultures, not about their past, their origin, or their change. Yet, since the present variety of cultures has not always existed—any more than humans have always existed—then we must assume at the very least that they must have come into being in an accountable way. Otherwise we end up believing in a sort of miraculous virgin birth of cultures.

These criticisms of the anthropology which I was taught, and which many still practice, are by no means original. What I have tried to do here is to synthesize an evolutionary and a social anthropological view. If in the first third of the book I show how our collective creativity is in fact grounded in our nature as a species, then in the second third I show what our species does with that creativity. I argue that change, creation and re-creation, interpretation and re-interpretation, are all part of the fabric of everyday experience. These are not processes which occur occasionally and exceptionally, but are rather the very stuff of human social life. Even when we do something that seems traditional, we do so in new conditions, and so are in fact re-creating tradition rather than simply copying it.

A third strand, and all strands together

In the final third of the book I turn to anthropology itself. Consider the plight of anthropologists trying to grasp an unfamiliar form of human life. It is an effort partly controlled by a methodical unease about the validity of any one conception of another culture. This unease is grounded in the reflection that we are likely to fail in understanding others by seeing them in our own image, not theirs. As a rule of thumb such distrust of one's native response is not only salutary but necessary: we need to devote tremendous time and energy to the study of other societies because our first, naïve understanding is almost bound to be wrong. But it is a long way from a humble testing of one's opinion to the assertion that people from one society cannot understand those of another society. For anthropologists do manage, one way or another, to forge a working understanding of other cultures.

Indeed, on more mature reflection, anthropologists are only a minor example of a greater theme in human life, namely the continual shuffling of people from one society to another, as visitors or settlers or converts, willing or unwilling. In these circumstances people do manage not only to deal with each other, but to achieve a mastery of skills native to another society, not only language, but music, art, science, and literature, in addition to the complex ways of politics and trade.

Let me take another step. I believe that these processes of learning and mastery are also very close to the underlying processes which make social variability possible. Think of the process of one generation following on from another. Those of the younger generation must, like strangers, acquire from their elders the skills native to their society. Their mastery—like that of the settlers and traders—will have to be flexible and applicable to ever new circumstances. They will have to deal with constant changes of an environmental, and a social environmental, kind. Hence the sense that the younger generation makes of things, and the sense they impress on events, must reflect their own situation and not be a mere parroting of their parents. If they were parroting then we would say that they did not understand, any more than a parrot understands what it repeats. A marker of real understanding is being able to do something new with what is learned, not just to copy blindly what others have done.

So I am suggesting that there is a common core to learning how a society works, knowing how it works, and knowing how to change it. Central to all these is the fact that people are social, that they exist and act in relation to each other. Learning, living together, and operating on common social life are all done with, through, by means of, and in the face of other people. Learning, living together, and changing the social world are done between people, not within them. To understand how we do any one of these things opens an understanding of the others. If we could understand more of how our world has come into being, we could come to understand more of anthropology. And if we could understand something of how anthropology works, that would help us understand more of how our world has come into being.

The view I take is that much can be discovered from looking directly at how people relate to each other. This is a venerable tradition in anthropology, especially in British social anthropology, and the ideas I set out here follow on from that tradition, or at least they do so to the extent that I take persons and relationships in society to be the basic stuff of human life.

It might, however, be useful to have a term to distinguish my approach here. I take a mutualist view, one which stresses that people are so deeply engaged with each other that we can only properly understand them if we understand even their apparently private notions and attitudes as interpersonal ones. I borrow the term 'mutualism' from the psychologists Arthur Still and Jim Good. In their usage, mutualism covers a broad stream of ideas and styles drawn from anthropology, sociology, and social psychology. Mutualist writers have regarded people as inextricably involved with each other in face-to-face relationships. They have understood the works of humans to be always achieved jointly. From a mutualist point of view there are great puzzles, and great enlightenment, in our apparently everyday ability to raise children or even to conduct a plain conversation with each other about the weather. In a mutualist perspective even the simplest human organization—the corner shop, your family—is an intricate thing with a subtle, delicate, and often uncertain way of working. Similarly, to understand even those we know best is an elaborate and difficult task, and one not always achieved successfully. As one of Woody Allen's characters remarked with a shrug, 'who can ever say that they really, truly, understand another person?' It is a surprise that these things can be managed at all.

2

The Great Arc

In this chapter I set out some of the ways in which anthropologists have thought about human diversity. I tell a story about how one version, one understanding, of that diversity is now giving way to another.

The first version became well established before the Second World War. Under its aegis anthropology as an institution—with funds, university departments, and a particular way of publishing in journal articles and books—gradually became what we know today. This first version of diversity, one which was largely ahistorical in its perspective, justified the expense and rigours of long periods of fieldwork in remote regions. Such fieldwork then revealed ethnography, that is, specific knowledge of hitherto uncontemplated versions of social life. These disclosures to the North Atlantic world, or at least to the world of North Atlantic anthropology, were mostly phrased in the present tense, the so-called 'ethnographic present'. There were good reasons for this. As I have pointed out, such a present tense need not imply an ahistorical point of view. There was an urgency to discover ways of life as they were then, not as they had been. And yet earlier anthropologists had squandered much of their credibility by speculating freely, but groundlessly, upon the past of 'primitive' peoples. So it seemed logical to found the new anthropology on what has come to be called a 'presentist' viewpoint.

But awkward circumstances and interpretations began to surface. The world as the anthropologists' first version found it did not always accord very well with the complexity of the world as found by, for example, historians or sociologists, or by anthropological fieldworkers themselves. Societies which had seemed isolated and untouched turned out, on second inspection, to be deeply affected by other societies, and especially by the societies of the anthropologists themselves. The effect of these fruitful disparities began slowly but surely to be expressed in general theoretical statements about diversity. A new and more difficult consciousness of human diversity came to seem desirable, one which is more thoroughly conscious of the historical character of social experience and of human relatedness across the globe. This new understanding is still in the making. It does not invalidate the older anthropological knowledge, but it does show that knowledge in a new light and gives it a fresh significance.

The great arc

The 'before' in this story has many well-springs, but for my purposes the richest single source is the second chapter, 'The Diversity of Cultures', in Ruth Benedict's *Patterns of Culture*, published in 1935 and continuously in print since then. The ideas were hers, but not hers alone. Most of them had come into being with the nascent discipline of cultural anthropology in the preceding years of the century in the United States at the hands of her teacher, Franz Boas, and his associates and pupils. But she expressed herself clearly and forcefully, and used an imagery that was widely influential.

I should point out here that when *Patterns of Culture* was published, deep disagreements marked the relationship of British social anthropology, and especially of the then influential Englishman Radcliffe-Brown, with American cultural anthropology. Yet, as I will show presently, they shared underlying assumptions which are well expressed by Benedict. I should also note that the two traditions later merged so closely that it is possible, at least for my purposes here, to regard them as variants of a single larger tradition. In any case, what they share most decisively is a commitment to fieldwork as the definitive source of knowledge.

Benedict used this anecdote to introduce and to epitomize her vision of cultural diversity:

A chief of the Digger Indians, as the Californians call them, talked to me a great deal about the ways of his people in the old days. He was a Christian and a leader among his people in the planting of peaches and apricots on irrigated land, but when he talked of the shamans who had transformed themselves into bears before his eyes in the bear dance, his hands trembled and his voice broke with excitement. It was an incomparable thing, the power his people had had in the old days. He liked best to talk of the . . . foods they had eaten. . . . [They] had eaten 'the health of the desert', he said, and knew nothing of the insides of tin cans and the things for sale at butcher shops.

One day, without transition, Ramon broke in upon his descriptions of grinding mesquite and preparing acorn soup. 'In the beginning', he said, 'God gave to every people a cup, a cup of clay, and from this cup they drank their life. . . . They all dipped in the water, but their cups were different. Our cup is broken now. It has passed away.'[1]

This is a rich and moving narrative, encompassing at once the trauma of colonization, the poignancy of anthropology among the colonized, and a more dispassionate but still felicitous reflection on ethnic diversity. In the ensuing pages Benedict uses both Ramon's imagery and his personal situation as basic material on which to embroider her own understanding. Her strategy is gradually to add comments and explanations, so that the reader is led gently from the fieldwork anecdote to the teachings of anthropology in general. *Patterns of Culture* is most emphatically not a fieldwork monograph, but in this passage at least it demonstrates how the particularity of fieldwork, and the typical use in ethnographic writing of personal encounters with those studied, might be turned to a more general theoretical use.

Thus she continues 'There were other cups of living left, and they held perhaps the same water, but the loss was irreparable. It was no matter of tinkering with an addition here, lopping off something there. The modelling had been fundamental, it was somehow all of a piece.'[2] So for Benedict the implication of Ramon's imagery is that each way of life is coherent and integral, just as a cup is integral. Indeed its integration is shown, for Benedict, by the fact that it can be broken. This is a central idea in her work, and it is elaborated a great deal further in the rest of *Patterns of Culture*. But note too that, so far as it is possible to reconstruct Ramon's story without Benedict's explanation, it amounted to a striking way of talking about two things: a sense of the loss of an irretriev- able past, and a sense of ethnic diversity. The extraneous addition, 'it was somehow all of a piece', did not contradict Ramon's version, but it was not necessarily part of it. It was her view, not his, which stressed the untinkerable wholeness of cultures: a culture, she wrote later in the book, 'like an individual, is a more or less consistent pattern of thought and action'. I make the point to emphasize that Benedict had a specific goal in mind, the setting out of a general view on human diversity as envisaged by the then relatively new and still struggling discipline of anthropology.

A further entailment of Benedict's gloss was that social and cultural separateness is (like a cup) hard-edged and mutually exclusive: one either has a culture, or one does not. It either survives, or it is lost. Ramon lives in one society, or in another. Thus Benedict further interprets what Ramon meant:

Those things that have given significance to the life of his people, the domestic rituals of eating, the obligations of the economic system, the succession of ceremonials in the villages, possession in the bear dance, their standards of right and wrong—these were gone, and with them the shape and meaning of their life. . . . [Ramon] did not mean that there was any question of the extinction of his people. But he had in mind the loss of something that had value equal to that of life itself, the whole fabric of his people's standards and beliefs.[3]

Benedict then remarks that 'he straddled two cultures whose values and ways of thought were incommensurable. It is a hard fate.'[4] This viewpoint was echoed by Benedict's close friend and colleague Margaret Mead, who wrote 'If we realize that each human culture, like each language, is a whole, . . . then we can see that if individuals or groups of people have to change . . . then it is most important that they should change from one whole pattern to another.'[5]

So in this perspective anthropology could be concerned with a man such as Ramon chiefly for what he had had in the past—a 'whole pattern' of life—or for what his descendants might have in future, the 'one cosmopolitan culture' of the

Anglophone United States. On this theory the human world is composed of separate, distinguishable entities: one society and culture might be dominant, but it is still only one separate variant among equals. As the historian of anthropology James Clifford has recently remarked, each culture is thus thought to be a 'natural kind', just as the entities of the physical world—kinds of plants, kinds of animals, kinds of minerals—are natural kinds.

The separability of cultures is tightly linked with a further feature of Benedict's vision, that of the tremendous, unpredictable, very nearly unaccountable variety of different ways of life. She writes:

In culture . . . we must imagine a great arc on which are ranged the possible interests provided either by the human age-cycle or by the environment or by man's various activities. . . . Every human society everywhere has made [a] selection in its cultural institutions. Each from the point of view of another ignores fundamentals and exploits irrelevancies. One culture hardly recognizes monetary values; another has made them fundamental in every field of behaviour. In one society technology is unbelievably slighted . . . ; in another, equally simple, technological achievements are complex and fitted with admirable nicety to the situation.[6]

So this 'great arc' consists of so many experiments in living, so many explorations of human possibility, so many selections from the infinite variety of what could be installed in a way of life. Benedict supported this view by observing—following her teacher Franz Boas—that just as the human mouth is capable of producing a practically infinitely varied continuum of sounds, yet any actual language selects only a few of these sounds as meaningful, so each culture chooses only a few of the possible arrangements of common life. The sense of selection or choice here does not at all imply any actual process by which sounds, or customs, were chosen in history. The emphasis lies rather on a sense of practically motiveless experimentation, of gratuitous or at least unaccounted variation which has nevertheless produced a panoply of well-knit forms of great beauty and value.

Sea shells

After a few pages Benedict leaves the images of the cup and the great arc behind, and concentrates upon adducing ethnographic examples to elaborate and clarify her argument. Yet as she does so, the appropriateness of the initial imagery becomes the more apparent. Indeed there is, in a sense, an underlying imagery, an imagery something like that of exhibits in a museum, where one finds an array of distinct, separate, integral objects, each unique and yet each sharing some essential attribute with the others. Benedict did not use such a figure of speech, but anthropologists, including Benedict, were closely associated with museums in America and elsewhere at the time. Much of her writing seems influenced by the underlying template of 'collection', a word then applied as much to customs, beliefs, and immaterial culture as to the pots and masks and material culture displayed in museums.

I now redeem my promise to show some consistency between this museum-like view of cultures and an apparently different view, that of British social anthropology. It is true that Malinowski, one of the two most influential British contemporaries of Benedict, was fundamentally friendly to the American approach. But Radcliffe-Brown, the other dominant British anthropologist of the time, was adamantly opposed to talk of 'culture', and in this he stiffened the resolve of many of his colleagues and successors in Britain. Nevertheless, he displayed an orientation to diversity which in important respects is fundamentally similar to Benedict's. Here is a passage by him which is ostensibly created through an image of the seaside, but in fact that same ghostly likeness of a museum shimmers in the background as well. He is writing about 'social structure':

When I pick up a particular sea shell on the beach, I recognize it as having a particular structure. I may find other shells of the same species which have a similar structure, so that I can say there is a form of structure characteristic of the species. By examining a number of different species, I may be able to recognize a certain general structural form or principle. . . . I examine a local group of

Australian aborigines and find an arrangement of persons in a certain number of families. This, I call the social structure of that particular group at that moment of time. Another local group has a structure that is in important ways similar to that of the first. By examining a representative sample of local groups in one region, I can describe a certain form of structure.[7]

Radcliffe-Brown's imagined museum was of natural history, not ethnology, but he chose to use as an analogy an object very similar to Benedict's cups. Sea shells are hard and frangible, each is clearly distinct from others, and they can be arrayed in a comparative order. They fall easily into 'natural kinds'.

It is true that Radcliffe-Brown characterizes these objects in a very different way than did Benedict. He is interested in an 'arrangement of persons', a 'social structure', and as he reveals elsewhere, his conception of a social structure concentrates on 'the political institutions, the economic institutions, the kinship organization, and the ritual life'.[8] This ordering and weighting is different from the catalogue of relevant matters in Ramon's society as laid out by Benedict, who was characteristically more interested in an arrangement, not of persons, but of ideas and values: 'the whole fabric of his [Ramon's] people's standards and beliefs'.[9]

Yet Radcliffe-Brown was, if anything, keener on the integral character of his found objects, and wrote of social systems on the analogy of organisms whose constituent organs work harmoniously together (as occasionally did Benedict). His task, as he saw it, was something like that of a comparative anatomist or other natural scientist. He wrote that 'the method of natural science rests always on the comparison of observed phenomena',[10] and the aim of comparison is 'to discover the universal, essential, characters which belong to all human societies, past present, and future'. Benedict was not nearly so insistent on the rhetoric of science, but she did use it occasionally, writing for example of the 'societies historically as little related as possible to our own' as 'the only laboratory of social forms that we have or shall have'.[11]

This language of science, like the underlying template of the collection, points towards another trait the two views share, which is an orientation away from history and towards timelessness. For both Benedict and Radcliffe-Brown the anthropologist is perfectly justified in comparing, say, the society of ancient Greece with that of present-day Pueblo Indians or Australian Aborigines, as if they existed in a bell-jar, cut off from their historical setting. In that great laboratory they are all equally valid as experiments in living (Benedict) or as specimens (Radcliffe-Brown). To the extent that they took the natural sciences as a model of knowledge—and Radcliffe-Brown did so more than Benedict—they accepted that such knowledge is in its character universal and uniformitarian, that is, equally applicable in all places and times. Moreover, to view societies in so grandly comparative a way brought with it a sense of loftiness, as of an enterprise whose grave purpose put it on a par with the natural sciences. Such an air was useful in debate with others, such as evolutionary biologists and psychologists, who at the time were (and still are) putting forward views of human nature which resolutely ignored the sort of evidence of diversity which the anthropologists stressed. To that extent, the timelessness had a rhetorical, combative character. But it was also fully consistent with, indeed necessary to, the notion of cultures or societies as bounded, integral wholes. For once mutability and the vicissitudes of history are allowed, the notion of the integrity and boundedness of cultures or societies begins to waver and melt.

Between

Patterns of Culture is a rich and complex book whose surface I have barely scratched. Much of it is social commentary. It treats then current controversies with social and even political import, and holds out ethnographic knowledge of the diversity of cultures as a good in itself, and valuable too as therapy for ailing attitudes and practices in North Atlantic society. Diversity shows that other forms of life are possible, that we are not bound solely by our own tradition or our own unreflecting view of human nature, and that we can and must learn to appreciate the validity of others' ways. Only then can a tolerant, pluralist civilization emerge. The fact that *Patterns of Cultures* is still in print after fifty-five years is a tribute to its enduring topicality and penetration.

But hindsight also allows us to see in the book ironies which may have been unintended or unconscious at the time but are now plain. Benedict shows a keen awareness that North Atlantic societies had come recently (on a scale of centuries) into contact with the societies usually studied by anthropologists, and that such contact had had profound and often painful consequences. She acknowledges, indeed stresses, that North Atlantic civilization itself was in the midst of deep historical changes. And she is clear that all the societies studied by anthropologists had themselves a long and productive history which had given rise to the very forms of life which anthropologists study.

Yet all these insights are sharply divorced from her conception of anthropology and its subject. As a social critic she used the fact of mutability easily and confidently; as a theorist of anthropology she ignored it. Much of the irony can be seen in her presentation of Ramon. He was on her account a respectable inhabitant of an actual social milieu, 'a Christian and a leader among his people in the planting of peaches and apricots on irrigated land'. But 'his hands trembled and his voice broke with excitement' when he spoke of the shamans in the old days. Surely all of this—the Christianity and the nostalgia for shamans, the growing of peaches and apricots in a market economy by a man still a member of his Amerindian people—is no less remarkable, no less striking an example of the human condition, no less peculiar a way of life, no less investigable a puzzle? But Benedict says only that 'he straddled two cultures whose values and ways of thought were incommensurable'. On the sea-shell theory of mutually exclusive and frangible cultures, they are perhaps incommensurable, perhaps even mutually unintelligible. Yet somehow Ramon was managing to get along, living according to some form or other. And Benedict herself was managing to talk to him, managing to learn something from him, managing even to participate to some degree in his life. If we take these criticisms seriously, then they point to very serious deficiencies in the sea-shell theory of culture.

My strategy is to move swiftly to the 'after' of the story, to anthropology's current answer to the sea-shell theory, but it is worth pausing briefly over the 'between': why did anthropologists move away from the notions shared by Benedict and Radcliffe-Brown?

Perhaps the most straightforward answer is that the worlds that anthropologists find are always like that of Ramon, a permanent half-way station between one condition and another, between a past and a future and between one society and another. Let me illustrate from my own fieldwork, reported in *The Forest Monks of Sri Lanka*. When I arrived in Sri Lanka to study Buddhism, my plan was to find out how the ancient precepts of that religion existed, in fact, in the daily practice of Buddhist Sri Lankans. A hidden assumption, something I had packed in my baggage without thinking, was that there would be something ancient and genuine to be found, but which contemporary Sri Lankans, like Ramon, had lost. And so I was excited when, in a remote corner of the island, I stumbled upon the existence of forest monks, who were barely known to the world of North Atlantic scholarship, and who seemed to embody the oldest and most authentic principles of the Buddha himself. There was only one problem: the movement of forest monks was not 2,500 years old, dating from the age of Buddhism, but scarcely more than 20 years old. Roy D'Andrade has somewhere remarked that studying culture in today's world is like studying snow in the middle of an avalanche. That was my experience, and there seem to be reasons for thinking that the avalanche of change is particularly swift and powerful today. But as I delved into the monks' way of life, I discovered that they had never remained unchanged. The avalanche has been going on a long time.

There are other reasons as well. Anthropology is part of a larger world of scholarship and thought, and cannot easily remain untouched by the conundrum of change as revealed by historians or sociologists. Anthropology has grown to be a more practical and more urgent subject, and applied anthropologists are called upon to understand people in exactly Ramon's position, not as Ramon might have been or might be in the future. Anthropology itself has grown a bit older, and the very peoples who had seemed, or been presented as, quite unchanged when they were first studied have now moved on themselves. Perhaps one of the most poignant of these changes is that chronicled by Colin Turnbull, who wrote movingly of the timeless world of the Mbuti pygmies of the Belgian Congo in *The Forest People*, published in 1961. But in *The Mbuti Pygmies: Change and Adaptation*, published 22 years later, he wrote:

I was first among the Mbuti pygmies of the Ituri Forest, in what was then the Belgian Congo, in 1951. I went back for something over a year in 1954. Even in that short space of time things had changed, and initial impressions had to be corrected. When I returned again in 1957–9 I had quite a hard time reconciling some of my earlier findings with what I found then. And on returning to the same part of the same forest yet again in 1970–2, it seemed as though I had to contradict myself all over again.[12]

But, as Turnbull is forced almost grudgingly to admit—and to admit against the deeply felt vision of a primeval, immutable happiness which he had evoked in *The Forest People*—this was not necessarily a matter of self-contradiction and self-correction, but of change going on before his very eyes.

I must not, however, give the impression that the inadequacies of the sea-shell theory have wholly dominated anthropological thought or practice. What anthropologists know is based on what anthropologists do, and the basic work of anthropology is ethnographic fieldwork: the intensive, fairly long-term study of a fairly small group through more or less face-to-face relations (often supplemented, it must now be stressed, by further historical research). The first task of an anthropologist in the field is to work out what is going on, and the first task of an anthropologist back at the desk is to describe what is going on. This description—or as anthropologists often think of it, this translation, this task of making the foreign familiar, the unintelligible intelligible, the incoherent coherent—does not necessarily require, in the first instance, a treatment of change. What readers of both *The Forest People* and *The Mbuti Pygmies: Change and Adaptation* need to know first is not that the inspiring *molimo* ceremony of the Mbuti has changed in this way and that, but rather what it is at all. There are many excellent, indeed beautiful, studies in ethnography that go no further than translation.

Europe and the people without history

Since Benedict and Radcliffe-Brown wrote, there have been many answers to the inadequacies of the sea-shell theory. We are still in the midst of the argument and it is harder to see clearly where and how it could be summarized than when looking back to Benedict's time. But in my judgement the work that best expresses anthropology's collective response is Eric Wolf's *Europe and the People without History*, published in 1982, very nearly 50 years after *Patterns of Culture*. This is the 'after' of my story. *Europe and the People without History* is a long book, a comprehensive book, not so approachable as Benedict's but bearing a great weight of deliberate argument and carefully marshalled evidence. Like Benedict, Wolf distills the work of other anthropologists while making his own contribution. Like *Patterns of Culture*, his is also a work of social and political criticism, one which contributes to a very different view of human diversity.

Like Benedict, Wolf puts forward ideas that are not palatable to all anthropologists. *Europe and the People without History* is in fact rather like the Super Deluxe pizza: it has as much as you can get on to a pizza, it is the best in town so far, it's a meal in itself and if you want something special this is it, but it's got anchovies. Some people like the penetrating flavour of anchovies, some don't. In this case, it has Marxism, or rather it has a perspective which is deeply informed by a lifetime of grappling with many of the same problems of change that engaged Marx, only in countries which we at present designate as belonging to the Third World, and with material and events that Marx could not have foreseen. The consequence is, on the one hand, that Wolf has a comprehensive view over both the largest scale of human life, the global system, and the smallest, the life of families and communities. On the other hand, he has a bias towards specifically economic and political dimensions of human life, and one would not look to him for an understanding of the often equally influential religious, linguistic, or artistic dimensions. Nor does he deal much with the forces of nationalism and ethnicity which have again pressed powerfully into our collective awareness while I have been writing this book. Within these limitations, Wolf's is both a persuasive reformulation of Marx's historical ideas for anthropological use and a cogent answer to the dilemmas raised by notions of integral, unchanging cultures. It is this latter accomplishment that I will concentrate on.

Wolf lays out his theme as follows:

Most of the groups studied by anthropologists have long been caught up in the changes wrought by European expansion, and they have contributed to these changes. . . . We thus need to uncover the history of 'the people without history'—the active histories of 'primitives,' peasantries, laborers, immigrants, and besieged minorities.[13]

He continues, 'If social and cultural distinctiveness and mutual separation were a hallmark of humankind, one would expect to find it most easily among the so-called primitives, people "without history," supposedly isolated from the external world and from one another.'[14]

This reflects an opinion set out by Benedict, who wrote that 'With their comparative isolation, many primitive regions have had centuries in which to elaborate the cultural themes they have made their own. They provide ready to our hand the necessary information concerning the possible great variations in human adjustments, and a critical examination of them is essential for any understanding of cultural processes.'[15]

But Wolf argues to the contrary that there was in fact no isolation, comparative or otherwise. He gives the following example, concerning the slave trade:

Since the European slavers only moved the slaves from the African coast to their destination in the Americas, the supply side of the trade was entirely in African hands. This was the 'African foundation' upon which was built, in the words of the British mercantilist Malachy Postlethwayt, 'the magnificent superstructure of American commerce and naval power.' From Senegambia in West Africa to Angola, population after population was drawn into this trade, which ramified far inland and affected people who had never even seen a European trader on the coast. Any account of Kru, Fanti, Asante, Ijaw, Igbo, Kongo, Luba, Lunda, or Ngola that treats each group as a 'tribe' sufficient unto itself thus misreads the African past and the African present.[16]

Indeed by far the greatest weight of *Europe and the People without History* is devoted to showing, region by region throughout the world, the ways in which apparently isolated, apparently local and unaffected, groups of people were in fact already deeply entwined in a growing world system of commerce, colonization, and the exercise of imperial power. For the sake of convenience he takes the beginning of this world history, or at least of this part of world history with which he is closely concerned, to be 1400, just before the great voyages of discovery. So when anthropologists came upon the scene four or five centuries later, they found a world which was not ancient or untouched, or primitive and insulated, but one already fashioned by extensive interplay with the very societies from which the anthropologists stemmed.

He stresses too that no known society is pristine and untouched, the product of its own history alone. 'All human societies of which we have record are "secondary," indeed often tertiary, quaternary, or centenary. Cultural change or cultural evolution does not operate on isolated societies but always on interconnected systems in which societies are variously linked within wider "social fields." '[17] Wolf applies an imagery of hard, impenetrable things, but uses it to describe the view he rejects: 'By endowing nations, societies, or cultures with the qualities of internally homogeneous and externally distinctive and bounded objects, we create a model of the world as a global pool hall in which the entities spin off each other like so many hard and round billiard balls. Thus it becomes easy to sort the world into differently colored balls.'[18]

The notion of 'people without history' has another implication as well.

We have been taught, inside the classroom and outside of it, that there exists an entity called the West, and that one can think of this West as a society and civilization independent of and in opposition to other societies and civilizations. . . . Ancient Greece begat Rome, Rome begat Christian Europe, Christian Europe begat the Renaissance, the Renaissance the Enlightenment, the Enlightenment political democracy and the industrial revolution. Industry, crossed with democracy, in turn yielded the United States . . . [It is] a moral success story, a race in time in which each runner of the race passes on the torch of liberty to the next relay. . . . If history is the working out of a moral purpose in time, then those who lay claim to that purpose are by that fact the predilect agents of history.[19]

In other words, those without history, the primitive and isolated, could, on this ordinarily accepted view, have no moral purpose. Moreover, they could have had no effect upon their own lives and destiny, because in the long run the only active agent is the civilization which, developing independently, now bears down upon them. They were passive, inert, waiting to be discovered. Wolf stresses to the contrary that all peoples everywhere have a hand in their fate, that they are not just patients but agents as well.

So the view of diversity that Wolf embraces is one which stresses the relationship between peoples or populations:

The central assertion of this book is that the world of humankind constitutes a manifold, a totality of interconnected processes, and inquiries that disassemble this totality into bits and then fail to reassemble it falsify reality. Concepts like 'nation,' 'society,' and 'culture' name bits and threaten to turn names into things. Only by understanding these names as bundles of relationships, and by placing them back into the field from which they were abstracted, can we hope to avoid misleading inferences and increase our share of understanding.[20]

Compared to Benedict's great arc, this view of diversity calls at once for a different focus and for an increase in subtlety. The change of focus is, so to speak, from the centres of cultures and societies to their peripheries and the relations between them; and from a more or less static description of their characteristics to a dynamic one of processes in which they are involved. For example, Wolf defines 'societies' as 'changing alignments of social groups, segments and classes, without either fixed boundaries or stable internal constitutions'.[21] This is very far from Radcliffe-Brown's view of a society, and it makes of a society something less like an object and more like an event or a series of events. Wolf treats culture in a similar way. He calls it 'a series of processes that construct, reconstruct, and dismantle cultural materials [such as social values or ways of categorizing the world]'. If we think of Benedict's imagery as being guided by the experience of contemplating an array of objects in a museum, then Wolf's is more a cinematic, a movie-goer's imagery.

Wolf's subtlety involves a process of disassembly and reassembly. He does not reject the old terminology out of hand, but regards it rather as a tool, or perhaps better as a stage in the making of the final product, which is understanding. On the one hand it is important to disassemble the global dynamic system and see how individual 'societies' or 'cultures' work. This is why Wolf's view, and the view I take here, does not reject the great collective work of ethnography which anthropologists have already achieved. But this step of disassembly must be followed by reassembly, so that in the end— he quotes from Alexander Lesser—we see societies as 'open systems . . . inextricably involved with other aggregates, near and far, in weblike, netlike connections'.[22] Many of the societies which anthropologists have disassembled still await a corresponding reassembly, some demonstration of how they have arisen and changed in the 'weblike, netlike connections' of our broader human life.

The reassembled system, ultimately the world system as a whole, is therefore a system of relationships, and Wolf thinks of relationships in a particular way. They possess force in their own right.

Relationships subject human populations to their imperatives, drive people into social alignment, and impart a directionality to the alignments produced. The key relationships . . . empower human action, inform it, and are carried forward by it. As Marx said, men make their own history but not under conditions of their own choosing. They do so under the constraint of relationships and forces that direct their will and their desires.[23]

I have already mentioned Wolf's use of the slave trade to illustrate what he means by this. Certainly the slaves were affected, but so too were all the other societies involved in slavery, from Britain itself, to the Americas, to the African slavers who sold other Africans to Europeans. However any individual may have experienced this trade, the aggregate effect was one of forces beyond anyone's control, forces which lay in the form of relationships between people: between the captured and the captor, between the African and the European slaver, between slave-trader and plantation-owner in the Americas. In fact these relations, hitherto most visible to scholars studying North Atlantic societies, were more than matched by the complexity and causal effect of relations in Africa itself. These relations gave rise to new predatory, militarized states, the founding of specialized organizations of slave-hunters, and the victimizing of societies which did not possess such forms of social organization. It has long been our habit to attribute large-scale change to technology, such as the use of guns in Africa. But before technology can be blamed we need first to look at the relationships within which the manufacture, acquisition, and use of guns makes sense. Guns do not enslave people; people enslave people, using guns.

Let me return for a moment to Ramon. Benedict was keenly conscious of the pathos of his plight, but her anthropology could not, in the strictest sense, describe or understand him. He lived in neither one culture or another, neither one society or another from her point of view, for Benedict's form of thought was calibrated only to static wholes, not to animated in-betweens. Wolf's thought, on the other hand, is designed explicitly for Ramon's condition. It is designed to understand the process of colonization, the reducing of native Amerindian populations to a new social situation in which they are partly a class and partly an ethnic group. Wolf could describe how

Ramon entered into new relationships, such as those of an agricultural debtor and a seller of agricultural goods in a market. He could describe, too, how new forms of social relations between Ramon and his fellow Amerindians had arisen. And he would be ready in principle—though this is in fact the weakest and least cultivated part of his book—to show how the new cultural form of Christianity had come to sit alongside or uneasily to replace an older shamanism.

Metamorphic life

That is the end of my story about how our conception of human diversity changed. What is the moral of the story? The first moral is that human life is metamorphic. 'Metamorphic' here is a term of art meant to capture the incessant mutability of human experience, the temporality woven into all human institutions and relationships. In contrast the sea-shell theory of Benedict and Radcliffe-Brown ignores temporality and mutability. There is an irony here, for the notion of cultural diversity exemplified by Benedict was one designed from the ground up to confirm that humans are mutable, varying tremendously beyond the narrow dictates of natural selection. But she and others had likewise rejected from the beginning the task of giving an actual account of variations: the notion of culture was not only ahistorical, it was in effect anti-historical. Each culture had its own causal and conservative power, stamping on each generation, on each plastic human individual, its own distinctive character. The consequence was, as I wrote elsewhere, that in such a theory 'social and cultural patterns have a determining character with little place for will, accident, change, or the commingling of circumstances. Somehow everything comes out looking the same every time.'[24] As J. D. Y. Peel observed, such an ahistorical view 'is inconsistent with a realistic concept of what society is and human experience within it' because it 'eliminates change, incompleteness and potentiality, memories and intentions—in a word, historicity'.[25]

The second moral is the one set out forcefully by Wolf: human life is causal, and it is relations between humans which form the causation. This point is made just as strongly, and more succinctly, in the following paraphrase of some words of Maurice Godelier, which I have already quoted in part, 'The fact is this: human beings, in contrast to other social animals, do not just live in relationships, they *produce* [*relationships*] *in order to live*. In the course of their existence, they invent new ways of thinking and of acting—both upon each other and upon the nature which surrounds them. They therefore produce culture and create history.'[26]

The phrase emphasized by Godelier, that humans 'produce relationships (or in his word, societies) in order to live', reaches a long way toward the heart of my argument. It bears, first, a material meaning, in that humans do not gain their livelihood individually but collectively. This is self-evidently true of contemporary urbanized societies, where people are dependent on each other for all basic material goods. But it is also true for the technologically simplest societies of the ethnographic record. 'Self-sufficient' has never meant that each individual can have a life apart from ties with other people, but only that a group can live by their pooled efforts.

The phrase 'in order to live' also bears a fuller sense. People live by means of relationships emotionally and intellectually. The speech we learn only makes sense in respect of the others we learn it from and to whom we direct it. The values in behaviour we acquire are sensible only in the perspective of others, or in our own imagination of others' perspective. Indeed culture, here meaning just largely mental goods, forms of knowledge and values to live by, which we have learned or created, is intelligible only in its use by people and in respect of other people. Cultures, in other words, presuppose relationships.

Wolf proposed that relationships work on a large scale, such that relations form an environment, the basic conditions under which life is conducted. Thus, for example, both the slavers of African predatory states, and the slaves themselves, faced an environment which was created by people, but which they nevertheless experienced as given, ineluctable, and all too inescapable. Perhaps an even better example is that of famine.

The great Bengal famine of 1943, in which perhaps 3 million people died, was created by people, not nature, and much of the starvation in Africa today has the same character: people are affected by war, steep prices, and other man-made disruptions of the man-made social and economic environment, and they therefore become vulnerable to scarcity or even starvation. Throughout this book I take for granted that such human—as opposed to natural—causation does occur and is important for understanding human nature.

But I shall want to argue that human relationships also have a fine grain, a small scale. One of the large changes in the human world that followed on, and was significantly associated with, the slave trade, was the industrialization of Britain. The export of manufactured goods to the West Indies and Africa helped fuel the development of manufacturing. Following Wolf's style, one can speak of the forces and conditions which gave rise to the Industrial Revolution and the development of a working class in England, and in so speaking one refers to a distinctive level of causation in human life. The language for such causation may be impersonal and it may be compelling to speak of movement in systems or of other large-scale patterns. But none of those changes could have occurred had people not been able to implement the new forms of relationship embodied in factory work, or later in the revised version of such work mediated through trade unions. People had to create these institutions, and they could only do so by forging new relations. Forging these relations entailed in turn the creation of mutual attitudes, mutual intentions, and mutual understandings—or misunderstandings—about each other. I shall want to use the word 'interactive' to denote this fine grain, this mutually constructive nature of human life.

The question again

Metamorphic, causal, interactive: these are traits very far from the character of human life as sketched by Benedict or Radcliffe-Brown. Yet these traits do not so much replace those earlier ideas as lend them further nuances. As Wolf said, it is a matter of disassembly and reassembly. If Benedict had asked the question about diversity it would have read like this: given the diversity of distinct, sharply bounded, traditional cultures, what must be true of humans in general? We cannot do without the notion of distinctiveness, for world history since she was writing has only confirmed its salience, quite despite what she might then have expected. As a salvage anthropologist of Amerindian societies, attempting to reconstruct the previous state of societies and cultures already transformed, she experienced the forgetting of a pre-colonial past. Anthropologists two generations later experience rather the creation and recreation of new cultural and social identities, whether among ethnic groups in the United States or in countries such as revolutionary Iran or the now defunct USSR. As Ulf Hannerz recently pointed out, 'the world system, rather than creating massive cultural homogeneity on a global scale, is replacing one diversity with another; and the new diversity is based relatively more on interrelations and less on autonomy'.[27]

So having disassembled the flow of human life to discern distinctiveness, we must reassemble it without the sharp boundaries or the unalterable tradition. The question we must ask of these peculiar animals is one which allows them not only to have a distinctive form of life with distinctive forms of relationship, but also to coin new forms, to participate in the flow of history. We must replace the question:

> Given the diversity of human forms of life, what must be true of humans in general?

with the question:

> Given the creation, metamorphosis, and re-creation of diverse forms of life, what must be true of humans in general?

We had thought that humans were just animals with cultures, so we had answered the first question by saying that they are intelligent, plastic, teachable animals, passive and conformable to the weight of tradition. Now we see that humans are also active, they are also animals with history. They are inventive and profoundly social animals, living in and through their relations with each other and acting and reacting upon each other to make new relations and new forms of life. Both the question and the answer are now a good deal more difficult.

3

Beginning to Make History

So what is it about humans that allows them to make history? Gananath Obeyesekere calls this an ontological question, by which he means a question about what really is the case, about what exists, about what lies at, in his words, 'the muddy bottom' of human nature.[1] For the late nineteenth- and early twentieth-century physical anthropologists, the opponents of Franz Boas, races were the real existents. They lay at the root of (what were supposed to be real) differences in intellectual and moral capacity between groups. Boas and his pupils quite effectively rejected the notion of races, and set out a different schedule of the real: human plasticity and cultures.

I here propose yet another ontology, a mutualist one, one which stresses 'sociality', which for the moment I define provisionally as a capacity for complex social behaviour. Many species and especially the social primates have their own form of it, but human sociality is conspicuous since we participate in such immensely varied and complex forms of life. My intention here is not to replace the notion of culture as culture replaced the rightly discredited idea of race, but rather to shift the emphasis. On balance, I argue, individuals in relationships, and the interactive character of social life, are slightly more important, more real, than those things we designate as culture. According to the culture theory, people do things because of their culture; on the sociality theory, people do things with, to, and in respect of each other, using means that we can describe, if we wish to, as cultural.

The significance of sociality stems partly from its ability to mend a failed aspiration carried within the idea of culture. On the one hand, anthropologists have stressed from the beginning that culture is public, a shared and common resource. To that extent, culture has been recognized as a social matter. But in fact the recognition has tended to stop at an uneasy half-way mark, at a position that still fails to grasp the thoroughly social nature of humans as a species, fails fully to accept that humans, in the first instance, relate to each other, not to the abstraction of culture.

The problem is an old one which has dogged both sociology and anthropology. Consider, for example, this dictum of the contemporary cultural anthropologist Clifford Geertz: 'man's nervous sytem does not merely enable him to acquire culture, it positively demands that he do so if it is going to function at all'.[2] The stress here is laid upon the relationship between an abstracted, idealized individual and that other abstraction, culture. Nothing else, and no one else, intervenes. A similarly flawed statement was made two generations ago by the sociologist and anthropologist Marcel Mauss: 'the contribution of collective representations [i.e. culture] . . . is so great . . . that at times we seem to want to reserve for ourselves [sociologists] all investigations in these higher strata of the individual consciousness.'[3]

Perhaps the difficulty can be seen more clearly in this purple passage from Leslie White's address at his inauguration as president of the American Anthropological Association in 1958:

Thus [with cultural symbols and meanings] man built a new world in which to live. To be sure, he still trod the earth, felt the wind against his cheek, or heard it sigh among the pines; he drank from streams, slept beneath the stars and awoke to greet the sun. But it was not the same sun! Nothing was the same any more. Everything was 'bathed in celestial light'; and there were 'intimations of immortality' on every hand. Water was not merely something to quench thirst; it could bestow the life everlasting. Between man and nature hung the veil of culture, and he could see nothing save through its veil. . . . permeating everything was the essence of words: the meanings and values that lay beyond the senses. And these meanings and values guided him—in addition to his senses—and often took precedence over them.[4]

On this showing the only significant, the only really real, features of the human species comprise 1) each individual alone, 2) the world of objects, and 3) that immaterial object, that veil between them, culture. For some purposes it might be reasonable thus to abbreviate the complexity of actual experience. Such ideas might be used by a psychologist, for example, to differentiate between animal and human perception. But if we restore what was abbreviated we see something much more intricate: humans living in a multitude of relationships with each other and managing jointly to understand and manipulate the physical world. In that perspective, culture, or what French sociologists have called collective representations, exists in and through such relationships, and the significance of the collective representations cannot be separated from the relationships.

Nor is it reasonable to regard culture or collective representations as some kind of object to which people relate. This assumption has had a use in placing cultural representations in the foreground so that we can begin to capture the distinctions between ways of life in an unambiguous way. But by restoring symbolic expressions to their actual setting a finer pattern emerges: collective representations have significance in their use by people in relation to other people and none apart from such use. The importance of these restorations is that they remind us of a setting in which change might be thought of as natural, the setting of actual social life with all its fluidity, uncertainty, construals and misconstruals, its laboriously achieved continuity, its planned and its inadvertent innovations. So long as we think of humans simply as individuals subjected to a collectivity, or to disembodied cerebration, change of the sort human history so richly evidences becomes curiously distant and difficult to comprehend. A more thoroughly sociological view places change, not permanence, at the centre of our vision.

Darwinian demands

I now put forward a notion of how sociality evolved. I say it is a 'notion' because I will not try to tie these ideas closely to particular times and places in an actual historical narrative of human evolution. This is partly because the direct information that is now available on human evolution—largely information drawn from fossil and archaeological finds—is too sketchy to support such a narrative. It is at present just too difficult to infer with reliability the subtleties of social behaviour and mental attributes from bones and rocks. But there are other sorts of evidence, evidence of a more indirect sort drawn from many fields, from primate ethology to cognitive psychology. This evidence also requires a great deal of inference, but it at least has the advantage of being rich and variegated. It now suggests a relatively new and quite different view of human evolution than the one—or ones—which have dominated biological anthropology so far.

Ordinarily we would not expect a socio-cultural anthropological understanding to be consistent, or commensurable, with a biological one. The dispute between Boas and the physical anthropologists of his time has continued, over different issues, right up to the present, and will continue into the twenty-first century. Indeed an important component of the collective identity of cultural anthropology in America—and British social anthropology has merely followed on in this respect—derives from a resolute rejection of biological and evolutionary explanations for human behaviour. These are bitter controversies and they ensure that it is very difficult to write, or to read, of such matters with equanimity or clarity.

I believe, however, that the two perspectives can be fruitfully reconciled. Indeed I hope to show that they can be reconciled even by sticking to a full-blooded, uncompromisingly evolutionary, perhaps quite blood-curdling description of sociality. Such a description might, at first glance, seem wholly inconsistent with, or wholly alienated from, the account I have so far given of human interrelatedness. The challenge is to make a biological language concerning organisms, genes, populations, and natural selection cohere with a language of persons, relationships, societies, cultures, and above all history. Or better—because this is really the point—to show clearly and decisively where one language ends and the other begins. I am, in other words, putting forward a new treaty for peace on the border between socio-cultural anthropology and biology. For what evolved was our capacity to make history, and once that happened, we could make history without the intervention of natural selection.

Let me begin with the word sociality itself. I use it—rather than other words such as intersubjectivity, say—because it is already in use among behavioural biologists. In effect, it forms the link between the two languages. Indeed at first glance it even appears to have a quite sociological or anthropological flavour: the behavioural biologist E. O. Wilson, for example, lists ten characteristics of sociality, such as group size, cohesiveness, compartmentalization, differentiation of roles, demographic distribution, and so forth.[5] In this usage, to describe the sociality of a species or a population of animals is to describe its society, albeit in a rather limited way.

What I want to do is reinforce this notion of sociality. One choice would be to make it more richly sociological—one could emphasize, for example, that among social primates it is also the quality and complexity of interaction that is important. But I am going to take the opposite tack. I want to make it more richly biological. I argue that this conception of sociality is not sufficiently biological, and in particular it is not sufficiently Darwinian. If sociality is to be any help at all, it must be given a strictly evolutionary description. That description is as follows:

> Sociality is an inherited trait or traits expressed in individual organisms, attributable ultimately to the frequencies of genes in the population of which they are members. Sociality is established through the force of natural selection on that population.

Note first that this introduces an ambiguity into the biological meaning of the word—or rather, it stresses an ambiguity that is already there. Ordinarily one could say that there is a difference in sociality between wolves in Canada and in Spain, or between chimpanzees in the wild and in captivity. Here sociality denotes the specific variant of social life among one population or another, and built into it is the recognition that different populations of a single species can have different kinds of sociality.

But a biologist can also speak of the sociality of one species— say of lions—as opposed to another—say of elephants. Though she may recognize that each such sociality actually contains a range of possibilities, nevertheless the range would be different for each species, and so she could talk reasonably about differences in sociality between species. Moreover, since sociality in this sense is attached to a species, then it must be reproducible. It must, in some way, be coded genetically so that it can be expressed in the behaviour of populations of that species. This is the idea of sociality I put forward here, and I understand it to be simply a logical concomitant of already existing biological ideas and practices.

This further implies that sociality, so defined, has evolved. In Daniel Bullock's words, 'there is to be something genuinely new in our chapter, just as there was something genuinely new in each prior chapter [of natural history]'. The chapters closest to us are those of the social primates, whose forms of sociality are, relative to other social mammals, very complex and in many ways very like our own. So the 'something new' is best seen as something different from the socialities of chimpanzees, bonobos, gorillas, baboons, and so forth. Of course these relatives are not our ancestors, but rather our cousins, who have their own lineage in which their own form of sociality has evolved. So our knowledge of the chapter before ours is indirect and must be inferred.

Darwinian biology offers various means by which evolution can occur, but I will assume that a change so substantial and far-reaching as the rise of human sociality could only have come about by natural selection. In other words, it could not have come about by evolutionary processes which are largely random, such as genetic drift or a simple event of mutation. So the question is, since humans are so similar to their near relatives, what selective advantage does distinctly human sociality have?

Evolutionary biology also lays down a general form that the

answer to such a question must take. The answer must show how the organisms possessing the trait—or, as in this case seems likely, more of the collection of traits—within a population were more successful. The criterion of success is straightforward: subsequent generations of the population would have more individuals with the traits, and fewer of those without them. Since what I am talking about here is the ability to fashion more complex and more varied forms of social life, then I think it reasonable to speak of an increase in the power of sociality among such a population. Such an argument must be accompanied by a health warning, however: from an evolutionary point of view this increase in power is in principle no different from another species' increase in, say, length of nose or size of testes. There are no evolutionary grounds for congratulating ourselves as a species.

Let me issue another health warning as well. Ideas cast in an evolutionary vocabulary have entered into the collective imagination of North Atlantic societies and lead a horrible life of their own, often far removed from their use in accountable biological research. These ideas suggest some powerful, compelling, and inescapable organic force welling up from within the darkness of the germ plasm to force us to commit inhuman acts. Not 'the Devil made me do it', but 'our genes made us do it'. Some writers have even depicted genes as if they were rather like little demons inside our bodies constantly pulling strings.

But the picture I put forward here is quite different, and is more in tune, as I understand it, with the real subtlety of Darwinian theory. Sociality is a capacity, a potential. It can only be realized by conception, birth, maturation, and growth in a suitable environment. The genes themselves are only a part of this process. In the perspective of the process as a whole they comprise not so much a blueprint of how an organism must look as a list of potentials that an organism might have. Their potentials may be differently expressed in different environments. Indeed a recognition that this is true for humans and other social animals is basic to the very idea of sociality as used by biologists. For sociality is recognized as a relatively plastic, rather than a fixed, endowment.

Such plasticity is basic to evolutionary ideas and especially to their application to humans. This plasticity is revealed by the way in which Darwinian theory differs from sociological and social anthropological styles of thought: it does not concern humans as persons, humans as realized and accountable agents in a social setting, but only humans as organisms. Evolutionary theory, in other words, does not pretend to explain the full detail of human life in all its dimensions. And because that theory speaks only of humans as organisms, then it can coexist with very different notions of, and practices concerning, human persons constructed in different cultural and social historical circumstances.

Finally let me say something about natural selection. As Elliott Sober has pointed out, natural selection is quite properly conceived as a sum of forces acting on a population.[6] All the forces taken together are nothing other than the environment in which each organism of a population thrives or fails to thrive. Most often, of course, the environment is conceived as external to the population, as consisting of other species, soil, water, climate, and so forth. But in the case of social animals, there is another, and an increasingly important, factor as well: the social setting itself. For each organism in such a social population, its fellows and their form of social organization comprise a vital part of the environment.

What follows is a sketch of some of the main patterns in the evolution of human sociality. The end-point is the presently known actual variation of human social life: whatever happened must be consonant with this outcome. We are not exactly the crown of creation, but here we are. The beginning point is the sociality of our ancestors in the hominid lineage. We cannot discern this sociality directly, but the evidence from other social primates is rich and varied, and gives us good grounds for inference.

The basic sketch

My reasoning is based on that of the psychologist Nicholas Humphrey, who argues for the primacy of social intellect—in my terms sociality—in human and social primate evolution. The core of his argument is as follows:

Social primates are required by the very nature of the system they create and maintain to be calculating beings; they must be able to calculate the consequences of their own behaviour, to calculate the likely behaviour of others, to calculate the balance of advantage and loss—and all this in a context where the evidence on which their calculations are based is ephemeral, ambiguous and liable to change, not least as a consequence of their own actions. In such a situation, 'social skill' goes hand in hand with intellect, and here at last the intellectual faculties required are those of the highest order.[7]

Humphrey argues that the adaptive advantage of the intellect associated with sociality does not lie in technical invention. 'Even in those species which have the most advanced technologies [such as the Gombe chimpanzees studied by Jane Goodall] the exams are largely tests of knowledge rather than imaginative reasoning.' Techniques are either trial-and-error, which are not very effective, or are learned from others. Humphrey emphasizes learning from others. He suggests that the possession of technology at first presupposed little technical intelligence. For the emphasis would have to lie in achieving and maintaining successful relations with elders from whom techniques are acquired, not on inventing the techniques. So society functions in the first instance as a sort of 'polytechnic school' to teach simple subsistence skills. Society allows a long period of dependence in which the young experiment and learn, in continuous contact with their teachers. And since this is an adaptively advantageous pattern, selective pressure will make for longer periods of dependency in childhood and greater age for the elders.

But, as a consequence of the growing diversity of ages and relative positions, there will be a growing complexity of differing interests.

Thus the stage is set within the 'collegiate community' for considerable political strife. To do well for oneself whilst remaining within the terms of the social contract on which the fitness of the whole community ultimately depends calls for remarkable reasonableness (in both literal and colloquial senses of the word). It is no accident therefore that [humans], who of all primates show the longest period of dependence . . . , the most complex kinship structures, and the widest overlap of generations within society, should be more intelligent than chimpanzees, and chimpanzees for the same reasons more intelligent than cercopithecids [monkeys].[8]

Note that the key idea here, that of social intelligence as the leading edge of social primate and hominid evolution, is strikingly different from the received wisdom of both earlier scholarly literature and the popular imagination. In this received wisdom there are, so to speak, previous episodes in the 'moral success story' of ancient Greece, Europe, and industrial democracy in the United States. Those earlier episodes involved man's bigger brain, his opposed thumb, his invention of the stone axe and fire, and then led triumphantly forward through technological innovation to the personal computer. But on Humphrey's showing we would want to tell a very different story. We might be impressed—if we are going to be impressed at all—not by the chunk of hardware, but by the incalculably complex web of social, political, and economic relations between people that created that computer and delivered it to the desk.

Social intelligence Mark II

Humphrey's ideas blend harmoniously with others in a wide river of continuing research in human evolution, psychology, behavioural ecology, socio-linguistics, social anthropology, and even philosophy. It is at present impossible to specify the larger ecological scene within which human sociality evolved, though there are some promising leads. Nor is it possible cogently to connect human intellectual and social evolution with the (relatively plentiful) fossil evidence. The real story of *Why Humans Have Cultures*, the story that will pin the answer down to a particular place, and a particular time, remains elusive and much of it will always remain so. Nevertheless, given the beginning and the latest chapter in the story, certain steps seem to have been logically necessary. In what follows I will try to bring some of this research together to explore Humphrey's insight.

Social and technical intelligence

Humphrey stresses the distinction between social and technical intelligence. There is some evidence to confirm this. One possibility is that technical intelligence could be present, but only as a more or less unimportant by-product of social intelligence. Thus Thomas Wynn has argued that present-day chimpanzees—assuming them to be at least as smart as our own forebears—have the intellectual capacity to have made the earliest identified stone tools.[9] They apparently do not make such tools, although they do occasionally use tools of an *ad hoc* character, such as pieces of grass to extract termites from mounds, or stones to break nuts. This might suggest that social intelligence, which is highly developed in chimpanzees, has indeed been far more important in the course of their evolution. It is this argument that Humphrey has applied to human evolution as well.

Another possibility is that social and technical intelligence are in fact related, so that the development of social intelligence has automatically resulted in the development of technical intelligence. Thus the philosopher Daniel Dennett has argued that a form of reasoning appropriate to understanding people could be usefully, indeed powerfully, applied to dealing with the material world. That is, social intelligence involves the ability to attribute to others various mental attributes: their plans, attitudes, intentions, and so forth. We can, to that limited extent, read minds: it is not a mystical achievement, but an everyday ability, used continually in everyday life, to grasp what others are planning and thinking with a fair measure of success. This ability, or rather set of mind, which he calls 'the intentional stance', takes for granted that people have more or less rational objectives and attitudes, that they plan to achieve those objectives, and that their actions reflect their mental states.[10]

Dennett then argues that we can also take what he calls 'the design stance', in which we think about how things work technically: how they are put together to achieve a purpose, how one piece fits together with another, how things must have a certain shape, how one part moves another, and so forth. The design stance works without attributing plans or intentions or attitudes to these things. This would be a set of mind equivalent to technical intelligence pure and simple.

The point is that it is possible to take many things which are designed from the design stance, and describe them from the intentional stance as well. Indeed, he argues, the intentional stance is a perspective which—for us at least—is particularly powerful. We are particularly good at imagining and understanding things, even material things, when we attribute intentions or, plans to them. This does not, of course, mean that we need really to believe that inanimate objects have minds. For example, a cabinet-maker I know talks of old wood as 'wanting to split', and a painter I know speaks of certain kinds of paint as 'wanting to lift' and even 'getting tired and wanting to let go'; yet they certainly do not believe that wood or paint are actually persons. Rather, we use a set of mind whose original focus was to make calculations 'where the evidence on which . . . calculations are based is ephemeral, ambiguous and liable to change' in order to do something relatively less difficult, and that is to manipulate the physical world. This suggestion is supported by recent psychological research that shows there to be an 'interactional bias' in human thinking.[11] That is, we do indeed tend to reason as if the inanimate world were human- or animal-like, made in the image of thinking, planning, intending beings.

The selective advantage of sociality

Humphrey's original argument stressed the transmission of technical skills from generation to generation as the chief advantage of sociality. This is a plausible line, but few subsequent researchers have followed it; they have concentrated rather on slightly different uses of being social and of sharing knowledge.

One form of knowledge is in a sense both more elementary and more important than knowledge of technology, and that is knowledge of the environment. The East African savannah in which hominids probably emerged had a particular set of characteristics: it provided foodstuffs which were highly seasonal, widely dispersed, concentrated in patches, and embedded in coverings or in the earth. It was a rich enough environment, but also offered many challenges. In such a setting a knowledge of the landscape is vital, and the ability to obtain and disseminate such knowledge would be of very great selective advantage. This line of argument still places stress on social intelligence, for it presupposes a group which is larger and better organized, which can monitor a larger territory collectively, and which can manage to share or exchange foodstuffs.

From this perspective it is not the sharing of knowledge alone which is important. Insofar as increased sociality goes hand in hand with an increased division of labour, that division of labour could itself have directly beneficial effects. It could directly enhance the exploitation of resources by distributing responsibility for foraging—always assuming the ability and willingness, themselves dependent on sociality, to exchange food. Not only would elders have acted as teachers and guides, but adolescents may have had a role as explorers for the group as a whole, and even children may have had a distinct part in infant care and in other necessary activities. These are characteristics which we find widely distributed among contemporary human populations. And it is also possible to discern from contemporary social primates how some division of labour based not on age or sex alone but also on different accomplishments and differential training might arise and persist.

An evolutionary ratchet

Humphrey argues implicitly that the possession of such a transmissible and increasing division of labour, combined with the sheer size of hominid groups, amounted to a selective force in themselves. How could this work? I think the selection must have had two features. First, the ecological and social history of the group rendered it relatively complex in its division of labour. There would also have been a further complexity in the fluidity of movement between groups or in relations between groups, as is attested for both modern humans and chimpanzees. In such a social setting any individual would have to have a great deal of what Humphrey calls 'reasonableness'. For in fact what was then emphasized was the ability to understand others and to move successfully in an increasingly complex social milieu.

Second, as some increased in 'reasonableness', others would follow. Or as Byrne and Whiten put it, 'any increase in Machiavellian skill by one "player in the game" will select for enhanced skill in the other, both in competitive and cooperative interaction. One can thus imagine an evolutionary spiral of Machiavellian cleverness'.[12] So we can capture something of the complexity of selection for sociality by saying that an organism faced two distinguishable problems: first the group configured in a complex way, and then the capacities of others to act more or less successfully than oneself in that group.

The phrase 'Machiavellian cleverness' apparently stresses the potential for deception and exploitation of others in such a setting. And it is true that the best evidence for the social intelligence of other primates lies in the fact that they deceive each other (and therefore have a sophisticated idea of what each other thinks). This harmonizes with notions of self-interest that behavioural biology has taken from neoclassical economics and the political theory of possessive individualism: each acts to his own immediate advantage. These ideas have been useful, but they also have a flaw, in that they obscure the basic fact of human sociality. They render it difficult or impossible to see how better co-operation beyond a range of close kin might redound to the benefit of one organism over another.

Recently, many writers have shown that a narrow conception of evolutionary self-interest is unnecessary and implausible, especially in the social primates. Perhaps the most persuasive— and against the background of a basic assumption that everyone is selfish, the most surprising—argument was set out by the social theorist Robert Axelrod, working with the biologist William Hamilton. They showed that co-operation can arise, persist, and spread in a population where there is no centralized control.[13] An organism which is basically inclined to co-operate, but which will retaliate if necessary, can prosper and even replace less friendly animals, especially if the animals are associated with each other over a long and indeterminate time. Theirs is a general argument which can be applied as effectively to the evolution of micro-organisms as to the United States Congress, and it is specifically relevant to social primates. In such species individual animals are markedly dependent on one feature of their environment, namely their fellows configured as a group. In those circumstances the more or less successful, more or less dependable working of social relations is vital to each animal.

So though we tend to think that deception or, in the language of games theory, 'defection' would automatically be the best strategy for all, in fact it could only be a minor theme, a departure from a basic consensus. And indeed it has been increasingly demonstrated by field observation of many animal species that co-operative strategies, especially strategies of reciprocal altruism, are very widespread. This need not imply that disinterested kindness and Utopian harmony prevailed alone in the human lineage, or in any other lineage for that matter. Faction and alliance, loyalty and treachery are also likely to have been perennial themes in our early, as in our more recent history. Rather, the challenge has always been to act 'reasonably', responsively, and on balance pacifically toward both close kin and others.

As Humphrey assumes, the production of more and more social complexity in hominid evolution must have been a gradual process. These groups slowly wove their own societies, supplemented by their relations with other groups and modified by the complexities of the other species and the natural setting in which they lived. It is not clear how long the evolutionary ratchet of increasing sociality lasted. (Indeed, it may still be going on; it is hard to investigate because the effects could only be seen over a period of time measured in tens or hundreds of human generations.) But while the process lasts, each increase in sociality would be more than matched by an increase in the intricacy of collective life. The notion of an evolutionary ratchet is consonant with the idea of co-evolution, which suggests that organisms may produce changes in the environment, changes which redound on themselves, creating a circle of positive feedback. The only peculiarity in human evolution was that human social arrangements and their unintended consequences became a selective force in themselves.

The invention of history

In this process the variety of relations between persons which we recognize as distinctly human must have arisen. There came into being different family and kinship arrangements, relations of production and long-standing relations of exchange between non-kin, domination and political power, and the capacity to manipulate these possibilities further through speech. There arose, that is, the exceptionally plastic ability for each person to enter into many forms of relationship, to coin new relationships and new forms of life. And with the appearance of these forms there appeared the forms of causation associated with them: not just the ecological causation, the selective forces which bear on all organisms, but now distinctly human social, political, and economic causation. These animals were, so to speak, released into history. I have progressively revealed parts of Maurice Godelier's programmatic statement of this point, and I shall now quote it in full:

In the course of their existence, [human beings] invent new ways of thinking and of acting—both upon themselves and upon the nature which surrounds them. They therefore produce culture and create history (or History).

Of course other social animals too are the product of a history, but it is one they have not made: that of the . . . evolution of living matter, and of the animal and vegetable species which [have appeared] in the course of the earth's existence. . . .

This fact is not just like any other, for an account of it involves an analysis of both the evolution of nature and the specificity of man within that nature. All else in this sense lies in its light or shadow. If we wish to explain the human race and its history, to develop the natural or the human sciences, we cannot but take this reality as our starting point.[14]

As anthropologists and archaeologists have increasingly demonstrated, such distinctively human social causation operates in circumstances far less socially differentiated than in an industrializing urban society. Social causation has been documented, for example, among both prehistoric and contemporary hunter-gatherers, who might otherwise be thought to be subject mainly to direct physical environmental influence. Among contemporary Australian Aborigines, for example, their band size and composition responds as much to the state of relations between individuals and between groups as it does to the necessity to live in a harsh environment. Analogous statements can be made about pastoralists and agriculturalists. Moreover the rise of the great and terrible inventions—kings, money, writing, printing, capitalism, nationalism—gave scope to ever new forms of social causation. We are capable, that is, not just of creating new forms of social life, but also new forms of causation. The historian Fernand Braudel, for example, has shown how the invention of instruments of credit in late medieval Italy gave rise to the new possibility that the manipulation of such instruments could affect the price of basic foodstuffs in far distant Holland or Germany. Certainly the modern world is well acquainted with such causation—in the form of the elusive yet powerful movements of money, resources, and influence across the world, which aim to benefit some but cause untold harm to others.

Three tales

In the next chapter I will explore further the nature of this peculiar animal who makes history. But for the moment let me draw breath and summarize what I have so far argued, in terms of competing stories of human evolution. In fact, any comprehensive account of how humans evolved would be an extraordinarily complex one, taking into account human bipedalism and other physical traits along with many mental and behavioural ones. The result might be extraordinarily intricate, and disappointingly so for anyone who would wish to find any plain moral import in our Darwinian history. But so far, as Misia Landau has pointed out, many ideas of human evolution have been relatively simple and straightforward, coming down to a few plain tales.[15]

One tale that has been at play in this chapter is the evolution of technical intelligence. This has been a constant theme in conceptions of human evolution. Here, for example, is a relatively late example of it, the biological anthropologist Philip Tobias writing in 1965 to describe the key event:

Sooner or later, some among the numerous Africa-wide populations of australopithecines [a forerunner in the human lineage] did acquire the mental capacity to overleap the highest implemental frontier. . . . Sooner or later, some of them did acquire the right quantity and/or quality of brain to be able to use a tool to make a tool. Initially, perhaps this would have been an isolated flash in the pan, but if it conferred a sufficient selective advantage, the capacity for it would have spread. . . . Now a new major breakthrough occurred. Stone tool-making . . . became feasible: new, virtually limitless possibilities opened up.[16]

As I have pointed out, such a story clips neatly on to the end of the story of the march of technological civilization from Greece to the United States. It is an earlier episode in that triumphal advance, the equivalent in soberer terms of the cartoonist's image of man inventing fire or the wheel.

A second tale was that of the sudden discovery of 'meaning', the sudden spiritual leap, the bursting through a barrier separating man from animal. In Leslie White's version, 'Nothing was the same any more. Everything was "bathed in celestial light"; and there were "intimations of immortality" on every hand.' This is a tale whose origins, as James Rachels has recently reminded us, lie very deep in our own, quite specifically Christian, past. Bishop Wilberforce, a contemporary of Darwin and his great opponent, wrote that 'Man's derived supremacy over the earth; man's power of articulate speech; man's gift of reason; man's freewill and responsibility; man's fall and man's redemption; the incarnation of the Eternal Son; the indwelling of the Eternal Spirit—all are equally and utterly irreconcilable with the degrading notion of the brute origin of him who was created in the image of God.'[17]

The Christian thinker Teilhard de Chardin later attempted to blend the story of the evolution of technical intelligence with this idea of some special creation for humans. He accepted that humans had indeed evolved, but he insisted that there was nevertheless at some miraculous point a leap which led, as White would have it, from meaninglessness into meaning.

Now on the face of it, the technical innovation and the spiritual stories are rather at odds, a rather materialist view versus a religious one. But in fact the two have often gone quite well together. Thus Tobias, writing in the same year as his explication of technical intelligence, quoted approvingly from Chardin:

As Teilhard de Chardin put it, 'evolution went straight to work on the brain, neglecting everything else, which accordingly remained malleable.' Somewhere, in the line of ever-warming consciousness, 'a flame bursts forth at a strictly localised point. Thought is born.'... Thus, although the anatomical leap from non-man to man is small and insignificant, it is a change marked by the birth of a new sphere, that of thinking. With man, we have entered 'the psychozoic era.'[18]

On reflection, it is not surprising that a tale of technological intelligence goes so well with a tale of spirituality, for the march to technological civilization is often represented as carrying with it enlightenment and a higher form of spirituality.

I have shown little enthusiasm for either of these stories. It is true that something of each of them might be reconciled with the mutualist story I have put forward. I do not, for example, deny that technical accomplishments have been important. Yet, following Humphrey, I have made them subsidiary to the development of social intelligence. Similarly, in the next chapter I admit that there is something extra in human speech that makes it much more intellectually powerful than any so far described form of animal communication. But, I will stress, speech too is dependent upon the prior establishment of social intelligence and of a social setting within which its special skills can flourish. It need not be thought of as some ineffable flame bursting forth or as the addition of some essential but mysterious quantum which leads from bestiality to humanity.

There are many differences between Humphrey's story and those that have gone before, but the key one is that Humphrey's is a gradual story and the others are not. On his showing, the 'something genuinely new in our chapter' arrived slowly, steadily, gently, step by step. The story began far back in the primate lineage and has led to a varied family of forms of sociality. Ours is the one of most interest to us, and it has some peculiar twists to it, but it is not a sociality radically different from the others.

One consequence of such a view is that the 'muddy bottom' of human nature is not radically different from that of other social animals. As Darwin put it, 'Man in his arrogance thinks himself a great work worthy the interposition of a deity. More humble and I think truer to consider him created from animals.'[19] This sharply contradicts an attitude of human specialness which is so deeply ingrained in North Atlantic thought that it need not acknowledge its Christian source. But Darwin's view is consistent with the views of other great ethical traditions, such as Buddhism and Jainism, which regard all sentient beings, human and animal, as existing on the same moral footing, though with different capacities. To the extent that stories of human evolution are motivated not by an encounter with bones, stones, and actual behaviour but by received ideas, then—as James Rachels has argued so persuasively—we might best receive a different set of ideas.[20] Certainly the moral and, as we now realize, practical consequences of conceiving ourselves as fellows with other animals, and with the natural world, could be very beneficial.

In the present context the gradual story of evolving social intelligence has another benefit as well. It is plausible. It does not depend on some quintessentially mysterious event. It leads on to a series of questions which can be soberly asked, even if not all of them can be answered. It leaves us room to wonder at our nature, to find it miraculous by comparison with what we might have been or with what others now are; but it also leaves the opportunity to learn more and more about how we became what we are.

4

The Anatomy of Sociality

I NOW turn to a more detailed description of the traits belonging to human sociality. The evidence is drawn from studies of living humans—both adults and, more fruitfully, infants and children—and social primates. Here the basic strategy is that of a comparison, either explicit or implicit, between humans and other primates. Such comparisons cannot show what happened in evolution, but they do convey vividly both the end result of that evolution and the mental capacities necessary for our complex social life.

When psychologists write of mental abilities they often try to distinguish one ability from another, on the (currently fashionable) assumption that mind is constituted of separate modules. I do not however argue as a psychologist. The mental capacities I now describe are very heterogeneous, and might best be thought of as circles overlapping the same area, which is sociality.

Intersubjectivity

The broadest circle, the most general way of talking about sociality, is as intersubjectivity, an innate human propensity for mutual engagement and mutual responsiveness. Some of this propensity is cognitive or intellectual, some of it emotional, but in any case human character and human experience exist only in and through people's relations with each other. Colwyn Trevarthen, who helped pioneer the study of infants' intersubjectivity, and his co-worker Katerina Logotheti describe it thus:

Now we possess evidence that the newborn can imitate expressions of persons and enter into an exchange of feelings. One year later the baby shows a specific need to share purposes and meanings and to learn how to denote common ideas by means of symbolic expressions. Human cultural intelligence is seen to be founded on a level of engagement of minds, or intersubjectivity, such as no other species has or can acquire. . . . Steps in early psychological development, while adjustable to different styles of upbringing that convey different social and moral principles, reveal universal powers and needs for emotion and communication that are essential to normal 'socialization' and to normal 'cognitive growth'.[1]

Jerome Bruner has described intersubjectivity from an infant's point of view: 'The infant's principal "tool" for achieving his ends is another familiar human being. In this respect, human infants seem more socially interactive than any of the Great Apes, perhaps to the same degree that Great Apes are more socially interactive that Old or New World Monkeys. . . . Infants are, in a word, tuned to enter the world of human action.'[2]

These are statements which must partly be understood against the background of an earlier ontology, an earlier view of what was really real and important in the growth and development of people. On the earlier view, a view shared in some measure by both anthropologists and psychologists, the real included individuals and their innate abilities to deal with the world of objects, including people. There was then culture, or what was learned on top of these basic existents. Here, however, the view is very different. There are individuals, but they are only understood in relationships with other individuals. When culture arrives, it is built on an already extant scaffolding, and indeed it is still intimately concerned with relationships and other individuals.

This ontology, this relative evaluation of what is more fundamental and what less, was set out firmly seventy years ago by the Russian psychologist Vygotsky: 'Any function in the child's cultural development appears twice, or on two planes. First it appears on the social plane and then on the psychological plane. First it appears between people as an inter-psychological category and then within the child as an intra-psychological category.'[3]

Only in recent years, however, has the collective effort of psychologists been directed to describing intersubjectivity. Here, for example, Trevarthen and Logotheti summarize a great deal of research on the first year of a human infant:

Newborns, even 10 weeks premature, can achieve direct engagement through hearing and seeing an affectionate 'other', and by feeling body contact and gentle movements.... The infant makes orientations, expressions and gestures and moves in concert with the sympathetic partner. Eye contact is sought and the baby can imitate movement of the eyes and mouth.... This is primary intersubjectivity or basic person–person awareness.... Development of the baby's brain [benefits] from emotions generated in such communication, the existence of which proves that the baby has a dual 'self + other' organization in its mind, ready for contact with the expressed feelings of a real partner.[4]

In subsequent development, these tendencies give rise to responses that are increasingly guided by the style of care-givers. Children experiment in play with different relationships, and different combinations of attitudes and events in relationships. In other words, the basic scaffolding, which consists of intensively attending to and responding to others, is given at birth. That scaffolding is then used to construct another scaffolding, namely the specific form of relationships peculiar to the child's society.

So from infancy humans are directed to other human beings as the significant feature of the environment. In an evolutionary perspective this must point to an emotive, cognitive, and conative change, an increasing dependency on, openness towards, and vulnerability to, one's conspecifics. Humans are available to each other, their abilities are only developed and transformed by others and in respect of a social setting. The capacities of sociality may be in individuals, but they are completed only between them.

There is a further implication of intersubjectivity, which concerns the way we know the world. Some writers now use the term 'distributed processing' to speak of human thought. The analogy here is with computers which have more than one central processing unit (in effect, more than one brain), or which carry out computations in co-operation with other computers. Similarly, what each of us learns and uses is, on this view, much more than each of us has in his or her head alone.

In a sense this is obvious. I have assumed from the outset that a larger group, with a more complex division of labour, can deal with a highly patchy, seasonal environment more effectively than the same number of unconnected individuals. Those in the group use each other's knowledge as well as their own. Similarly, I am now using a very complicated machine to write these words. I must have at least some personal knowledge of it, but I also depend on others. For example, I rely on more complicated machines, maintained by other people whose job is to know those machines, to preserve what I write against electronic mishap and to print out the results. Moreover when something goes wrong with this machine, I am helpless and need a specialist. So I depend on, and assume, other people's knowledge. Or as an example of distributed processing on a smaller scale but with much more intensity and interaction, we may consider a pilot and co-pilot in a cockpit. In any emergency they depend on each other's knowledge and each other's information in the midst of swiftly changing, highly complicated, and potentially fatal events. And on a far larger and more leisurely scale, the knowledge that each one of us has of an organized discipline, say anthropology, exists in the eyes of, is published through the good offices of, is based on the efforts of—and is useful eventually in the thought of—other anthropologists and other people. What Michael Innes calls the 'examination-passing classes' may imagine that the repository of knowledge is individuals alone, but that is simply not the case. The implications of this basic set of ideas have only begun to be explored in the human sciences. For the present at least, it is just plain hard for scholars and researchers to think in these terms.

Mind-reading

One of the ways of dealing with this difficulty is to hold one of the variables, one of the participant's attitudes and beliefs, still for a moment and concentrate on the other. This is what is done by psychologists and philosophers interested in higher-order intentionality. The notion of intentionality begins from the premiss that animals such as primates and humans represent the world to themselves, and intentionality just means that some state of affairs is thought about, is an object of intention or representation. This representing is reflected in such common forms of speech as 'Michael *imagined* that he still had the key', or 'Amy *hopes* that she will see her grand-mother', or 'Elizabeth *expects* that the roads will be slippery tonight'. The first part ('Amy hopes') shows that what follows is someone's representation.

Utterances such as these correspond to first-order inten-tionality. Second-order intentionality appears in the following: 'Amy *felt* that Michael *wanted* her to eat her egg properly at breakfast'; 'Elizabeth *feared* that Michael *thought* she was working too hard'. Here one person represents another's representation, i.e. Amy represents to herself Michael's representation to himself. It is possible to take such inten-tionality a good deal further. Here, for example, is fourth-order intentionality: 'I *believe* that you *recognize* that I *think* you *understand* that higher-order intentionality is a pretty everyday affair among humans.' Higher-order intentionality can get very complicated, but at base it is no more complicated than playing scissors–rock–paper. The key is that when people think about other people, they think about them in a certain way, as having thoughts, plans, ambitions, and knowl-edge like themselves. This is Dennett's 'intentional stance',[5] but here it has an extra wrinkle, namely the possibility of representing mutual attitudes and mutual knowledge of each other. Andrew Whiten refers to higher-order intentionality as 'mind-reading',[6] and as long as we realize that nothing beyond everyday, fallible experience is involved, that is a handy way to talk about it.

The literature contains well-documented cases of mind-reading among social primates.[7] It seems that even third-order intentionality—'I have some representation of her representa-tion of my representation of her'—might be the best explanation of some scattered observations, but the evidence is hard to interpret. These are mostly cases of intentional deception, and so point to the Machiavellian side of the social primate character. But so far it seems unlikely that other primate species ordinarily, as a matter of course, have such complex representations of the world.

Humans are another matter. Perhaps one of the best explored uses of mind-reading among humans is in conversation. Humans use third-order intentionality routinely as the basis for the turn-taking that is necessary in conversation, as the philosophers Paul Grice and Jonathan Bennett have pointed out.[8] As they might put it, Utterer intends Audience to recognize that Utterer intends Audience to produce response such-and-such. On the one hand, such turn-taking is based ultimately, at least as far as development is concerned, on those original propensities to attend to others and to respond which characterize infants. Moreover much of conversation may be conducted in a matter of fact, relatively automatic mode. But on the other hand, the ability to take part in an extended, complex conversation—and especially to take part reasonably and appropriately in a conversation in a language and setting learned in adulthood—are matters of monitoring finely and with great concentration the flow of others' attitudes and intentions. Many of us may take it for granted, but it is still a very hard thing to do.

Politeness

The notion of intentionality is relatively bloodless, but it leads immediately to another, indeed to the central, matter of human life, and that is the way in which we are not so much self-aware as self-and-other-aware. Consider the following ethnographic example which, like many ethnographic examples, is lightly fictionalized to protect the guilty. Ben and Nigel, who are colleagues in an office—is it a university in England?—walk down a long corridor towards each other. Though at first, when they were at opposite ends of the corridor, Ben may have been unaware of Nigel, each step brings them closer, and as it brings them closer Nigel's presence dawns on Ben. But Ben's awareness does not stop there. If he, Ben, is aware of Nigel, then Nigel must be aware of Ben, or this at least is the feeling which rises in Ben, perhaps as a vague unease that he should not have worn those silly Christmas socks today. And of course Nigel too has a corresponding feeling, perhaps one directed to himself as one who dislikes Ben, but who wants to foster harmony.

As they approach more closely, the mutual awareness heightens. If Ben greets Nigel—whom he wants to impress— from too far away, it will seem awkward and sophomoric. Or that at least is Ben's vague instinct. He holds himself back. As for Nigel, if he waits too long to greet Ben, it will seem cold and forced, but he is having a hard time compelling his face to smile. And so, second by second, they draw nearer, looking everywhere but at each other, aware of self, aware of other, aware of other's reaction to self. Will they manage to speak?

Or consider this analogous case, from Ivo Strecker's study of the Hamar of Ethiopia.

In Hamar the [recognition of others' needs] is remarkably slow in coming forth when a visitor is to be greeted. The reason for this lies in the . . . pattern of Hamar social organization, where small domestic groups are on perpetual guard against each other. Therefore greeting only occurs after a *fait accompli*, that is, when it is already established that a guest is going to stay, be lodged and fed, etc. With people who are not closely related the right to hospitality is an open question. . . . When a male guest arrives he will first, without comment, sit down on the small stool he always carries, either in the shade of a tree if it is during the heat of the day, or close to the kraal fence if it is early morning or evening. No one in the homestead will seem to notice him at this stage (an irritating experience, by the way, for a European visitor who has been culturally conditioned to expect his [evident needs] to be attended to immediately). But after a while the visitor may realize that a woman, somewhere not too close to him and yet not too far from him, has begun to sweep the ground. This is the first indication that he is not going to be snubbed. If, after all, he has come only for some limited business he now makes a move and asks for a drink of water, asks to talk to someone about a goat that has gone astray, or says whatever else he has come about. In this way he indicates that he does not wish to be invited to stay for long, and so the hosts know now not to invite him more expressly and he avoids having to refuse such an invitation which would be [an insult]. If, however, he wants to stay he simply continues to wait in silence for the next sign which will probably be the woman spreading out a cow hide on the spot she has just swept clean. She nods to him and he takes off his sandals and settles down on the cow hide. There he rests for a while and then at last the proper greeting takes place. One by one the male members of the homestead stroll casually over to where the guest rests. Each one sits down on his stool neither too close nor too far from him, and after pausing for a moment, address him.

These examples are of apparently trivial events, but the matter is great, for they point to a quality of human life which seems decisively to separate humans from other social primates. In everyday encounters of this sort, people may routinely feel embarrassment or pride, insecurity or confidence, and a multitude of other emotions and attitudes that have been finely tuned into the local variant of human sociality. Hamar can *oblige* or *disoblige* each other, *foster* or *obstruct* each other. Nigel can *insult* Ben, or *compliment* him, and Ben can *impress* Nigel, or *disgrace himself in Nigel's eyes*. In either case people have needs and wants that are not immediately physical, but have to do with their 'face', to use Erving Goffman's term, their awareness of self in respect of others.

Compliment and insult may seem peculiarly immaterial. Yet these events, these very real events, can have long-lasting consequences: the situation may develop into a friendship, or into an office vendetta if Nigel does not manage to unfreeze his face. In Hamar more serious things can happen. These can come about because of an initial event—an insult, for example—which had no actual immediate physical effect upon either party, no immediate prejudice to either person's nutritional or health status, and no immediately evident consequences for their reproductive success. As Penelope Brown and Steven Levinson have shown to such tremendous effect, the phenomena of politeness and impoliteness absorb a tremendous amount of human energy and effort.[10] This is because humans are delicately attuned to one another, and to themselves in relation to others, in a taut web of interaction. The maintenance or destruction of that web are matters of absorbing interest and overriding importance.

Pedagogy and aesthetic standards

The learning of a local variant of sociality—of how to greet people, how to part from them, and how and how not to attend to their 'face' and their other needs in between—is therefore central to human maturation. The psychologist David Premack has shown that humans have one special trait in regard to this educational requirement, a trait that he calls 'pedagogy'. Pedagogy arises from the sense of self-and-other, but it has a particular slant: it is a set of abilities through which an individual 'observes another, judges him or her according to some standard, and intervenes to bring the novice's behaviour into conformity with [that] standard.'[11] Premack argues that the set of cognitive capacities which we can impute to chimpanzees in their transmission of material techniques are not pedagogy proper, but rather imitative learning, albeit of a high standard. Chimpanzees practice a form of training, but such training does not involve an aesthetic standard, and Premack is careful to differentiate training from pedagogy. In chimpanzee training there is always some direct pay-off to the trainer, since the novice is trained to perform some service for the trainer.

In contrast, full-blown human pedagogy presupposes, first, the disposition to invest time in training without any immediate return. Second, pedagogy involves a sophisticated aesthetic judgement of what constitutes a good performance, whether in using social or technical skills. Third, it involves representing the difference between the pedagogue's own ability and that of the novice, and therefore higher-order intentionality.

The deferred pay-off of pedagogy is its most striking feature from a Darwinian point of view, for it achieves what the evolutionary biologist John Maynard Smith models as 'the social contract game': 'I will [co-operate]; if any other individual [defects], I will join in punishing him; if any other individual fails to join in punishing, I will treat this as equivalent to [defecting]'.[12] Maynard Smith assumes that such a strategy could only be found among humans, who—to put it in Premack's terms—possess an aesthetic standard on which to judge behaviour. But the social contract game is only a functional equivalent of pedagogy because 'punishment' and 'joining in punishment' are achieved by pedagogy chiefly in the upbringing of the young, not through transactions between fully formed adults. Moreover strong emotional dependence on others in both infancy and adulthood makes such an unselfish trait more comprehensible, and its power more gently persuasive, than the idiom of game theory would suggest.

The consequences of pedagogy lie in the capacity among humans of transmitting an 'aesthetic standard', to use Premack's term. Among humans such standards apply in the first instance to interactions between people, for that is the first—if not the final—focus of our interest as a species. An aesthetic standard is specifically interactive.

It is tempting to translate the notion of aesthetic standard into a more familiar idea, such as that of social rules or morality or just culture. But I think it important to resist the temptation, because those other terms may convey an inappropriate certainty or predictability. An aesthetic standard is best thought of as essentially flexible, and as requiring some judgement and imagination. Aesthetic standards underdetermine actual action: whatever they are, they are not like a blueprint to be followed or a computer algorithm. If aesthetic standards were not flexible, and therefore capable eventually of being diverted into new standards and new sensibilities, there could be no history: we would always have reproduced the same pattern of behaviour over and over again.

It is possible to see evidence of this underdetermination in contemporary ethnography. In her monograph on the Ilongot of the Philippines, for example, Rosaldo writes of what I call an aesthetic standard as 'emotionally oriented themes and images' which 'maintain for Ilongots a sense of consistency in things that people do, thereby permitting them to see over time that people act in more or less familiar ways for more or less well-known reasons.'[13] The sense of 'more or less' here is just that themes and images are powerless in themselves but are empowered by people using them to interpret their relations to each other in specific situations.

An analogous point is made by Edward Schieffelin concerning the Kaluli of Papua New Guinea. He writes of 'cultural scenarios', which evidence how people 'work reality into intelligible forms'.[14] Schieffelin maintains a lively sense of human agency labouring on and through an aesthetic standard, and of people improvising their interactions according to a feeling of what seems appropriate and what does not. By his account it is easy to see how such a standard is fundamentally flexible. It comes as no surprise, for example, that the Kalulis' elaborate Gisaro ceremony is recently acquired, yet in a relatively short period has been naturalized and is now vitally important to the Kaluli form of life. The notion of an underdetermining aesthetic standard allows for both the approximate predictability and the innovation, the repetition with constant variation, that are embodied in such history, such change of culture.

Of course other matters are also taught and learned: making arrowheads, weaving, reading, gardening, driving, playing the flute. These are not social aesthetic standards. Many of these procedures, or parts of these procedures, might best be called automatisms, because once learned we do them without thinking. The creation of automatisms makes for new forms of human causation, such as the effect of the past on the future, or of one person on others at a distance, allowed by writing and reading. But however important in human history, technical skills and automatisms are still dependent for their existence on a social aesthetic standard, just as—on Nicholas Humphrey's argument—simple technology among other social primates is dependent ultimately on reliable social relations.

Indeed it is possible to go further, because skills and tools exist not merely in a relationship between people and the material world, but are components of activities carried out in respect of other people. You, dear reader, now hold this physical object, this book, a product of many automatisms and of many relations between people and the natural world. But it is also the product of many social relations, and its present purpose, its existence—its ontology, if you will—in your hands is interactive and social, not physical: through it you relate to me, and beyond me to Ruth Benedict and Eric Wolf, to the Kaluli, the Ilongot, the Hamar, to Ben and Nigel, and perhaps again to yourself.

Creativity and repetition with constant variation

As I remarked, the underdetermining character of aesthetic standards, their nature as essentially fluid and re-interpretable, rather than closely controlling and pre-programmed, leaves an essential role to invention and creativity. This point was already implicit in Humphrey's argument. When he wrote of society on the analogy of a school, he used imagery of calculation or of exams, and therefore of social intellect working like an algorithm. But when he wrote of the sheer complexity of life in a shifting social setting he fell back on words such as creativity and imagination. Similarly the psychologist Sylvia Scribner writes that 'beneath the surface of [practical thinking] lie continuing acts of creativity—the invention of new ways of handling old and new problems'.[15] She considers relatively simple social and technical problems in the organization of work for a well-defined end. But the social world offers far more variegated, and far more ambiguous occasions in which people must devise a relationship, and so the capacities of sociality must be correspondingly more creative.

One way in which people are evidently both creative and concerned to get things right is in accounting for events in the recent past, in telling stories about what really happened. In those circumstances, as Rosaldo writes of the Ilongot, it is not just a matter of their applying 'schematic programs', but of using 'associative chains and images that tell what [events and motives] can be reasonably linked up with what'.[16] The force of 'reasonably' here is that more than one narrative line, and more than one identification of narrative with actual circumstances, are possible, are indeed defensibly true, so in any particular case the associative, creative linking may take one of many forms.

Creativity is a strong word, but in the sense I use it here it is connected with other, related cognitive acts that people commit in trying to grasp their complicated interactive experience. Not just Humphrey's 'calculation', but interpretation, evaluation, and inference might also be arrayed with creativity in the same spectrum. Thus one of the ideas which has accompanied the discovery of the traits I designate as sociality is a new notion of human communication. According to the old model: I first think my thoughts, wrap them in words, send them out through my mouth as vibrations which are received in your ear, and then they travel to your brain where you unwrap my thoughts from the words in which I wrapped them.

On the new mutualist model, even acts of common, everyday speech involve a crucial step of interpretation and inference. On this model two interlocutors do their best to establish with each other that they are having a conversation, that they are talking about the same thing, and that one wishes to hear from the other. To put it in Grice's terms, Utterer and Audience have to establish a relationship. Utterer utters, but what he is in effect doing is something rather different: he is placing his words in the public domain, and Audience still has to make a leap, to infer, to interpret, that they relate to previous topics in conversation, that they are meaningful, that they are directed to her, what they mean, and so forth.

The sense of interpretation, evaluation, inference, and even creativity on the one hand, and of effective communication on the other, is captured in this vivid example offered by the Russian philosopher Mikhail Bakhtin:

Two people are sitting in a room. They are both silent. Then one of them says, 'Well!' The other does not respond.

For us, as outsiders, this entire 'conversation' is utterly incomprehensible. . . . Nevertheless, this peculiar colloquy of two persons, consisting of only one—although, to be sure, one expressively intoned—word [the word in Russian is *tak*], does make perfect sense, is fully meaningful and complete.

In order to disclose the sense and meaning of this colloquy, we must analyze it. But what is it exactly that we can subject to analysis? Whatever pains we take with the purely verbal part of the utterance [i.e. however we try to unwrap the meaning from the words], we shall still not come a single step closer to an understanding of the whole colloquy.

. . . What is it we lack then? We lack the 'extraverbal context' that made the word *well* a meaningful locution for the listener. [We lack what they jointly know, and what they jointly know each other knows.] At the time the colloquy took place, both interlocutors *looked up* at the window and *saw* that it had begun to snow; *both knew* that it was already May and that it was high time for spring to come; . . . *they were both looking forward* to spring and *both were bitterly disappointed* by the late snowfall. On this 'jointly seen' (snowflakes outside the window), 'jointly known' (the time of year— May), and 'unanimously evaluated' (winter wearied of, spring looked forward to)—on all this the utterance *directly depends*, all this is seized in its actual, living import. . . . And yet all this remains without verbal specification or articulation. The snowflakes remain outside the window; the date, on the page of a calendar; the evaluation, in the psyche of the [interlocutors]; and nevertheless, all this is assumed in the word *well*.[17]

One way to think of creativity in this everyday sense is as play, the play of images, associations, feelings, symbolic tokens and their relations, such as might be found in music or mathematics or myths or plastic art. The point here is that play is not defined by its pointlessness. For, first, play with symbols, their relations, and their meanings, as for example in mathematical play, leads to genuine discovery, to ideas and assertions that can be validated intersubjectively. And second, play can be very serious: the word- and sound-play of children when they are learning to speak is not 'mere' play, but is experimentation and exercise with the very material of which speech is made.

The fundamental pattern here is that of making variations on a theme, as Douglas Hofstadter has so persuasively explained. That is, the patterned rhyming and alliteration of a four-year-old, as well as the repetition with constant variation in the music of, say, Bach, depends on there being a perceived theme which is then varied. In this respect creativity does not mean so much creation out of nothing, but rather embroidery on an already existing fabric. So creativity hovers very close to the way things actually are, and represents a 'slippage', as he puts it, from what is to what almost is. Hofstadter gives the following example of what he calls the ordinary, but still quite brilliant slippability of everyday life:

I overheard [the following variation on a theme] one evening this past summer in a very crowded coffeehouse, when a man walked in with a woman. He said to her, 'I'm sure glad I'm not a waitress here tonight!' This is a perfect example of a subjunctive variation on the given theme—but [unlike a laborious and deliberately made slippage] this one was made without external prompting. . . . [A deliberate slippage] looks positively mundane next to this casually tossed-off remark. And the remark was not considered to be particularly clever or ingenious by his companion. She merely agreed with the thought by saying 'Yeah.'

   I found this example not just mildly interesting, but highly provocative. If you try to analyze it, it would appear at first glance to force you as listener to imagine a sex-change operation performed in world record time. But when you simply *understand* the remark, you see that in actuality, there was no intention in the speaker's mind of bringing up such a bizarre image. His remark was much more figurative, much more abstract. It was based on an instantaneous perception of the situation, a sort of 'There-but-for-the-grace-of-God-go-I' feeling, which induces a quick flash to the effect of 'Simply because I am human, I can place myself in the shoes of that harried waitress—therefore *I could have been* that waitress.' Logical or not, this is the way our thoughts go.[18]

More than that, we can say that the man had understood the situation, and we have evidence that he understood it, because he made this slippage, this slight but vital movement from what is to what might have been. The slippage was the understanding.

   The next step is a short but necessary one, and that is from this routine understanding in a routine situation to those slightly more crucial occasions, namely the learning of a new theme and the discovery of new variations. Hofstadter gives us no reason to see the man's understanding as being, for him, a discovery. But nor is there in principle any difference between the first time one discovers that 'There-but-for-the-grace-of-God-go-I' feeling and the hundredth. Here learning and understanding are in effect the same thing. Both adults and children bring imagination and creativity—slippage—to learning, and especially to learning about situations. So do immigrant workers, captives and slaves, out-marrying women and in-marrying men, travellers and even anthropologists. These are all people who begin from scratch in a new society, who need to make the leap from ignorance and incompetence to understanding. So this everyday creativity suffices for everyday life, an everyday life that seems always the same but actually is always different; it suffices for children being inducted into that life; and it suffices for strangers.

But having taken that step, we cannot avoid taking another. At the core of my concern here is the question of, how humans manage to make history. What is it that allows them to make, say, their present society into another one? And the answer must in part be this: they do so using the same abilities that allow anyone to understand and deal with a situation which is new and unprecedented. This assumes, of course, that new situations do arise, that the common life which our social inventiveness creates will run beyond anyone's power wholly to control and guide it in familiar channels. This fact is enshrined in in Max Weber's perennially useful phrase 'unforeseen consequences', and I take it to be basic to the causal and metamorphic nature of social life. So making history is very often a matter of dealing creatively with already accomplished metamorphosis, a metamorphosis that presents itself as an accomplished fact. Moreover metamorphosis comes not individually, not atomically, but in a flow of action which is 'ephemeral, ambiguous and liable to change, not least as a consequence of one's own actions'. How else would we understand such a flow, and how else would we devise ways to respond to it? Only by moving subjunctively, by making what was not, but almost was, into what actually now is. Using the same creativity that lets them understand and recreate the old, the already given, people also create the new, new forms of relationship and new forms of common life.

Speech and stories

I turn finally to speech, and I stress that my concern is speech, not language. The distinction between the two was drawn early in the twentieth century by the French linguist Saussure, who took the main concern of linguistics to be language (*langue*), the abstract mental structure, the set of relations between different words in a vocabulary, and between kinds of words in syntax. This abstraction may be made to show a degree of clarity and certainty not so easily found in the messier realities of actual speech (*parole*).

For most of the twentieth century this view of speech, namely that it is to be studied as a largely or purely formal system, as language, has dominated. In recent years the influential linguist Noam Chomsky has even argued that the knowledge of language is quite different from other kinds of knowledge. It is specifiable as a system of grammatical rules which ultimately have a deep structure which is innate in human individuals. This deep grammatical structure underlies the surface structure of the actual grammar of any given language. Moreover he argued that this is shown by the speed with which human children learn the complexities of language, compared to the relative slowness with which they learn other skills. To this inherited mental mechanism he gave the name Language Acquisition Device, abbreviated as LAD.

Yet many of the same charges could be laid against the LAD idea that I earlier laid against notions of culture. It is fundamentally asocial and individualistic, taking no cognizance of human sociality. Consequently researchers are beginning to explore more interactive and social perspectives. Here, for example, is Jerome Bruner, who is still willing to use the LAD notion while putting it in a different context:

Language acquisition 'begins' before the child utters his first lexico-grammatical speech. It begins when mother and infant create a predictable format of interaction that can serve as a micrcosm for communicating and for constituting a shared reality. . . . [The infant] could not achieve . . . language acquisition without, and the same time, possessing a unique and predisposing set of language-learning capacities—something akin to what Noam Chomsky has called a

Language Acquisition Device, LAD. But the infant's Language Acquisition Device could not function without the aid given by an adult who enters with him into a transactional format. That format, initially under the control of the adult, provides a Language Acquisition Support system, LASS. . . . In a word, it is the interaction between LAD and LASS that makes it possible for the infant to enter the linguistic community—and, at the same time, the culture to which the language gives access.[20]

But the psychologist Michael Tomasello takes this argument much further, and in the process rejects the notions of a special LAD and of a universal and innate grammar:

Language and its acquisition obviously rely crucially on basic processes of perception, attention, categorization, learning, memory, and other general cognitive processes. But in most cases it is the social versions of these—social perception, social attention, social cognition, and social learning—that are of crucial importance in acquiring the unique aspects of language that distinguish it from other human activities. Once human language, and particularly its systemic properties as expressed in grammar, is viewed within the framework of these social/cultural skills, its learnability becomes no more difficult to conceive . . . than the acquisition of many other cultural skills and conventions.[21]

These issues are far from settled. But in what follows I take the view that the capacities for understanding grammar and for understanding a world jointly, interactively, with other people, are inseparable from one another. Together they amount to speech.

Speech is therefore a mutual, intersubjective activity, and central to this mutuality is the fact that people do things to, for, with, and with respect to other people through speech. With speech we promise, threaten, ask, pronounce, warn, reassure, and agree, amongst many other things. The sense of work on and with people being done by speech can be seen in the business of agreeing. At first glance, we might imagine that agreeing is, say, a matter of some state of affairs in the world. First one knows it, and now both know it. And of course, when Nigel agrees with Ben (it turns out they did manage to greet each other, even to stop and chat) that it is a pretty foul, typically English day, there is certainly some information in the agreement. But that information does not, in fact, concern new data about the physical world, to the effect that the cold rain is slanting in from Siberia. Neither Ben nor Nigel imagines that the other is anything but painfully aware of that. Rather the agreement affirms, to start with, a piece of second-order intentionality, that they both know, and know that the other knows all too well, that it is raining. Here of course we are back with Bakhtin's 'Well!', but the interlocutors are less in sympathy, have more work to do to achieve harmony. And in fact the information, and the mutual action, does not stop there, for what is actually on the way to being achieved, step by step, is further mutual understanding: about each other's willingness to chat, to be friendly, to open up a space for further interchange. From one point of view this is information, no doubt, but such information is the stuff that relationships are made of. So from another point of view, Ben and Nigel are actually working on, and with, each other, not on their mutual knowledge of meteorological matters.

In the recent history of our ideas of language such 'speech acts'—the phrase is that of the philosophers Austin and Searle[22]—seem to be special cases which are secondary to the primary function of speech as the outward garb of inward, disembodied, representational, descriptive, propositional thought. On this old view of communication, thoughts are things that are true or false propositions about the physical world, and speech is just used as their wrapping. But if speech is viewed as a component of human sociality such disembodied thought seems, on the contrary, a special and peculiar case of speech: unuttered speech in a descriptive mode without an explicit interlocutor. It may very well be that such internal speech, such thinking to oneself more or less in words, does exist and has deep roots in our evolutionary past. But it could only come to seem the norm, the essential form of an inner language, after many developments. One such development, which I have described in *The Buddha*, is the invention of a generalized mode of speech which is directed to a general, rather than a specific, audience and to the future. Such disembodied, apparently contextless, abstract philosophical thought was invented, evidently quite independently, in both ancient India and ancient Greece. These ideas and practices were then given new life in a new form of social relationship by the use of writing, and of printing, to allow writers to address anonymous strangers and posterity.

The sense of simultaneously informing and acting on others is combined powerfully in what is arguably the most information-laden speech activity of all: story-telling. Story-telling, as I use it here, can refer to very minimal occasions, such as a glancing remark which reveals to my wife that I did, after all, go to the bank today. But it can also refer to the narration of the *Iliad* or to the writing and reading of *The Decline and Fall of the Roman Empire*. Indeed, story-telling points to what is perhaps the most powerful human capacity, which is to understand one's own and others' moods, plans, and beliefs, and the metamorphosis of those mental states, in a long flow of action. From this perspective humans can understand a complex social setting with a long time dimension, they can understand changes in that setting, and beyond that they can also urge on each other particular information about, and interpretations of, that flow. Such narrative thought lies at the heart of sociality, and I devote the next chapter to it.

Putting it back together

These abilities into which I have anatomized human sociality are not necessarily irreducible, nor do they cover every characteristically human capacity. The actual tools by which cognitive ethologists or psychologists might explore the differences between primate species might have to be a good deal finer and less encompassing. Nevertheless I want to make an anthropologist's point, and urge that these capacities do work together, that they produce a unitary effect, namely the power to create, maintain, and change forms of social life.

This chapter comprises my fundamental answer to the question of how people came to have history. In what follows I leave biological and—except for some parts of the next chapter—psychological matters behind, and explore some of the implications of sociality. I look at narrative thought and how it forms action, at an actual example of people understanding a great metamorphic movement in social life, and at the character of anthropology. For though anthropology is only a minor theme, a footnote to human sociality, it does depend crucially on one facet of sociality: the ability to come to imagine the stories of others, others with whom one has at first no imaginable connection.

5

Reading Minds and Reading Life

IN *Actual Minds, Possible Worlds* the psychologist Jerome Bruner sets out a contrast between what he calls the paradigmatic mode of thought and the narrative mode. The paradigmatic mode is that of philosophy, logic, mathematics, and the physical sciences, whereas the narrative mode concerns the human condition. He remarks that the narrative mode is little understood and speculates as follows:

Perhaps one of the reasons for this is that story must construct two landscapes simultaneously. One is the landscape of action, where the constituents are the arguments of action: agent, intention or goal, situation, instrument, something corresponding to a 'story grammar.' The other landscape is the landscape of consciousness: what those involved in the action, know, think, or feel, or do not know, think, or feel. The two landscapes are essential and distinct: it is the difference between Oedipus sharing Jocasta's bed before and after he learns from the messenger that she is his mother.[1]

The notions of a narrative mode and a dual landscape are, I think, potentially very fruitful. They go to the heart of the human capacity to imagine, to construe and misconstrue, others' mental states, and beyond that they point to the fuller amplitude of human sociality as a whole. But these, and other ideas I refer to in this chapter, are also distinctly psychological in their character. That is, they answer to psychology's burning question: what is the nature of mind? I do not in fact think that anthropology and psychology are, or should be, so clearly separated as this may imply. But I do want to suggest that some movement from psychological ideas to anthropological ones is necessary. This movement is very like that of disassembly and reassembly as described by Eric Wolf. The psychological ideas disassemble the complexities of human interaction into plainly investigable parts; but the anthropological need is to reassemble those parts into something that corresponds more closely to the complex flow of human social and historical life.

In *Actual Minds* Bruner was concerned chiefly with the landscape of consciousness and with the narrative mode as exercised by adult competence, especially in literature. Janet Astington has taken the ideas in another direction, towards 'Narrative and the Child's Theory of Mind'. She confirms that a crucial change occurs between 3 and 5 years of age, when children begin to understand the difference between the two landscapes, the difference between what is true and what someone thinks is true, between 'the weaver knows that the loom is empty' and 'the Emperor thinks that the loom must have cloth on it'.[2] These issues she approaches from a theory-of-mind viewpoint, a psychological perspective that regards children as forming their own, so to speak, folk psychologies, theories of mind, about how their own and other minds work. Her conclusions are drawn from a deliberately impoverished experimental setting, in which one experimenter relates to one, or at most two, children, giving them narrowly defined tasks to perform. But even in this closed setting the children's performance hints at something more as well. Astington notes, for example, that the placing of an experimental task in a narrative frame facilitates children's understanding, quite apart from any additional information conveyed.

This implies, I think, that the narrative mode might amount to something more, to something beyond the individual theories or competences into which it might be analysed. We might usefully think of a distinct capacity, narrative thought, a property of the human species which differentiates it from other species. Mind-reading or higher-order intentionality is a necessary foundation for narrative thought. But that is not the end of the matter, for narrative thinking provides a yet more powerful form of mind-reading. Such thought allows humans to grasp a longer past and a more intricately conceived future, as well as a more variegated social environment. Narrative thinking allows people to comprehend a complex flow of action and to act appropriately within it. In other words, narrative thinking is the very process we use to understand the social life around us. It supports directly the more elaborate and mutable sociality which differentiates humans from their cousins, the other social primates. In this perspective the link between the landscape of consciousness and the landscape of action cannot so easily be disjoined for purposes of exposition, as Bruner and Astington disjoined them. For in our evolutionary past, as in our later history, the landscapes of action and of consciousness have been part of one real and determining flow of deeds and mortal consequences.

Some sense of the reassembly, the reinstatement of atomic abilities to their living setting, is conveyed in these remarks by the psychologists Trevarthen and Logotheti, writing of that same crucial period in children's development:

In every culture, the period of 3 to 5 years is one in which children begin to discover wider opportunities for co-operation as well as the harsher aspects of human conflict and aggression. They begin by imitating and comparing, and then gain *imagination for real co-operation in a narrative drama where pretended roles complement each other*. Emotions of liking and disliking are strongly expressed in play. When play breaks down, fights can become mean and bitter. Friendships and antipathies last, but are open to negotiation and change. Confident and joyful sharing of experiences, and of the motives that give them significance, depends on acceptance of rules and the exercise of communicative skills that facilitate agreement.[3] [*My emphasis.*]

This child's world as described by Trevarthen and Logotheti is an altogether more intricate, risky, and entangling place. It is in fact more like human social life, and certainly more like the threshold to an adult social life that adult competence must match. To think of people as holding a theory concerning others' ideas and beliefs is perhaps a reasonable first step in trying to understand how we master social complexities. But in order to enter into play, pretend roles, or negotiations over friendship and antipathy, the child—and *a fortiori* the adult—

must build a more sophisticated understanding of a social setting than mind-reading in a narrow sense can provide.

Research programmes

In the following list I have tried to convey the anthropologist's aspiration to reassembly and integration by contrasting some anthropological research programmes with those of psychology and primate ethology. I do not want to make these comparisons invidious: psychologists and behavioural biologists are building a view of humans from the simple to the complex, whereas anthropologists begin from the complex. But I will nevertheless want to argue that some features of the human mind—or better, of human 'distributed processing'—appear only when the complex is taken into account.

Consider the following 'primal scenes'. These are, so to speak, the stage directions which determine what will be considered of interest to one discipline or another.

1. A generic individual (with theories or mind modules) confronts the environment. (This model underlies experiments with animals, for example, or people working with experimental apparatus rather than interactively with other people.)

2. Generic individuals confront each other and their environment in a shifting social setting with a narrow temporal horizon. (This more social setting is characteristic of Nicholas Humphrey's view of primate interaction, and of many theory-of-mind experiments.)

3. Individuals typed by age, sex, and rank confront each other and the physical environment in a face-to-face community over some period of time. (This is characteristic of longitudinal ethological studies, as of the chimpanzees in Gombe or at the Arnhem Zoo.)

4. Role types, based on named individuals but distinguished by achieved and/or marked social statuses, relate to each other and the physical environment in a face-to-face community with a weighty cultural tradition and complex social organization. (This is the traditional characteristic view of ethnography of Benedict or Radcliffe-Brown.)

5. Named individuals with shifting role types relate to each

other and the physical environment in a face-to-face community with complex social organization, a long past, an uncertain future, and a rolling cultural heritage. (This is the sort of historically oriented ethnography that anthropologists have gradually come to pursue.)

6. Those listed in point 5 join with others, and against others, in interest groups, ethnic groups, and classes to remake their heritage (of role types and groups) in the face of shifting global social and social environmental forces. (This is the ethnography of Wolf, the fully reassembled picture, which is in many ways still unachieved.)

I have surely over-simplified, but this list will help me to make three important points.

The first concerns the difference of temporal perspective between the top of the list and the bottom. Humphrey, for example, writes that social primates inhabit a world where, as I have already repeated, 'the evidence on which their calculations are based is ephemeral, ambiguous and liable to change, not least as a consequence of their own actions'. The key word is 'ephemeral'. This is not, as I first thought, a world without time, but one whose temporal horizons are very close and which does not, at least so far as the social primates are concerned, suffer the burden of a laboriously planned future or a long-remembered past. Similarly, experiments in the theory of mind are usually very brief sets of actions. But in contrast the settings studied under the rubric of no. 4 above, and even more so those under 5 and 6, are ones with broader views on time, bringing into consideration the lifetime of individuals and the longer continuity or discontinuity, over generations or centuries, of families and other institutions.

Second, the perspectives at the top of the list are socially simple. The experimental settings reported in this volume have at most three roles: experimenter, subject, and perhaps one other. Even the experimental stories have only two or three characters. On the other hand humans considered by anthropologists are socially variegated on many dimensions. Within a family or small community different kin relations distinguish one person from another: mothers, mother's brothers, grandparents and great-grandparents, daughters, cross and parallel cousins. Besides these relations, and often involving the same people, other social, political, or economic distinctions might be made: woman and (uninitiated) girl, healer and patient, judge and plaintiff, headman and villager, queen and subject, host and guest, customer and trader, master and slave.

Finally, the temporal and social perspectives are intimately involved with each other. For in human societies regarded as such, the types or characters are frequently ones arrived at over a large part of a life cycle: a doctor or healer trains for years, a woman becomes a wife after being initiated and achieving her society's version of the age of reason, a peasant son succeeds to his patrimony as head of household only with age and his father's retirement or death. Moreover, these gradually attained characteristics of persons occur in a mutually construed flow of events extending beyond any one person's life cycle into the past and the future. The acquisition of his patrimony by the peasant son, for example, is intelligible because of, indeed is constituted by, the previous inheritance by his father, and his father's father, and so forth.

Such a flow of events includes performative acts—the vows of marriage, initiation into manhood, conferral of a degree, coronation as a king—which are constituted by ceremony and a form of words which bring about a change in the status of a person or group. Such acts are constituted by, and are only conceivable within, a wider social and temporal setting: a church, a community, a university. In the larger evolutionary perspective the peculiarity of this human trait is highlighted if we ask how such roles differ from those we might attribute to a social primate of another species. For example, ethologists are clear that the role 'newly immigrant adult male' is an important one in other primate societies. Such a role appears among ourselves in many ways: a new commander is appointed to your unit; an immigrant doctor joins your local medical practice; a new apprentice gets a job with your company; a new prisoner arrives in your cell. Such characteristically human movements are only intelligible in the light of, and indeed are constituted by, a much larger and more complex social background than those found among our primate cousins.

And finally there are other and larger events which may not be performative alone, but which all the same create a new and long-lasting state of affairs and set of characters. A murder takes place, a feud begins, and new identities with new relations of enmity spring into being. Famine strikes and the populations of whole regions are rendered refugees and dependants. A colonial power arrives and society is transformed from top to bottom.

Anthropologists, sociologists, and social historians have one way of conceiving such events and arrangements, while the people involved have another. Different participants have different understandings of the action. But what I take to be ineluctably true is that human beings have an effective capacity which enables them to create, to understand, and to act within these ramifying complexities, complexities extended through social rather than physical space and unfolding in an event-filled rather than abstract time.

Narrative thought

It is this capacity which I want to designate as narrative thought, a capacity to cognize not merely immediate relations between oneself and another, but many-sided human interactions carried out over a considerable period. We might say that humans understand characters, which embody the understanding of rights, obligations, expectations, propensities, and intentions in oneself and many different others; and plots, which show the consequences and evaluations of a multifarious flow of actions. So narrative thought consists not merely in telling stories, but of understanding complex nets of deeds and attitudes. Another way to put this would be to say that human beings perceive any current action within a large temporal envelope, and within that envelope they perceive any given action, not as a response to the immediate circumstances or current mental state of an interlocutor or of oneself, but as part of an unfolding story. (I owe this latter formulation to Paul Harris.)

I use both 'plot' and 'character' here as terms of art. I think it essential that character be conceived very broadly, since it must comprehend simultaneously individuals as having statuses and roles—that is, as standing in well-precedented relation to one another—and individuals as having idiosyncratic histories and propensities. There must be some room for abstraction, so that people can be understood as acting with a generic set of obligations and rights: as, for example, a lawyer, or a king, or a mother acts with obligations and rights towards clients, subjects, or sons and daughters. But the particularity of one person rather than another, of Hannah rather than Amy, must also be grasped at the same time. We must understand not just the type of the grandfather, for example, with all the relevant expectations about how he should act within a family, but also this grandfather's individual propensities: mellowness or irascibility, friendliness or aloofness, wisdom or foolishness, and so forth. In this respect the notion of character resembles that of the social philosopher Alfred Schutz's 'type', which combines both individual and generic characteristics.[4]

I pause for a moment to mark something very important about this idea. To combine an idea of generic social role with that of individual characteristics goes very strongly against traditional practice in social and cultural anthropology and in sociology. There the idea has been to abstract and discard the particularity of individuals in order to stress their generic character. But if we are to have a notion of people being able not just to understand things in general, but to grasp and act on particular circumstances, then we need narrative thought to have more than merely generic power. We need to know what to do in this conversation with this particularly difficult colleague, not just what to do with people we call 'colleagues' in general. This is, I think, a necessary corollary of the sense of reassembly that I am advocating, and I will write more about it later.

Characters with their relationships are also set in a flow of events, a plot, with its sense of plans, goals, situations, acts, and outcomes. As Bruner puts it, narrative thought concerns 'intention and action and the vicissitudes and consequences that mark their course'.[5] Plots embody what a character or characters did to, or about, or with some other character or characters, for what reasons, how people's attitudes, beliefs, and intentions thereby changed, and what followed on from that. To comprehend a plot is therefore to have some notion of the changes in an inner landscape of thought in the participants as well as the outer landscape of events. Indeed the two are inseparable, because the metamorphosis of thoughts entails the metamorphosis of social relations and vice versa.

This metamorphosis arises from the fact that people do things because of what others feel, think, and plan. I may apologize *because* she was *angry*. Or I may buy her a Michael Innes thriller *because* she will *enjoy* it. I may explain why I made that remark in a department meeting *because* my colleague apparently *misunderstood* it. Government policy may be changed *because* a rival party *plans* an effective campaign on some issue. Many, perhaps all, forms of law are based upon the attribution of intentions or knowledge to those held accountable. In war deeds are done because of what the enemy think or believe or desire or plan. And it is difficult to conceive of conducting the most elementary interaction of everyday life without attribution of intentions and knowledge to others: for example, even the simplest conversation is based on mutual attribution of states of mind to each other by interlocutors.

So when we understand a plot, we understand changes of mind and of relationship, changes brought about by acts. Moreover, we are able to link acts, thoughts, and their consequences together so that we grasp the metamorphosis of each other's thoughts and each other's situations in a flow of action. In this perspective character and plot are indivisible, for we understand character only as it is revealed to us in the flow of action, and we only understand plot as the consequence of characters acting with characteristic beliefs and intentions. With such narrative understanding people orient themselves and act in an accountable manner, sensibly, effectively, and appropriately, creating and re-creating complex skeins of social life.

Oedipus Rex

Let me use Bruner's example, *Oedipus the King*, to illustrate what I mean. On one hand, Sophocles' play could be no better example of the power and intricacy of immediate and temporally simple human mind-reading capacities. From the beginning the drama plays on the difference between the audience's received knowledge of Oedipus' actual condition of incest and parricide and the false state of mind of Oedipus on the stage. To cast the situation in a form which emphasizes the layers of mind-reading involved we could write:

> We *know* that Oedipus *believes* [falsely] that he is innocent, and is not the cause of the city's pollution.

And even during the early scene with Teiresias, whose prophetic knowledge of the real state of affairs is not accepted by Oedipus, this configuration is wound more tightly until:

> We *know* that Oedipus *believes* [falsely] that Teiresias seeks to *deceive* Oedipus and the citizens; but we also *know* that Teiresias *knows* that in fact Oedipus *deceives* himself.

Sophocles drives this interplay of ignorance and knowledge further and further until just before the revelation, when Jocasta, beginning to realize the truth, implores Oedipus not to pursue his enquiry into his origins: 'I beg you—do not hunt this out—I beg you, / If you have any care for your own life / What I am suffering is enough.'[6]

> We *grasp* that Jocasta *fears* that she might *know* what Oedipus *hopes/fears* the herdsman might *know* about Oedipus' birth.

In this case we even have Jocasta reading her own mind, fearing that she might know something. Looked at in this way, the play is constituted through its use and manipulation of humans' abilities to construe and to track complex states of mind in themselves and others. The drama is literally made of mind-reading. Moreover, action is set out as taking place in a very narrow time-span, a few hours perhaps, and only with few characters, so that the plot is a good deal closer to the experimentalist's chronological and social simplicity than to the anthropologist's complexity.

But it is misleading to think that the story of Oedipus is circumscribed by mind-reading alone. Narrative thought is no less an ingredient of *Oedipus the King*, and indeed the wider envelope within which the action takes place covers most of an ordinary human life. It includes the union of Laius, Oedipus' father, with Jocasta, his mother, Oedipus' own birth, his exposure on the hillside and rescue, Oedipus' murder of Laius, his accession to the throne and marriage to Jocasta, and the begetting of his children. Without this framework the short-term play of mind-reading would be senseless. And indeed, since the story of Oedipus also looks forward to his death and apotheosis at Colonus and to the fate of Thebes in later episodes, for a Greek audience the temporal envelope extended into the future as well.

So if *Oedipus the King* is unintelligible without mind-reading, it is equally so without understanding the notions of a king and queen, a husband and wife, a mother and son, without the conception of a human life-span and its proper stations, and without the notion of what constraints and possibilities govern long-lasting relationships. It would also be unintelligible without some notion of Oedipus' idiosyncratic character, including the intelligence and heroism which allowed him to confront the Sphinx and solve its riddle. Nor could we grasp the action without being able to conceive such a change in statuses as Oedipus' taking of marriage vows or being crowned king, or Jocasta's giving birth to legitimate children. And finally, I suggest, it would be incomprehensible were not statuses, changes in status, and the transformation of relationships, attitudes, and beliefs knitted together into a larger, developing, narrative whole. The fate of Oedipus, to blind himself, and of Jocasta, to hang herself, would seem poorly motivated had not the tempo and relation of events, both on stage and in the larger context, led inexorably to that outcome.

It is for this reason that the separation of a landscape of consciousness from a landscape of action is finally unviable: for the tale is made indissolubly of Oedipus' relations to others, of the characters' beliefs, feelings, and intentions in regard to each other, of public events, and of their unfolding together in a compelling sequence. Only this reassembled whole, this integrated consciousness, can explain the audience's understanding of events, or the ability of the characters themselves to act accountably in the plot.

Making events

However, it is misleading to conceive narrative thought only after the pattern of an audience understanding Oedipus. For that example sets narrative thought in a passive mould, as a capacity which enables humans to comprehend successfully a social world which is already formed, already given, and immutable. For purposes of research into mind-reading or narrative thought it may be easier to take this view, since to consider the social environment as shifting introduces complexities that are very difficult to reckon. But in an evolutionary perspective narrative thought must have been important as an active competence as well, one which enabled humans to shape events, and indeed society, through plans or projects. I suggest, in fact, that the human capacity for planning and for having long-term projects is at base not different from narrative thought.

A plan may be conceived on a short or a long scale. A plan on a very short scale, such as those envisaged by Humphrey or in some more complex psychological experiments, may perhaps be directly grasped as an immediate intention, belief, or attitude through mind-reading in a narrow sense. Ben's intention as he busies himself with his kettle to offer a cup of tea to his colleague Nigel might be read by a Nigel equipped with higher-order intentionality. But a long-term plan, such as Ben's design to woo Nigel and get him to help Ben displace Angela as head of department, appears only through a grasp of Ben's character and through a casting of events in a long enough perspective. Only then might Ben be understood as a schemer and Ben's actions be revealed as a campaign, not a random series of interactions. More important, Ben could only be a schemer if he could project the unfolding of his scheme over a considerable period of time and in the face of vicissitudes. This dimension of human life would appear more clearly if we read *Macbeth* or *Othello* rather than *Oedipus*.

Let me look at the example of Ben more closely. On the one hand there are the larger narrative assumptions which are part of Nigel and Ben's setting, assumptions analogous to those which enable an audience to understand Oedipus. Ben and Nigel understand what a chairperson is, what it means for a university to have a relatively democratic structure, and therefore how a chairperson might be chosen or elected. More to the point, they connect these larger assumptions with an actual history, the development of the power of the chairperson in their university and Angela's appointment as chair several years ago.

Moreover for Ben there is a yet larger history as well, one which he tells both himself and others. Angela epitomizes what Ben regards as an unfortunate and backward influence in (shall we say) the discipline of anthropology. She is steering the department towards an emphasis on biological and evolutionary interests. Ben, as the faithful student of the celebrated Professor Zehetgrueber, represents a concern with cultural symbols. This is indeed the department Zehetgrueber founded, the one which should carry forward his project of symbolic anthropology. Ben could not understand what was going on, let alone act, if he could not put characters together with plots: he could not understand himself as the student of Professor Zehetgrueber or Angela as an abidingly deleterious influence. It is the casting of Angela as a villain in the developing story of Zehetgrueber and his apostles that furnishes him with orientation and direction. And as action develops and circumstances change, he will be able to orient himself according to that narrative understanding, or according to some new and further understanding which develops out of it. Narrative thinking would be pretty poor stuff if it could not adjust to changing circumstances, to the metamorphic character of human life.

There is a finer-grained story too, one which concerns the patterning of events on a day-by-day, even hour-by-hour scale, and the forming of action on that scale. The meeting to arrange the election of the new chairperson is next month. Ben's close friend and ally, Lotte, has agreed with Ben that things have gone too far and that they need to change the direction of the department. They must work quickly. They cannot count on everyone agreeing, but there are some who might come around, among them Nigel. Ben agrees to approach Nigel while Lotte approaches others. Indeed—and now we are back with Ben about to offer Nigel a cup of tea—Ben will not mention his conversations with Lotte, for the fastidious Nigel does not wholly approve of Lotte: for one thing, she brings her knitting to department meetings. Rather Ben will address Nigel directly and appeal to his shared concern with symbolic anthropology. And as Ben now hands Nigel that cup of tea, he looks very closely to see Nigel's reaction as the topic of the chair is raised. Ben will be able to narrate to Lotte the course and timing of his conversation with Nigel. From that they will measure Nigel's inclinations and decide how next to move. So far events go according to plan, that is, according to narrative consciousness.

Note further that in such circumstances informing and knowing can amount to doing. Suppose that Nigel reacts with unexpected warmth to Ben's veiled suggestion that he, Ben, might be willing to stand. The situation changes. Ben, by their mutual knowledge of his proposed candidature, actually comes a step closer to being a candidate. Ben could go back to Lotte with a very different prospect than the one he began with. In this respect a change in the landscape of consciousness— namely the knowing by Ben that Nigel agrees and the knowing by Nigel that Ben is willing—would be a change in the landscape of action. The action might have been unintended as such by either party, though it fits well with Ben's unfolding plan.

It is possible to get a sense of this active character of narrative consciousness by asking a diagnostic question, suggested to me by the anthropologist Esther Goody: to what extent does narrative understanding happen in individual heads and to what extent is it constructed by social action?

Perhaps the best way to answer the question is to change the imagery. I argued earlier that people are connected to one another as in a taut, reverberating web. Because of their elaborated self-and-other awareness, events, feelings, and knowledge in one part of the web affect other parts of it. As a psychologist would disassemble the web, the understandings of the web might be in individual minds. But because the understandings are mutual and reciprocal, they are not really to be understood as individual phenomena, but as being in their nature interpersonal or intersubjective. In that respect the reciprocal knowing that Ben and Nigel have just shared is a joint construction which changes the character of the web, moves it forward into a new state. It will move a great deal further forward, of course, when the knowledge of Ben's candidature shakes the department as a whole. Then the reciprocal knowing that, say, Ben and Angela share, that he is going to oppose her, will demonstrate something else: how intersubjective narrative understanding has the potential to be neither friendly, mutually agreed, nor agreeable.

I think the notion of the taut web can do more work as well. First, everyone in Ben and Nigel's department is, whether they wish it or not, part of that web: they are responsive to each other by virtue of being *colleagues* in a *university department* with a *chairperson*. These are some of the generic characteristics of their situation as a social anthropologist would disassemble them. Department members have a social contract, though in fact no one ever signed it or would agree on its contents, and that social contract is renewed or altered by each interaction between members of the department. In this respect even a lackadaisical ignorance of events, or a wilful refusal to participate, count as attitudes directed towards others and oneself. These too make the web vibrate, or shift a thread here or there.

But—and this is another implication of the web imagery— this commonality, this mutuality of the web does not mean that there is only one single story about the web and its history to be told. Academics are at least as likely as anyone to look back and recount events as if everyone's motives were transparent, and as if events flowed naturally and explicably on. But in fact such a story will be only a partial one, told from a perspective for a certain purpose. No one at the time could have had access to all the information that would make such a story universally correct or absolutely encompassing, nor could anyone in retrospect tell such a thing, the ultimate story. All actually narrated stories are really only the story so far from X's point of view. Many different versions might agree on some points, as on who is now chairperson, but they could diverge widely on others, such as who the best candidate for the chair will be in the election. Some stories might have a great deal more thoroughness and comprehensiveness than others. So far as I can tell, Ben knows more than Nigel, who remained forever unaware of Ben's complicity with Lotte. And Angela's is a very different version of events again.

Recapitulation

So we need not think of narrative thought as being infallible, or as producing a canonical or impersonally correct and universally accepted account. All that I have asked of narrative understanding is that it enable humans to interact with complexity. They need only agree and understand each other to the extent that they work more or less reliably together, to keep the social flow moving; and of course it is often the misunderstandings that keep things moving all the more energetically.

The challenge was to produce a view of humans that makes them out to be something more than robots performing according to the programme of culture, but something less than omniscient and omnipotent beings with knowledge and power to make the social web just as they like. There must be room for the causal character of things, so that events can take a turn intended by no one. To make these points I have so far used fiction, and a fictionalized account based on experience, rather than an ethnographic one, because it has allowed me to reach into otherwise inaccessible corners of consciousness. I now turn to ethnography.

The Bull and the Saint

IN this chapter I relate and interpret a story in its setting. I encountered the story while doing fieldwork among Jains in Kolhapur, Maharashtra State, India. So one thing I want to do here is move from fiction to something which has the great advantage of actually having happened. The story itself, taken in isolation, is very striking, and has fascinated me for a decade since I first heard it. It concerns the heroic act, about a hundred years ago, of a spiritually heroic man, and reveals in a vivid way the view that Jains have of their religion and of the nature of sentient beings. It is an ethnographic gem, the sort of illustration of a way of life that ethnographers happen across with pleasure and use in their books with immense satisfaction.

That is the story in isolation. The story in the setting of its telling, however, meant a great deal more. For one thing, it was told as a contribution to a subtle dispute, an argument over how to present Jainism. Its import, so far as I could see, was that a tale of such heroism is worth a thousand words of abstract doctrine. Or, to put it in Jerome Bruner's terms, the teller of the story seemed to imply that narratives are superior to reasoning, that narrative thought is not just an alternative form, but is actually better than paradigmatic thought. This is one theme in what follows.

For another thing, the actual circumstances of the telling of the story seemed to be tightly bound to the meaning of the story. The very fact that the story was narrated by a particular someone to a particular someone else added something that was not, strictly speaking, to be found among its actual words. This is another theme. Indeed as I thought about it I came to realize that its telling was very simply part of its meaning and its meaning was part of its telling. I could extricate neither without either dragging the other along or else doing violence to the sense of the whole. So the story was also coloured by those present at its telling: by me, the foreigner and listener, by its narrator, and by others involved.

Now in one sense this may seem to have rather dizzying implications. Does it mean that the translator must intrude, that every ethnographic picture of a society must include an anthropologist in the foreground, cluttering up an otherwise clear and interesting scene? In another sense it merely repeats a point I have already made and which I believe to be unexceptionable. In the last chapter I pointed out that stories such as the one told by Ben to Lotte about his meeting with Nigel, or the story told by the messenger to Oedipus, are part of a flow of action. They are interpersonal and intersubjective. Each story has, no doubt, a series of possible meanings that could be parsed by writing the story down and sending it through a hatch into a roomful of linguists. But each story's real meaning arises directly in relation to the state of the web of persons who are concerned with the narrative. Similarly, if I rush into a police station with my shirt torn and a bleeding lip and blurt out to the desk sergeant a garbled story that I have just been robbed in the street outside, there is no disjunction between the flow of action and the account of that action: the setting and the story are one. Not just the garbled and perhaps incomplete words, but matters such as who is speaking to whom, make all the difference, just as it made all the difference when one Russian said 'Well!' to the other.

In one respect the story I am about to tell is no different from the stories of the last chapter. It and the others are about characters and their states of mind in a plot. They are all the sorts of things we must understand in order to act accountably in a flow of action, and they all require narrative thought. But there is a pivotal difference. The present story was not, or at least not explicitly, about a present flow of action but about something that happened a hundred years ago. Moreover, as I later learned, it is a story pretty widely known among Jains in Kolhapur. Indeed I found it in print as part of a biography of the hero. So in that respect it has a more general character. It has had, and will have, other tellings or writings-and-readings in other settings. This draws our attention away from the story in its setting to the story itself, as a disembodied plot or perhaps as a series of words. It appears in this light to have a life of its own, as a legend or a myth has such a life.

In fact, it appears to be part of what anthropologists would with ease and assurance call Jain culture; it is one of the myriad, very variegated, items that make up the common knowledge and practice of Jainism as held by Jains in the area. Now from the beginning of my argument I rejected an ontology of human life which regards individuals as relating directly to some mystically shared object, culture. But here is a case—and a case of a very common kind, for there are a great many other things as well that all Jains know or know how to do—which would seem to be best and most easily explained in just such terms. It seems that we could draw a thought bubble above the heads of the, say, thirty thousand Jains who happen to know the story, fill the thought bubble with the story and all the other related shared items, and call it Jain culture. After all, the story is one among many common items which exemplify Jain attitudes and values. It can be catalogued among the mental objects which distinguish Jains from others. So why labour to show that the story has an intersubjective, interactive significance when it fits so nicely into a known category?

I will answer the question only briefly now. It is necessary, as I have already suggested, to be able to specify how one way of life differs from others. The concept of culture has proven immensely useful in this, as a way of disassembling the complexities of actual social life. Indeed I will shortly be offering a typical description of Jain notions in just such a disassembling style. But I also want to reassemble social life, and such reassembly requires among other things that we have a clear idea of just what or who is doing what to whom in the flow of events.

Here, I suggest, the concept of culture cannot suffice, or at least it cannot suffice if we think that people do things just because of what they have in their thought bubbles. Few anthropologists would express their notion of culture so grossly, but many do in fact practice as though culture makes people do things, rather as some biologically oriented writers have asserted that genes make us do things. In the study of India, for example, the great French anthropologist Louis Dumont has stressed that it is a structure of ideas in the minds of Indians that makes them act as they do.[1] This is just one example of a tendency among all us anthropologists, a tendency to go some way, or a long way, farther than our evidence will permit in lending reality and autonomous causal force to culture.

The philosopher and the story-teller

I now turn to the story. The Digambar Jains of Kolhapur, or at least those whom I knew best, are urban businessmen. They were eager to speak of Jainism, and I was frequently offered a long impromptu religio-philosophical lecture. It is a well-marked local communicative genre, a way of speaking favoured by some, in which one speaker discourses at length on a morally uplifting topic to another. I may add that I saw a similar treatment being accorded by Jains to each other, usually by an elder to a younger man or to women.

On the occasion in question I was sitting in the office of a dealer in agricultural supplies, whom I will designate simply as 'the philosopher' or 'Mr P'. The following is abridged from my field notes. I have left out some passages which were repetitious. Mr P the philosopher spoke in English.

He began treating me to a sermon. Did I know about Jainism? Not much. He told me that the essence of Jainism is *ahiṃsā*. This is non-violence, and Gandhi was really a Jain. Did I know what *ahiṃsā* means? I did not. *Ahiṃsā* is the essence of all religions, he said. We must do no harm, we must help all beings. Did I eat meat? I used to, but no longer. Good, he said, that is *ahiṃsā*. *Ahiṃsā* is always a profit to yourself. *Ahiṃsā* means that we must say ill of no one, because we might harm them, but we would anyway harm ourselves. Why? Because to speak ill or to lie is to speak out of greed and hatred, and these harm ourselves. *Ahiṃsā* means no harm to others, and that means no harm to yourself. Did I think fasting was bad for health? I hesitated. No! he said. Fasting is good for self, fasting is *ahiṃsā*, because it harms no one and helps only self.

He seemed to be hitting his stride when someone called on a business matter, and the philosopher asked me to stay for tea, saying that he had to go out but would be right back. He left, and after a pause a shabby older man who had been sitting in the corner spoke in Marathi. He was a farmer perhaps, perhaps a poor relation or had come about a loan. Did I speak Marathi? A little. This, he said, is a story my grandfather told me. This is very important. Write this down, he said, pointing to my notebook. There was a great man, a hero, a *mahāpuruṣ*, who lived right near here, and one time that man went out to the bulls. While [doing something unknown to me] to the bulls one of them stood on his hand. What did he do? He did nothing! He waited and waited, and finally the bull's owner came and saw what was happening! The owner struck the bull to make it move, and the great man told him to stop, that the bull did not understand! *That* is *dharma* [true religion], he said, that is genuine *jainadharma* [Jainism]!

I will call the man who told the story just 'the story-teller' or 'Mr S'. I never learned his name. He told the tale with marked fervour, but fell silent when the philosopher returned and did not speak again. I took it that he was rebutting or improving on Mr P's account.

I later discovered a printed biography of one Siddhasagar which contains the episode of which the story-teller spoke. Siddhasagar lived into the first decade of this century. Late in life, after many notable religious deeds as a layman, he became a *muni*, a naked ascetic, and continued to live an increasingly ascetic life until his death. He died by ceremonial self-starvation when his senses began to fail and he was no longer able to avoid injuring insects while walking or eating. His printed biography informs us that he had been removing dung from beneath the bulls when the accident happened.

Let me fill in some of the background (in a disassembling sort of way). Jains are a severely ascetic minority sect who hold that souls cycle in endless torment from birth to birth. The cause of this eternal suffering is the physical and mental pain we inflict on other beings, for by such deeds we cause defilements to adhere to our own souls, and these defilements lead inexorably, with law-like regularity, to further painful rebirth. We may prevent defilement by adopting practices which prevent harm to others. Indeed the central doctrine of Jainism is *ahiṃsā*, harmlessness or non-violence, which encompasses both a general attitude to life and specific religious practices. Such practices include vegetarianism and truthful, kindly speech. But Jains also stress other practices which involve self-control, such as celibacy and non-attachment to material goods. These are not such obvious expressions of *ahiṃsā*, but for Jains they do indeed amount to the avoidance of harm: celibacy, for example, avoids the violence of sexual intercourse, which in Jain thought would cause the death of countless tiny life-forms inhabiting a woman's vagina.

The counterpart to these principles of harmlessness and self-control is self-mortification, the process of cleansing oneself of already accrued defilements. Thus Jain *munis*, monks or ascetics, live lives of extraordinary austerity. The *munis* of the Digambar sect (the sect with whom I worked in Kolhapur) go permanently naked, eat once a day, walk constantly from place to place (they are forbidden transportation), and from time to time remove their head hair by plucking it out with their own hands. Jain lay people also cultivate austerities, chiefly by fasting for various periods, sometimes as long as a month.

Now in one perspective this potted outline of Jainism is enough: it is enough to render the story intelligible, to fill in gaps of comprehension, such as what is meant by *ahiṃsā* and what notions justify such counter-intuitive deeds. This is just the kind of effectiveness we expect of cultural translation, of a disassembly of the flow of action. Now I will gradually put the flow back together again.

A short, sharp story

Let me begin by considering just the central story of Siddhasagar. And for the moment I will treat it as if it consisted just of these words:

... There was a great man, a hero, a *mahāpuruṣ* ... and one time that man went out to the bulls. While [cleaning the dung out of the stalls] one of them stood on his hand. What did he do? He did nothing! He waited and waited, and finally the bull's owner came and saw what was happening! The owner struck the bull to make it move, and the great man told him to stop, that the bull did not understand! ...

Mr S the story-teller (unlike the philosopher) spoke entirely in specifics, entirely in particular cases, not at all in generalities. It was a short sharp, story, and in fact it was very much the narrative equivalent of the Russian's 'Well!'. But it nevertheless had everything that we might reasonably expect of a story. 1) It showed a flow of events, 2) it concerned specific characters, 3) it displayed the attitudes, beliefs, and intentions of the characters, and 4) it revealed the relationship between events and those intentions and attitudes. We learn more in the written version—for example, that Siddhasagar must have been pinned to the ground for several minutes, that he was at the time a bonded servant, and that the bull's owner was his master—but these details add nothing essential to the narrative framework which I heard from the story-teller. It conveys with great brevity, but with great force, an unmediated and embodied sense of just how far a Jain might go.

Indeed the story's brevity is one of its most salient characteristics. The aim of the story is to demonstrate the attitudes and states of minds of its characters. Siddhasagar is in pain, yet intent upon compassion and *ahiṃsā*. The owner is concerned, eager to save Siddhasagar. Yet the only actual explicit attribution of a state of mind in the story is to neither of them, but to the bull, who 'did not understand'. What is going on here?

I think that this observation leads on to some very profound and important consequences. For it suggests that a story as understood is something a good deal more than a story as recorded. A story, as Mary and Kenneth Gergen have pointed out, can even be very minimal: in the right setting even the words 'I thought she was my friend' will do.[2] For when the relevant details are filled in—that it is said, for example, by a woman in an established relationship which has been upset by some apparently inconsiderate act—these words capture just that change in the landscape of consciousness that is so important to the flow of social life. A full explanation of the remark to a relative stranger might involve a very long narrative indeed.

So a story points beyond itself, to a situation with its accompanying states of mind. It is not just the words that are spoken or written. And indeed this is recognized as a pervasive problem in linguistics: the topic of any discourse, taken just as a slice of talk or writing, may in fact be many things. There is a whole series of topics and meanings, perhaps an unlimited one, which the room of linguists might pass back out through the hatch in response to any one story. What might such an alternative meaning be in Siddhasagar's story? Well, one meaning is that Siddhasagar was either insane or extraordinarily stupid for letting an Indian bull, more than six feet high at the shoulder, stand on his hand without protest. This is a meaning I have elicited by telling the story to people unsympathetic to Jainism, both Europeans and Indians. And one Jain to whom I told the story felt that Siddhasagar's act was unnecessarily self-endangering. Siddhasagar could, on these accounts, be a 'hero' either in a bitterly ironic sense, or as a misguided but well-meaning Quixotic figure.

I do not advocate either interpretation, but they are far from fanciful. Throughout history Jains have had to defend themselves against many negative interpretations. Jains frequently began their discussions with me on Jainism by defending some practice, such as the nudity of the ascetics or fasting to death. And there is a certain amount of scepticism spread about the edges of even so devout a community as the Digambars of Kolhapur. So as I continue reassembling the story I will bear in mind the question: what happened to justify my taking Siddhasagar to be a hero in a straightforward, non-ironical sense? This is not a merely academic question, for it really amounts to asking how I, or anyone, could be sure of understanding what was going on.

Ambiguities

Now the simplest answer to this question is borne in the words
which followed Mr S's narrative. He capped the story with
this: '*That* is *dharma* [true religion], he said, that is genuine
jainadharma [Jainism]!' This seems to certify that Mr S was
keen to portray Siddhasagar as a real, proper, exemplary Jain,
a standard for all to emulate. But if we look at even these
words from the ironist's point of view, we can see that they,
too, do not necessarily justify the interpretation more favourable to Jainism. The remark 'that's a typical Jones thing to
do' could be very negative as well as very positive. Once we
take 'hero' to mean its opposite, then Mr S's following words
could all too easily be scornful as well.

So where can we look for some confirmation that Mr S's
story was seriously meant? Well, in my field notes I had under-
lined the word 'That', in the above quotation, and that under-
lining was meant to capture an emphasis in what Mr S said.
Moreover, I believe—and I believe that I can show—that his
emphasis pointed back to things that happened and were said
earlier that had already established that this was a sincere
conversation complimentary to Jains and to Siddhasagar.

So let us go back to the beginning. The whole encounter
began with the philosopher's lecture. But it would be useful to
go back even before that and say a little about how I under-
took such encounters. By a stroke of luck I had been intro-
duced to the Jains at an annual general meeting at a local
temple at the very beginning of my fieldwork, and they had
undertaken formally and collectively to help me. So though
such help was not universally offered, I could usually depend
on co-operation.

Moreover, whenever I approached someone to discuss
matters with him—and it was almost always a 'him' because I
had little access to Jain women—I did so in a particular way.
I asked for help, and when I met a favourable response I
questioned my interlocutors eagerly, all the while writing
rapidly in my notebook and glancing frequently back at my
interlocutor to show that I was attending to his every word.

This was not exactly a method, and I did not arrive at it through art. It was an approach that had arisen spontaneously when I was doing some fieldwork in Sri Lanka that had some of the character of solving a whodunnit. I did not just appear eager and interested; I was eager and interested, and that interest continued in Kolhapur. I should note that I was the surer that it did work, and that it did draw sincere answers, by contrast with occasions when it did not work. For I soon discovered that when I asked Jain businessmen about their businesses rather than their religion the notebook and the eagerness were definitely unacceptable.

This background did something to establish a general atmosphere within which I could work, but every encounter had to be started more or less afresh (like all encounters, to one degree or another). Sometimes my evident interest sparked nothing, sometimes a more or less mutually engrossing, interesting, and egalitarian dialogue. But often, too, as with Mr P the philosopher, I ran into the religio-philosophical lecture format. The encounter with him was more like a forced dialogue, for I was required to play a particular narrowly defined part, that of a callow youth or an ethically ignorant stranger.

My field notes give some sense of how this came about. The tone of the whole encounter with Mr P the philosopher was dominated by his rhetorical questions, questions which expected only a narrow range of brief answers. Indeed some of his questions were rather in the style of 'have you stopped beating your wife?'; the sort of question that requires an answer but from the outset ignores that answer.

> 'Do you eat meat?'
> 'I used to, but no longer.'
> 'Good. That is *ahiṃsā*. *Ahiṃsā* is always a profit to yourself.'

Now we come to one of the key points of this whole discussion. Quite apart from what was being said, the acts of both Mr P the philosopher and myself conspired towards a particular end, which was the establishment of a relationship. The relationship that came about was guided very much by Mr P,

with my acquiescence. It was set in the mould of a strictly
ranked pedagogy, with the philosopher, the teacher, speaking
in effect from the lectern. This hierarchy was achieved subtly
but with great effectiveness. It was, for example, appropriate
for Mr P to take a high moral line, and to make comments
which reflected on my social and cultural background, but it
was not appropriate for me to do so. It was appropriate that
I reveal details about myself, laying myself open to such
comment. But Mr P offered no corresponding information
about himself, for he was establishing a position of domination.
Within that relationship, a morally and spiritually pedagogic
one, Mr P's personal details were not in principle necessary,
for the relationship was not, for example, one of personal chat
or egalitarian hospitality.

He arranged the setting, in other words, so that the content
of his message would be taken as august, impersonal knowledge handed down *de haut en bas*, a wisdom for the ages. The
relationship itself provided the necessary clue for knowing how
to take the message. Now in one sense I am saying nothing
more here than that I knew from the outset of the encounter
that we were all taking things seriously. It is just the sort of
thing that people, even anthropologists, know. But by asking
just how that seriousness was established, we can actually see
that it has a particular form. It is possible to have other forms
of serious conversation, as in the more egalitarian conversations which I struck up with both Jains and Buddhists. But
this seriousness that Mr P had arranged had a particular
flavour to it: it is the sort of seriousness that concerns things
so important that the instructed must be dominated by the
instructor. There is no questioning these teachings, as there
might be questioning in a conversation with more give-and-
take. And this of course added something to Mr P's words that
we might not have found there if they had been appeared, say,
on a page torn out of a book and lying on a subway seat.

Indeed we can see that his words might not only have had a
meaning established upon the relationship, but also a use: they
might have been part of a more concerted attempt to demonstrate the ethical superiority of Jains and Jainism to all others,

and particularly to Westerners. This encounter did not develop that far, so I will never know. But it was a common theme in other encounters with Jains.

Siddhasagar again

I turn now to the message of Mr S the story-teller. When the philosopher was called away he stepped temporarily out of this flow of action, and out of the shop, and the story-teller stepped forward. Our exchange began as follows: 'Did I speak Marathi? A little. "This", he said, "is a story my grandfather told me. This is very important. Write this down", he said, pointing to my notebook. "There was a great man . . . who lived right near here". . .'. So Mr S began by establishing that we could communicate in the first place. Then he straightaway picked up the relationship where Mr P had left it, and he did so explicitly. He demanded that I take what he was to say with the same seriousness that I had shared with Mr P, and I complied. Moreover he echoed the elder-to-younger, wise-to-ignorant, nature of the encounter by mentioning that his grandfather had told it to him. So in that sense the proper interpretation of his story had already been prepared by the solemnity of the philosopher: we were just following on in the same vein.

But the mention of the story-teller's grandfather, and that what happened occurred nearby, combined with the homely, modest setting of the story itself, had a very different effect than the philosopher had had. In the first place it was, however minimally, a revelation about Mr S, about his life, family, and opinions. This was a very different tack than the one taken by the earlier speaker, who revealed nothing of himself in his teaching. It subtly changed the relationship, establishing a more direct and less alienated engagement between the story-teller and myself. Moreover because of the relative intimacy of the narrated setting, it persuaded me at the time that this event occurred very much within the world of lived experience of the story-teller and his grandfather. In other words, this was not a legendary tale, set in some far-off kingdom as are so many Jain tales. It was not impersonal

knowledge. It was an everyday tale of everyday, if extraordinarily heroic, folk. And my later discovery of the pamphlet
about Siddhasagar confirmed this: the incident happened quite
nearby, well within what must be supposed to be the lifetime
of Mr S's grandfather, who must himself have been told by
others.

Just this proximity, this nearness of the heroic incident and
those who celebrated it to us interlocutors sitting among the
bags of fertilizer, was—or I took it to be—part of the story-
teller's message and part of what he was trying to achieve.
It went with his vehemence, bringing Siddhasagar out of a
remote past into a line which connected me to him, him to his
grandfather, and his grandfather ultimately to Siddhasagar
himself. We lived in the same world, and the actions of
Siddhasagar were to be as relevant in the present as they had
been in the past. I had the feeling of Mr S slapping a winning
card on the table, or producing a decisive wad of banknotes.
As Jains shout in unison, 'Muni Maharaj Siddhasagarji ki jai!',
'Siddhasagar lives!' Or as Mr S said, '*That* is true religion!'
This was not the august pedagogy of the philosopher, but
something more.

So I want to stress a quality of the story-teller's talk, which
was its sense of drawing me into a plot along with other already
established characters. These included not only Siddhasagar
and the bull with its owner, but the story-teller's grandfather
and those around him, the story-teller himself, and now me.
These were not characters in the frame of the story, but rather
part of both the story itself and our (briefly shared) lives.
What he said had something of the quality of that notorious
beginning, 'Well, now that you mention it, I know a story
about a ghost. In fact, it happened exactly a hundred years ago
tonight, at this very hour, in this very room.'

Of course the philosopher could have spoken more intimately, could have adduced ancient or recent sages who
asserted such ethical propositions as he was now subjecting me
to, but he could never have done so as effectively as the story-
teller. And the reason for that is quite straightforward: the
story-like character of Mr S's narrative fitted like a glove with

the story-like character of what was happening in the shop. The movement from one to the other, from the past to the present, from narrated characters in a plot then to experienced characters in a plot now, was easy, automatic, and compelling; it was, supported on a chain of people instructing others through story of the lived meaning of Jainism.

Let me review the wider significance of what I have argued here. In a disassembled perspective it is possible to find the narrative of Siddhasagar intelligible according to an abstract schedule of motives. Those motives form an explanation in terms of culture. They are the sort of thing that anthropologists produce when they fill in the background. So in this case the abstracted motives of self-mortification and *ahiṃsā*, fill in, in a sort of blanketing, indiscriminate way, the states of mind that we attribute to Siddhasagar. We do not need, when we use these abstractions, to question the setting in which his story is told.

Let me refer to such an explanation in terms of culture as a 'cultural gloss'. By agreement, by a sort of social contract built into a disassembled perspective, we assume that the cultural gloss provides all we need to know. We may not—and I suspect many of you do not—agree that self-mortification and *ahiṃsā* would be enough for us to regard Siddhasagar as quite such a hero as Jains do. But as part of the contract of the cultural gloss, we give them the benefit of the doubt. We agree that a cultural gloss tells us what Jains take seriously. And so we go for the sincere, rather than the sarcastic, interpretation of Siddhasagar.

When it comes to reassembling Siddhasagar's story something rather different appears. The interlocutors involved were not just talking to each other against a comfortable shared background, a common thought bubble. We, the interlocutors at the time, did not just assume that each knew what the other knew. Nor did we simply package up our meanings in words and send them back and forth to each other. On the contrary, the meaning of what both Mr P and Mr S wanted to say had to be negotiated along with the negotiation of a relationship. Only by negotiating the relationship could the story itself be taken in the spirit in which it was meant. Without that negotiation the story's interpretation would have been out of Mr S's control, however clear his words and however deep his convictions concerning it.

It could, of course, be said that this was true only because of my peculiar status, as an ignorant stranger. But since adult Jains themselves do more or less the same to their children and to each other all the time, that will not do. The relationships between Jains, or at least between speakers discoursing on Jainism, are a necessary accompaniment to the particular way they have of·talking about Jainism. Just as the Language Acquisition Device of the infant requires a Language Acquisition Support System already in place, so the truths of Jainism must be imparted in a proper social setting. On balance, there tends to be a particular flavour to these settings among Jains, as among Indians generally. There is a bias towards the authoritative pronouncement, that is, towards a relationship of unquestioning domination by the instructor. But in any case, the establishing of the relationship is necessary to the proper interpretation of the story.

So in fact I am putting forward this brief encounter in a faraway city as an example of a more general human truth: everyone negotiates relationships in order to negotiate meanings. If we subtract the authoritarian flavour, the telling of Siddhasagar's story still retains an essential element, the creating of a common meaning by working jointly, interactively, to establish which interpretation is to be accepted. In this perspective, the case of the anthropologist relating to those studied is just one example, and a not very special one, of a wider series of cases which ultimately embrace all human interactions. The sense of all stories, indeed all utterances, is dependent on the character of the human relationships that bear them. All meanings, like the 'Well!' of the Russians, are interactive.

What does this mean for a story like that of Siddhasagar, which, unlike the stories in the last chapter, has a life of its own in different settings and different media? Well, I do insist that all meanings are interactive, so on that showing, the dif-

ferent tellings or writings-and-readings must therefore depend
on their setting. Such a dictum is widely acceptable, even
banal, for most anthropologists, and for that matter historians
and literary theorists. But note that, if it is accepted, then
many implications follow. One implication, which I will
explore in the next chapter, is that such things as the story
of Siddhasagar participate in the metamorphic character of
human life. On the one hand, the story appears to be the very
type of a cultural good which is preserved, and which itself
preserves cultural values. On the other, it is fully subject to
the vicissitudes of the actual historical relationships within
which it is recounted. No story has only one true meaning,
as we might naïvely think it does if we were to take the
anthropologist's disassembled cultural gloss as a comprehensive
explanation. We need cultural glosses, but we need to be wary
of them.

A disagreement

Let me now explore the other theme of this chapter: the
apparent superiority of narrative to paradigmatic thought.
For I believed at the time, and still believe, that Mr S also
intended an implicit criticism of Mr P the philosopher. This is
part of the meaning of the emphasis placed at the end of
Siddhasagar's story: '*That* is true religion, . . . *that* is genuine
Jainism!' It is as if he had added, 'and not what he's been
telling you.'

Certainly what the story-teller said was altogether sterner
stuff than the urbanized, middle-class, rather over-educated
line that Mr P was giving me. Mr P was typical of a sort of Jain
protestantism which has evidently arisen in the last century,
bestowing authority on better educated lay people as independent arbiters in the interpretation of Jainism. The story-
teller's story, to the contrary, came out of the less well-educated
but more ascetic and intensely religious countryside, the
villages around Kolhapur which, in fact, have produced the
great majority of Digambar Jain *munis* in the twentieth
century.

But there was more as well. If Mr S the story-teller meant

simply to say that real Jainism involves stricter self-mortification
than the philosopher indicated, then he could have said so
directly. Why did he use the story? Is there something special
about story, something which simply cannot be conveyed
in any other way? I think the writer of the preface to
Siddhasagar's biography can give us a start here. He wrote:
'It is our experience that the life stories of great men are
attractive, *informative*, and inspiring to people. . . . The
readers' minds are so concentrated that they attend to nothing
else'[3] [*my translation, my emphasis*]. I have already remarked
that a story is attractive because it draws one in, engaging
one's attention. But in what sense are the life stories of great
men 'informative'? Does this mean any more than that they
just flesh out general ideas, giving concrete instances to
illustrate the abstractions of Mr P the philosopher? I think it
does.

First, the knowledge I received through the story comprehended more than just what happened to Siddhasagar and
the bull. As I have already remarked, I learned a bit, but a
very important bit, about the story-teller and his grandfather,
and with that information I also suddenly acquired a different
orientation, not to an ideal world of abstract injunctions but to
a real flow of relationships and interactions in the villages
nearby. In that sense the brevity of the encounter was more
than matched by a startling glimpse into a different world.

Let me pursue this further. As I eventually learned just by
hanging around a neighbourhood temple in Kolhapur, the
local Jain world often reverberates with stories of great or
minor religious deeds. It is, I suppose, just what occurs to
people to talk about at the temple, a sort of religious gossip.
What John Haviland has to say of ordinary gossip goes for this
religious gossip as well:

We ordinarily have thought of one's cultural competence as composed of codes: schemata for, say, plants and animals, kinship
systems, political structures, [religion,] and so on. The conceptual
schemata have, we assume, an independent existence prior to any
particular configuration of animals, any set of actual kin, any actual
political operation. But in gossip the nonparticular is irrelevant before

the actual; the contingencies determine the general principles—for they are all there is. In gossip, the world becomes more than ideal schemata and codes; it rests on the Who's Who, much expanded, on history, on reputations, on idiosyncrasies, on exceptions and accidents. Gossip exalts the particular.[4]

The mention of 'schemata' refers to one very vigorous and fruitful sub-school of American cultural anthropology, namely cognitive anthropology, whose practitioners do often tend to lend an independent reality to culture. For the moment, however, let me look more closely at this exaltation of the particular. At the centre of Jain lay religious life lies a rich culture of ceremonial self-mortification organized in the home and in elaborate ceremonial and story-telling at the local temple. This is not the *muni*'s life, but the ground from which *munis* spring. The basic act of self-mortification in lay asceticism is the taking of a vow of fasting, which is done amidst a more or less complicated, colourful, and sometimes quite expensive act of worship. This involves, for example, circumambulating the temple, placing fruits, rice, flowers, lamps, and so forth ceremoniously before an image, reciting certain formulae, and undertaking to fast in a certain pattern, for example on full-moon days for a year. The explanation for such action comes to the worshipper in the form of a story, to the effect that such and such a legendary figure took the vow on such and such an occasion. Thus each vow is rendered intelligible not by an abstract ethical statement, but by a narrative which attaches to it and to it alone. So in the first place the taker of the vow understands what she—and indeed it is most often lay women who undertake vows—is doing by identifying directly with some legendary figure. There is no intervening explanation to break the unmediated identification between what she does now and what was done then.

Second, the vows are taken in a setting of relationships that are vital to their understanding. The vow is taken from a priest—that is the first relevant relationship—who tells the story and describes the performance of the vow. Thereafter the fasting is carried out at home. Meals in Jain households, as in most Indian households, are fairly ritual affairs which dramatize relationships: men eat together, men and children are fed before women and are served by them, and so forth. Hence—as has been remarked to me by more than one Jain—the effect of not eating, and especially of serving excellent food which one is not going to eat oneself, can work powerfully on the imagination and the relationships of all concerned. The nuances of superiority and reproach, of submission and envy, of admiration and guilt that might thus arise have been called by Arjun Appadurai the 'gastro-politics' of the Indian household.[5] Moreover, because of the closeness of intermarriage and relatedness in such a community, this gastropolitical and gastro-religious knowledge one has of one's own household extends throughout the community. One knows intimately a local history, a social and psychic geography with its fault lines and upthrusts, just as one knows the landscape through which one moves daily. Such knowledge is particular and narrative in nature: it is just like—indeed often is—gossip.

My argument, then, is this: in so far as we are concerned with the understanding that Jains have of Jainism, then their understanding is basically a local, personal, particular, and narrative one. This is a point I made earlier when I stressed that, in the midst of social life, people's knowledge of the generic and the particular are inextricably mixed. Local Jains know of Siddhasagar, who lived 'right near here', but they also know of Mrs Patil, who took that long vow last month, and they may know, vaguely, of the legendary figure who was the first one to take such a vow. They know of Mrs Chaugule (these are pseudonyms), who died by fasting some years ago, and of Jinappa, a distant cousin who became a *muni*. There is more to Jainism than stories but, I argue, it is through stories, through characters with states of mind living in a flow of action, that Jains first and foremost understand Jainism.

Paradigmatic thought again

What, then, of Mr P the philosopher? Though what he said was not packaged as rigorous argumentation, it was nevertheless a form of abstract reasoning. It fulfils, so far as I can see, all the requirements of Bruner's paradigmatic thought. It is generalizing rather than particularizing, and it uses logic rather than story-telling. And in fact I suspect that what Mr P said was largely influenced by the work of a medieval Jain moralist and philosopher, Amṛtacandra, a translation of whose work enjoys some currency among the Kolhapur Jain intelligentsia.

To a large extent this chapter is an argument between my mutualist point of view and the mentalist one, or a collection of mentalist ones, taken by many anthropologists. I have stressed that it is people in relationships who make things happen, whereas the mentalist view holds that ideas or images or schemata do so. It would appear that much the same argument occurred, at least implicitly, among Jains themselves, between Mr P and Mr S. I have suggested that Mr S the story-teller had the better of it. But does that mean that Jains do not behave according to the paradigmatic precepts of their religion? There is one very strong reason to believe that they do in fact behave according to precepts, and that is the very existence of Mr P with his reasoning. This reasoning provides abstract and general motives for acting according to the principles of self mortification and *ahiṃsā*. In other words, here is a Jain providing his own cultural gloss. And here, too, is a Jain who would apparently argue that Jains actually do follow precepts rather than stories!

This is, I think, a strong point, and not one which can be easily, or in the end totally, dismissed. Let me begin by noting that it is possible for people to conduct their common social life, and their religion, without learned specialists and without the sort of systematic paradigmatic thought put forward by Mr P. It is just the case that many of the societies studied by anthropologists do not indulge in, or do not elaborate so greatly, a paradigmatic knowledge concerning their aesthetic standards. Thus, for example, Rosaldo's Ilongot, or the Kaluli studied by Schieffelin, just have not had the religious specialists to elaborate an edifice of reasoning about the conduct of social life.

In Jainism, on the other hand, there have been such religious specialists, and they have created a particular style of reasoning. A latter-day development has been that some devout lay people, mostly but not entirely middle-class, educated men, take up the burden of studying such thought: which explains the philosopher. For the rest of devout Jains, however, such learning may come a distant second or may not be relevant at all. They know of such things and trust them to be true, but show little evidence of using them as a matter of course.

What are we to make of this? Well, let me perform the thought experiment of imagining Jainism without its philosophical, paradigmatic, or schematic, propositions. Many Jains apparently conduct their religious life without such propositions. Such a Jainism would keep its stories and its naked ascetics who display in their very appearance the negation of ordinary indulgence. It would keep the statues of ascetics from the legendary past, statues which are so evocative yet so impervious to merely literal thought. Images of the legendary hero Bahubali, for example, depict a naked figure so firm in his vow to mortify the flesh by standing still in one place that vines have grown up around his legs. It would keep its habit of deep obeisance before such statues. And such a Jainism would certainly preserve its elaborate rites of lay asceticism.

What would it lose? To answer this, let me first ask how it got its paradigmatic thought in the first place. The answer to that is difficult, but it seems clear that, for India at least, the habit of generalizing thought grew up in a particular milieu, a rapidly urbanizing civilization which flourished on the plains of North India in the first millennium before Christ. Among the earliest records of this world are those that reflect the arrival on the scene of the Buddha and his near contemporary, Mahavira, the founder (or one of the founders) of Jainism. It was a fiercely competitive, rivalrous environment for religious aspirants—'Strivers' as they were called—each of whom was keenly conscious of the alternative ways of life offered by the others. These differences were aired in public debate, in debating halls apparently provided for just such occasions. In this setting it was invaluable to possess the ability to generalize, to speak for and to more people, and to have a larger, a more encompassing, more abstract and therefore (in a limited sense) more powerful description of things. This ability was assiduously cultivated, year after year, century after century, by Jains and all their rivals.

So in a sense the Jains' version of paradigmatic thought arose in just such a setting as the one which the philosopher subjected me to, a setting in which the superiority of Jains' way of life was being asserted to a non-believer or a novice. Without the abstracted set of ethical ideas focussing on *ahiṃsā* and self-mortification, without the universalizing language in which to explain these practices abstractly, Jains would have lost the ability to maintain their claims in the unforgiving arena of Indian religious and philosophical thought. Nor would they find it as easy today to assert themselves and dominate others, as Mr P did to me, or as Jains try to do when they move to North Atlantic societies and found associations to preserve and promulgate Jain learning.

What this suggests is that we must think of paradigmatic thought as something which is cultivated, invented, or discovered, and therefore as being of many different types. Jain philosophers evidence one sort, cognitive anthropologists display another, and there are some very widespread habits of generalized thinking ingrained in North Atlantic education that make possible the writing and reading of this book. But there is no reason to believe that such thought goes especially with literacy. We can be quite certain, for example, that Jainism's great rival, Buddhism, arose and was elaborated with rigour and clarity for several hundred years before being reduced to writing. And the anthropologist Edwin Hutchins, writing as a cognitive anthropologist, has shown how careful and ordered is the thinking of Trobriand Islanders (a people of Melanesia) when they come to contend over the ownership of land.[6]

This suggests that human thought is in fact more powerful and more creative than schemas or paradigmatic thought can compass. We can invent or discover new forms of paradigmatic thought, new schemas, as for example in Jain logic, Trobriand legal reasoning, computer programming, or mathematics; but such thought does not invent or discover us, or lead the conduct of our lives—except, that is, where we let it do so, as in subjecting ourselves to the reasoning of a legal system. The giving of cultural glosses by anthropologists is in fact one such form of paradigmatic thought. But it is important to reassemble such thought, to restore it to its social nexus. It is possible that Mr P does reason according to his precepts and act according to his reasoning. But it is not necessary to Jainism that all Jains do so.

Imagery

There is, to be sure, much more to Jainism as thus experienced than narrative alone. There is the schooling of the senses in the elaborate imagery of worship, the schooling of the body in acts of supplication and fasting, and the schooling of the sentiments in relationships in the home and temple. These are closely entangled with narrative consciousness, but run beyond it in a different direction than does paradigmatic thought. Such aesthetic and corporeal thought is often expressed through imagery, either mutely acted out or uttered in poetry and ritual song and speech. Thus every Jain temple has one central image, a statue in stone or metal of some former ascetic founder of Jainism (in some past aeon), which is the focus of a tremendous elaboration of figurative acts, speech, and the manipulation of ceremonial offerings.

Much writing in anthropology—called generally symbolic anthropology—has been in a mentalist vein devoted to considering such figurative forms of thought. James Fernandez, for example, says that the use of imagery by people 'makes a movement and leads to a performance'.[7] There is great insight in this: the metaphors of poetry and ritual, and of everyday speech, carry a great deal of the motivation and the slippability of human creative intelligence. Consider, for example, a feature set prominently before many Jain temples: a pillar perhaps 40 feet high with four small statues of ascetic founders at the top, facing the four directions. The pillar is called a *mānastambha*, a 'pillar of pride', and this seems a reasonable designation since it marks out the temple across a cityscape of roofs, or above the trees in a village. But I was told by a pious Jain layman that it really means 'pillar against pride', since the building and ritual dedication of such a pillar entails great financial sacrifice on the part of the donor. This slippage, from one designation to its opposite, is only one of many ways in which figurative thought works, but it is especially typical of the religious imagination in Jainism.

But note too that further slippages are possible as well, in particular social settings. The very man who told me it was a 'pillar against pride' was himself paying for a large part of such a pillar. So far, so good: he was representing himself to me as doing so for purely pious reasons. He was, however, desperately eager to have his family name inscribed as the only donors at the base. This became a very contentious matter, since he was not paying for all of the pillar. And so in the midst of the controversy another slippage was offered to me when someone remarked, 'a pillar of his pride.' This is the sort of remark we commonly make, and it is in such play of imagery that we see the creative side of human intelligence doing its daily work.

Anthropologists working in this symbolic style have revealed, and continue to reveal, an astounding wealth of human inventiveness. But figurative thinking alone cannot achieve the depth of motivation or the comprehensive consciousness of a social flow that narrative can. Thus, for example, I met Jains who spoke of some story or other, a legend or a tale like that of Siddhasagar, as being the key to their devoutness or even to their joining the company of naked ascetics. Figurative thinking is no doubt deeply involved in such stories, and in that respect the bareness of the narrative of Siddhasagar as told to me is certainly exceptional. But the relevant slippage, the slippage that makes people do things, is not from one image to another, as in figurative thought, but from one plot to another and from one character to another. Where motivation is concerned, it involves the ability to see oneself, to reinterpret oneself, in the light of someone else's life and plot. So, to adapt the words of Douglas Hofstadter, we achieve an instantaneous perception of the situation, a sort of

'There-but-for-the-grace-of-God-go-I' feeling, which induces a quick flash to the effect of 'Simply because I am human, I can place myself in the position of that Jain hero Siddhasagar'. For me the mental movement was not one of understanding and sympathy, such as the man observing the harrassed waitress might have felt. It was rather a movement of awe, imagining what it would be like to have an Indian bull, six feet high at the shoulder, standing on your hand, and still not to move. The performance, on the other hand, became one of trying to convey that understanding to you.

But for a Jain the movement and the performance might be altogether more transforming. It could move a Jain to become an ascetic, or to take vows at the temple. In the end it is the story, with its sense of what happened, why it happened, and what happened next, that makes all the difference. For what anyone really needs to know is what happened, why it happened, and what to do next. So story consciousness has an active as well as a passive side. People can not only grasp emotions and attitudes through it, they can also be moved to act. Stories, in other words, compass the element of the will, of conation, and of creation, as well as cognition and emotion. And that, in the final analysis, is why Mr S's tale of Siddhasagar is more powerful than Mr P's reasoning.

7

Metamorphosis

So far I have concentrated on the small scale of social experience. In so doing I have been influenced by the many
currents in the social sciences which I have summarized as
mutualism. One current was especially important in the last
chapter, namely the one concerned with the finest possible
analysis, from second to second, of interactions between two
or more people. In sociology such analysis is conducted by
ethnomethodologists and conversational analysts, and in
linguistics by interactive socio-linguists. That their titles are so
polysyllabic reveals, perhaps, how recondite their interests
are. Indeed they have tended to form a special, separate, and
rather distant cell among scholars in general. But their studies
have nevertheless cast a new and powerfully illuminating light
on how humans live together.

These scholars have not been very influential in anthropology. There might be many reasons for this. One was given
by Ernest Gellner, who wrote of ethnomethodology as 'the
Californian way of subjectivity.'[1] By this he meant that such a
concern with immediate happenings between individuals is,
in fact, a failure of sociological apperception, a form of inappropriately individualistic thought. It ignores, on his account,
the very real forces and events which shape the larger social
and historical world in which we live. I, however, have assumed
from the very outset that Gellner's—and more to the point,
Wolf's—macroscopic view and the microscopic view of
'California sociology' must both be part of how we understand
human sociality. On the macroscopic view we evidently do
create a great variety of social forms featuring 'weblike, netlike connections' with each other and within themselves,
patterned on a very large scale indeed. On the microscopic

view we can see how people actually create, manipulate, and transform the connections.

I move now from the micro- to the macroscopic scale. In the first chapter on narrative thought I distinguished the aspirations of psychologists from those of anthropologists. I pointed out that we anthropologists have already moved towards a more historical perspective. We are now writing of people 'with shifting role types as they relate to each other and their environment in a face-to-face community with complex social organization, a long past, an uncertain future, and a rolling cultural heritage'. And we are gradually moving on to write also of such people as they 'join with others, and against others, in interest groups, ethnic groups, and classes to remake their heritage in the face of shifting global social and social environmental forces'. In this chapter I set out an argument in this latter style of anthropology.

I follow two themes. The first concerns the way in which a particular large-scale metamorphosis was understood by some of those participating in it. Their understanding of those events was, I suggest, intersubjective and interactive in much the same sense as Mr S and I understood Siddhasagar interactively. In other words, people grasp the larger flow of events in which they live in much the same terms, and through much the same means, as they grasp their immediate setting. The second theme is this: the understanding of these particular participants was, at base, creative. It represented a new viewpoint, a new perspective which was relevant to the new circumstances in which they found themselves. Furthermore, by urging that viewpoint on others they contributed to the flow of events and helped to create new institutions which took part in the process of metamorphosis itself.

The case-study here is drawn from a Buddhist text of tremendous antiquity. We are used to thinking of our modern world as changing rapidly but, as Wolf pointed out, 'All human societies of which we have record are "secondary," indeed often tertiary, quaternary, or centenary. Cultural change or cultural evolution does not operate on isolated societies but always on interconnected systems in which societies are variously linked within wider "social fields." '[2] The metamorphosis in question occurred in the interconnected system of societies stretching along the banks of the Ganges river in North India 2,400 years ago. The text, the *Aggañña-suttanta*—or *Aggañña* for short—reveals far-reaching changes in their stream of social life.

It shows, too, a keen awareness of the relationship between its creators and speakers on the one hand, and its audience and their wider world on the other. Here, as in Siddhasagar's story, the frame is part of the picture, and the circumstances of the *Aggañña*'s telling are part of its meaning. And like the story of Siddhasagar, it was used by people to affect other people, and so was one of the instruments of change itself.

The *Aggañña*'s world

I begin with a very rapid survey of the social historical setting.[3] The Buddha—like Mahavira, his contemporary, the founder of Jainism—flourished about 400 BC on the Gangetic plain. A collection of small heroic warrior societies had spread along the river centuries earlier, and these societies had now developed into centralized monarchical states. There was a traditional list of sixteen of these 'great countries', but already by the Buddha's time some had swallowed others and were on the way to further conquests. One, Kosala, conquered the Sakyas, the Buddha's own people, in the Buddha's lifetime. Another, Magadha, already ruler of western Bengal, was to engulf the Vajji confederacy of tribal republics shortly after his death. In less than two centuries it would form the nucleus of the Mauryan empire, at the time the largest empire in the world, and the greatest power India would see until the height of the British Raj, 2,300 years later. A grand metamorphosis was in progress, one with no less important consequences for the people of the Ganges basin than the spread of capitalism and colonialism had for peoples along the coasts of the Atlantic.

At the heart of these states appeared new cities which contained the kings' courts, and to the courts and cities were drawn the makings of an urban life: merchants and craftsmen with new skills, soldiers and labourers, conquered lords to render tribute, the displaced, the foreigners, the opportunists. The court and the city drew the countryside into relation with the city, through force wielded by the king's soldiers and tax collectors, and through the subtler effect of long-distance commerce. There came into being a more complex division of labour, and of power and status, and those of different languages and cultures were now thrown together to get along as best they could. Wolf would be concerned with the forces leading forward to empire. I am concerned with a different matter: how did people understand themselves among these unprecedented forms of common life?

They began with one very old intellectual tool: a conception of the different estates in society. This tool was the property of the old heroic warrior societies, and is reminiscent of the medieval European division of society into three orders: those who pray, those who fight, and those who labour, or Church, nobility, and peasants. In the Indian scheme there were four estates. At the top were the Brahmans, priests of the sacrificial religion and intellectuals. Despite their rank, however, they did not wield power. That was left to the second estate, the Khattiyas, Kshatriyas or warriors, whose duty was to fight, to rule, and to pay for sacrifice. Into this category fell kings and nobility. The third estate were the commoners, the producers or Husbandmen. And the fourth estate were the Menials, those ineligible for the benefits of sacrificial religion and compelled to a life of servitude under the other three orders. This conception prescribed an orderly and hierarchical relationship between the estates, but it seems probable that it also more or less described that older warrior society, which had indeed been ranked, with a warrior élite and their priests ruling over commoners and others.

This old conception had been a pervasive way of seeing the human world, and in its light that world had been divided into what were, in effect, different species. To call someone a Khattiya, for example, was not just to designate him as a bearer of arms or a ruler, but also to attribute to him qualities as a person: generosity, heroism, nobility. A Brahman was not just a priest by vocation but inherently endowed with wisdom, virtue, learning, personal purity, and purity of birth. It was a view which had some of the divisiveness and simplicity of apartheid, where there are no people, only Blacks, Whites, and Coloureds.

As we shall see from the *Aggañña*, the estate scheme continued to be a common idiom, a sort of lingua franca, for talking about social divisions. (Indeed, after many repairs and rambling additions, it survives until today as a Brahman's view of the caste society of India.) Yet it had come to have a less certain purchase on the new societies along the Ganges than on the earlier heroic warrior societies, and it could not be understood in quite the same way. It did not comprehend the new variety and complexity of occupation and position. In pre-Buddhist texts, for example, we read nothing of merchants, but in the Buddhist and Jain texts they are a very prominent part of the scene. In the older texts the only ones to exercise power are Khattiyas, but in the newer there are paid soldiers and salaried officials as well. In the same vein, the Buddhist texts—among them the *Aggañña* itself—make clear that rank by birth had now a very uncertain relationship to status in fact. People who were not Khattiyas could become kings; Khattiyas could be punished as common criminals; and anyone, Brahman or Khattiya even, could fall to the position of servant. Such eventualities, part and parcel of the experience of the brave new Gangetic world, were simply not envisaged in the old estates scheme.

Finally—and here we come very close to the *Aggañña*—that old scheme, fostered by Brahmans, had no place for another prominent feature of the new world, the religious 'Strivers'. Strivers were religious mendicants, a loose and internally contending company of spiritual seekers who, like the merchants, wandered at will from kingdom to kingdom. It was from this intellectually fecund if vocationally celibate fraternity that Buddhism and Jainism arose, and with them, as I have observed, their several forms of paradigmatic thought. Anyone—Khattiya or Menial, Brahman, or Husbandman—could become a Striver. Moreover, in the Strivers' eyes, the ordinary, worldly, lay people were all equally subject to further, other-worldly laws, such as the law of acts and their consequences in rebirth which is so similar in Buddhism and Jainism. In the severe and censorious sermonizing of these men, rank meant nothing in the face of the iron decree of transmigration. From their point of view, the Brahmans' pretensions to pre-eminence were risible. The Brahmans' scheme painted society as harmonious, if unequal. But the Strivers gave voice to opinions which revealed how contentious and cacophonous society actually was. Thus, in the Buddha's world everyone was a Ramon, everyone was caught up in the currents of change, of actual conflict and of conflicting interpretations.

The mysterious Aggañña *temporarily disassembled*

The basic ideas of the *Aggañña* were probably current in the Buddha's time and many of them could perhaps have passed the lips of the Buddha himself. But the text as we now have it in its full form most probably came into being a little further downstream, some time after his death and closer to the rise of the Mauryan emperors. By then the Buddhist Order of mendicant monks was well established and had begun the laborious work of preserving—and amending or improving—the words of the Buddha. The origins of any single such text are always a disputatious matter, but I will treat the *Aggañña* as a collective work, forged by the Buddha and/or his followers into a powerful unity, perhaps from originally different pieces. (The version I use is that of the Theravada Buddhists of Sri Lanka, Burma, and Thailand and is preserved in the Pali language. Some versions of the text in other languages are also close to the Theravada version.)

The *Aggañña* has great beauty and piquancy, but it also has complexity, ambiguity, irony, and mystery. In it the Buddha appears to recount the origin of the world and society, and to assert, from a Striver's perspective, the superiority of the spiritual to the social order. Hence the name of the discourse, which means something like 'the discourse pertaining to origins'. But it is not that simple. The text's uncertain, or at least delicately nuanced, character was captured by Rhys-Davids, its translator into English. He wrote that it is 'one of the most interesting and instructive of all the Dialogues . . . a kind of Buddhist book of Genesis'.[4] But he went on: 'a continual note of good-humoured irony runs through the whole story . . . and the aroma of it would be lost on the hearer who took it *au grand serieux*.'[5]

For the moment let me ignore the irony and mystery and disassemble the *Aggañña* by paraphrasing it in brief, as though it were a straightforward sermon that could have a straightforward précis. I do so simply in order to orient you to the shape of the text as a whole.

The discourse begins with a conversation between the Buddha and two Brahman youths who are residing among the Buddha's monks with the intention of becoming monks themselves. In the course of talk the youths reveal that their relatives, proud of their rank, hold the Buddhist monks in contempt. The Buddha responds in kind. He implicitly ranks the Khattiyas above the Brahmans by always mentioning them first, but he points out that, in any case, the highest rank is held by Strivers and monks who renounce the world to seek salvation. The Buddha then points out that even King Pasenadi of Kosala—who had conquered the Buddha's people, the Sakyas—treats the Buddha with reverence because of his spiritual accomplishments.

The Buddha then recounts the myth. Eventually the universe will pass away, and when it reappears, sentient beings within it begin as beings of radiance, subsisting on joy alone. Gradually a flavourful skin forms (as on boiled milk), and beings then begin greedily to taste it. But through this and further acts of avarice and folly, the world, the beings, and their subsistence grow coarser, until finally they end by having bodies and being forced laboriously to grow rice to live. As the world thus develops various customs originate, and the last to originate are the estates. The Khattiya estate began first, when one being was chosen king in order to keep the others in line. The other estates followed. On this account the Khattiyas, not the Brahmans, are accorded the highest rank in worldly terms.

The lesson of the discourse—Khattiyas are the highest estate, but Strivers and monks are supreme—is then certified in a final verse.

> Khattiyas are supreme among this folk
> who believe (merely) in lineage
> But supreme among gods and men
> Is the one replete with wisdom and virtue.

(If my translation seems unpoetical, the original does not seem very catchy either. The *Aggañña*'s beauty does not lie in its verse.)

Reassembling the Aggañña

However, as I now argue, there is much more to the *Aggañña* than social and spiritual doctrine. Let me begin at the beginning. The *Aggañña* is a complex affair of frames within frames. The outermost frame consists merely of its first three words: 'thus have I heard'. This phrase precedes all Buddhist texts, but to call it a formula would be to miss its tremendous resonance. In purpose it resembles Mr S's beginning statement to me that he was told Siddhasagar's story by his grandfather: it locates what follows in a specific and warmly felt social milieu, that of the Order of Buddhist monks.

Yet these words also point to something else as well, to a far more deliberately established project of transmission and dissemination than Mr S's *ad hoc* narration. As K. R. Norman has shown, Buddhist monks organized themselves intricately into groups, each of which was responsible for memorizing, and teaching others to memorize, one section of the *buddhavacana*, 'the Buddha's word'.[6] Moreover these texts were subjected to mnemonic and literary elaboration—repetition of phrases, use of verse, alliteration and assonance—so that they could be more easily retained in memory and more accurately recited. And finally, the monks developed an extensive vocabulary of textual criticism in order to discuss and certify the fidelity of transmission and the accuracy of a text's contents. Consequently the great mass of early Buddhist literature—several library shelves' worth in their printed version—was preserved orally for perhaps several centuries before being reduced to writing. I remarked earlier that the social organization which supports one form of technology or another is at least as remarkable as technology itself. But here is a case where the technology is entirely immaterial, entirely intellectual, linguistic, and social, a case all the more remarkable for its complete lack of a material basis.

The sense of the texts belonging to a social milieu also needs some explaining. In my experience in Sri Lanka, monks do indeed regard words prefaced by 'thus have I heard' as the words of the Buddha himself. The words represent a tie directly to their heritage, a tie which is deeply felt, extending contemporary monks' perception of the flow of social life far into the past, into the Buddha's lifetime. And in the case of the *Aggañña* this tie is enriched by what, later in the text, is clearly a sense of performance, of a speaker playing to, and upon, an audience in a particular setting. It is now difficult to retrieve the original setting of such performances in any detail. But such texts evidently were recited for their sense as well as for their preservation, chiefly by a monk to other monks. In this respect the *Aggañña*—and the *Aggañña* especially—must have had some of the same evocativeness to the monastic assembly as, say, *Oedipus the King* had for a Greek audience. It creates that sense of mutual knowing and mutual mind-reading that allows for irony, for humour, and for words to mean much more than they actually say.

Brahmans 0, Monks 1

Within that outer frame we immediately meet the second frame, one which is a story itself and which carries on some way into the discourse. I paraphrase the beginning, following the order of the original as closely as possible:

Thus have I heard. While the Buddha was staying for a while in a house in the eastern suburbs of the city of Savatthi, there were among his accompanying monks two youths, Bharadvaja and Vasettha, who aspired to join the company of his monks. They spied him walking in the open air after meditation and approached, hoping to hear from him some talk of wisdom. After an exchange of civilities, he asked them whether they were Brahmans who had left home to take up the way of the wandering monk. They replied that they were.

So the story is a story of a conversation, located in a particular place at a particular time. The extra details—that it occurred at Savatthi, when the Buddha was staying for a while—has some of the same force as Mr S the story-teller's remark that the story of Siddhasagar happened 'right near here'. The conversation is a lop-sided one, between teacher and pupils, and in that respect is a stronger, more formal version of the dialogue between the paradigmatic, philosophical Mr P and myself.

The focus of the conversation, however, is not philosophical, but concerns the social situation of Bharadvaja and Vasettha. Indeed the topic is given away when their very names are mentioned, for these are plainly Brahmans. The Buddha asks Vasettha (who does the talking) whether their Brahman relatives do not revile them 'richly, roundly, with typical abuse' for having left home to become Buddhist monks. Vasettha replies as follows:

Sir, the Brahmans say this: 'the Brahman is the highest estate, the others are low; the Brahman is the brightest estate, the others are dark; Brahmans are well-born, not non-Brahmans; Brahmans are own sons of Brahma, born of his mouth, born of him, made by him, his heirs. But you have fallen from the highest estate, gone over to the low-born . . . the shaven beggars, the hired help, those blacks like something your kinsfolk shook off their feet' [my translation].[7]

And the Buddha makes this famous retort: 'Surely, Vasettha, the Brahmans . . . forget their own heritage? For the women of the Brahmans are seen to have periods, to be pregnant, to give birth and to suckle babies, and yet those very Brahmans, born out of vaginas, say that they are . . . born out of the mouth of Brahma.'[8] Thus the scene for the rest of the discourse is set, and what a scene it is: the Brahman boys have run away from home to become 'sons of the Buddha' (*buddhaputtā*). Their families have not got a good word to say about them or the Buddha. The Buddha, on the other hand, takes the view that the best defence is a good offence.

Let me look at the exchange more closely. There is comedy here, but high seriousness as well. The notion that Brahmans are born of the mouth of Brahma, the supreme god, is part of the myth of the primeval man set out in the *Puruṣa-sūkta* of the much older Brahmanical text, the *Ṛg Veda*. The myth lays out the origin of the estates. The Brahmans are highest, born of the mouth; the Khattiyas (in Sanskrit, Kshatriyas) are next, born of the breast; the Husbandmen are born of the loins; and the Menials are born of the feet. The Buddha's physiological realism in the face of this myth is very much a part of his style in this dialogue and elsewhere in Buddhist literature.

But I want to emphasize especially the sense of quotation which begins here and runs throughout the discourse. Sometimes, as we shall see later, the Buddha quotes Brahmanical ideas, sometimes Brahmanical styles of thought, and sometimes actual phrases from Brahmanical scriptures. For such quotation—here ironical quotation with a satirical edge—to work effectively, the speaker must presuppose that the audience has knowledge of that background.

Such quotation then serves as both a description and an interpretation of the surrounding social world. It brings from shadow into light a particular topic—in this case Brahmanical lore—while simultaneously sharing with the audience an evaluation of that topic; for the mention of a Brahmanical myth by a Buddhist monk to other monks could hardly be favouble to the myth. And that sharing with the audience amounts to what the linguist Deborah Tannen calls an 'involvement strategy'.[9] Involvement strategies simultaneously establish a relationship with the listener and create in him or her, not just an understanding, but an understanding which he or she knows to be shared. This extra piece of information makes all the difference, for it points to the setting of the discourse at the same time as providing an interpretation of the discourse. Thereafter it is possible for the interlocutors—or in this case, the speaker alone—to play either on the relationship established with his listeners, or on the meaning, or on both. The meaning affects the setting and the setting affects the meaning.

The narrated exchange between the Buddha and the youths has another dimension as well. The claims of the Brahmans are drawn as a contrast between their own position and that of others. This is gross vituperation, but in fact the language also has a subtlety not reflected in translation. The word for 'estate' in Pali is *vaṇṇa* (Sanskrit, *varṇa*), and this word is rich in implications. Its most ordinary meaning is just 'colour', and originally colours were used as emblems of the estates, though originally the colours were not skin colours. *Vaṇṇa* also means 'outward form' or even 'beauty', and all of these meanings receive some play here or later in the discourse. In this passage the contrast is between the whiteness, beauty and superiority of the Brahmans and the blackness and inferiority of the monks. And here skin colour must be involved in part. Perhaps a contrast is intended between those who work and live out of doors and those who do not need to. Thus the itinerant, begging monks might well be dark, but (rich) sedentary Brahmans need not be.

There is more. The Buddha was a Sakya, and the Sakyas were a distinct ethnic group whose *vaṇṇa* was that of Khattiyas—or at least they so regarded themselves. Here, however, the Brahmans evidently regard the Buddha and his followers as being in effect servants, as having the *vaṇṇa* rank of Menials, the dregs of society. So there is an edge to the Brahman's remarks which we would think of today as being racial, as being comments not only about colour but about social worthiness in general. They manage to insult the Buddha, his monks, and his people all at once.

But the Buddha's reply sets the Brahmans' pretensions and their much vaunted knowledge against another sort of knowledge, a basic biological one, with which it would not usually be associated. It is, to my mind, not only extraordinarily apt (if crude), but also effective. This is part of the creativity of the discourse: it urges a particular interpretation on its audience, and to the extent that that interpretation is effective, it changes people's minds, or at least confirms them in the face of opposition, diversion and distraction.

In the ensuing passages the conversation, which now takes a

turn more to sermonizing than to dialogue, explores these themes of rank. The Buddha points out that people of every rank can do evil deeds, just as people of every rank can refrain from them. In so saying the Buddha enumerates the estates repeatedly, and each time Khattiyas are pointedly placed first, a theme which is later recapitulated and which, as I have pointed out, caps the discourse as a whole. If we are to speak of rank in society—so the Buddha might have said—then the Khattiyas come first, not the Brahmans.

In these passages, too, the Buddha gives the other reason against the claims of the Brahmans to superiority. He goes on to assert that real wisdom, real virtue, and real superiority adhere not to worldly rank, but to those who become monks and pursue their salvation to final liberation. 'Supreme among this folk'—a foreshadowing of the phrase which is completed in the last verse of the discourse—is the spiritual truth, and here 'this folk' refers to the Order of Buddhist monks. So the ordering 'monks first, Khattiyas second, Brahmans nowhere' is laid out here quite explicitly. And indeed, if the discourse amounted to no more than the disassembled paraphrase, the final verse could be put here and the whole brought to a close.

Kings and Brahmans o, Khattiyas and Monks 2

But then the discourse takes a rather surprising twist. To illustrate his point, that those of spiritual accomplishment are 'supreme among this folk', the Buddha says:

King Pasenadi of Kosala is aware that the Striver Gotama [i.e. the Buddha] has gone forth into the monk's homeless life from the adjacent Sakya people. The Sakyas moreover have been annexed by King Pasenadi. So the Sakyas do obeisance to him and address him with honorifics, they rise when he enters and flatter him with ceremony. Now just as the Sakyas treat King Pasenadi, so he treats the Buddha, doing him obeisance, addressing him with honorifics, rising when he enters and flattering him with ceremony. For Pasenadi of Kosala thinks, 'is not the Striver Gotama well born? Am I not ill-born? Is not the Striver Gotama important, while I am not? Is not the Striver Gotama handsome, and I am ugly [lit. 'of bad *vaṇṇa*']? Is not he influential, while I am little heeded?' Thus, Vasettha, does one know that spiritual truth is supreme among this folk [my translation].[10]

And the Buddha goes on directly to say:

Vasettha, you [and the others] are gone forth from homes into the homeless life from various peoples, various names, various clans, and various families. If asked who you are, you reply, 'We are Strivers, sons of the Sakya'. And he who is well settled . . . and firm of faith in the Buddha may properly say, 'we are own sons of the Buddha, born of his mouth, born of the Truth, made by the Truth, heirs of the Truth'.[11]

One could say that these are simply amplifications of the point already made, about the superiority of the spiritual life and of those embarked upon it. But that would be doing scant justice to the Byzantine complexity packed into these few words.

Consider the theme of rank and mutual relationships. The Sakyas do obeisance to the king and the king does obeisance to the Buddha. But the Buddha is himself a Sakya, so the king finds himself doing obeisance to (one of) those whom he has conquered. Moreover the king's position is rendered more humiliating by the thoughts attributed to him: he regards himself as ill-born, ugly or of bad *vaṇṇa*, unimportant and uninfluential beside the Buddha. What is going on here? This is more than just elevation of the Buddha and his monks: it is positive abasement of the king, who is being treated even worse than the Brahmans, and its motive is not immediately clear.

I think that the speaker of the *Aggañña* and his audience here share another a thrill of recognition. The most obvious reference is to the conquest of the Sakyas, and the insults to Pasenadi give voice to a perception of injustice and oppression at Pasenadi's hands, and of Pasenadi's own unfitness for power. If he is ill-born and 'of bad *vaṇṇa*', then by contrast the Sakyas are well born and of high *vaṇṇa*. This is consistent with the line already pursued in the face of the Brahmans, namely that the Khattiyas take precedence of rank. Indeed the Sakyas appear to have had a partly republican rather than a purely monarchical form of government, so their rank as Khattiyas was evidently collective and they were marked off from the monarchical world in this further sense as well. Some of the Sakyas' *esprit de corps* seems also to rub off on the 'sons of the Buddha', his monks, who on this account are also 'sons of the Sakya'. Hence they are identified not with the Brahmans and the order of new monarchical power but with the Buddha and implicitly with the Sakyas and with Khattiyas.

But this link of the Order with Khattiyas and Sakyas is always relative to a more important link, namely with spiritual truth. In contrast to this world of rank and differentiation, their Order is a melting-pot in which all share a higher purpose and all estates merge into one: they are 'from various peoples, various names, various clans, and various families'. Later, in the fanciful origin myth, this theme will be repeated in reverse: all the estates will be seen to emerge out of a humanity essentially single in nature.

The historical specificity of this narrative—the mention of the historical Pasenadi and of the Buddha's people—is also consistent with a more general and perdurable commentary on kingship. Kings in general are not always treated very well in the early Buddhist literature. They are put into a list of disasters to be avoided at all cost, ranking with flood, famine, pestilence, and bandits. And this is quite understandable, both in the local historical circumstances of expanding monarchies and in the universal perspective of how kings exercise brute power. Nor do kings come off very well when they are shown in dialogue with monks: they are frequently depicted as capable of any cruelty and stupidity, and receive stern admonition from monks about the consequences of their brutality for their fate in the next life. In this respect kings are often set out as the very type of worldly folly and destructiveness. It is true that some kings, in other contexts even Pasenadi, are treated well ... just to the extent that they support the Buddha and his Order. And the early Buddhist literature contains, too, a representation of good or justified kingship, the *cakkavatti* or 'righteous conqueror'. But the view of kingship closest to the view which dominates the *Aggañña* is the sceptical, deeply suspicious one.

Still, the *Aggañña* itself does not moralize directly on kingship. It comments rather indirectly and ironically on it, portraying it in a world in flow, a world made up of mutual relationships, mutual attributions, mutual mind-readings. The sense of taut, alert responsiveness of one party to another, of speaker to listener, of Brahman to Striver, of Sakyas to Pasenadi, is vividly captured by the *Aggañña*'s peculiarly oblique approach. It could not so faithfully be captured by declarative, paradigmatic statements as by narrative and by quotation, irony, indirection, and multi-vocality—in other words, by the art of saying many different things in few words.

This is illustrated nicely when the Buddha lets his monks assert that 'we are own sons of the Buddha, born of his mouth, born of the Truth, made by the Truth, heirs of the Truth'. These words are immeasurably enriched by the underlying quotation, the variation on the theme of the Brahmans' earlier utterance. The words bring into view not just the absolute quality of the monks' way of life, but also the loyalty and pride of their relationship to the Buddha and the mutual hostility of their relationship to those other contenders in the disputatious arena of ancient Indian life, the Brahmans.

A delectable skin of earth

The Buddha then starts to tell the story of the origin of various customs, of kingship, and of the estates. This is the portion of the *Aggañña* that has so captured the imaginations of North Atlantic commentators, and there is no doubt that, as a whole, the story is powerful and beautiful. Its overall shape is that of a deterioration, from the original perfection that the universe possesses when it is (re)created down to the state of decay and moral turpitude which occasions the institution of kingship and the estates. Indeed it is characteristic of the monks' perspective that the story has such a shape, with kings and the estates being a consequence of increasing moral depravity. The narrative does not, however, have the shape of a simple parable to which a moral can easily be attached. On the contrary, it is more richly structured, and even less amenable to paraphrase, than the rest of the discourse.

One feature of this complexity is the tale's episodic nature. Let me begin with the first episode, which gives a fair flavour of how the others work as well. The Buddha begins by pointing out that, habitually, this world passes away, and then begins to evolve anew. At the beginning, sentient beings, people-to-be, are made of mind, subsisting on rapture, living in glory. Then—and here the Buddha changes abruptly to the past tense—things began in earnest. I use Rhys-Davids's translation to set the tone:

Now at that time, all had become one world of water, dark, and of darkness that maketh blind. No moon nor sun appeared, no stars were seen, nor constellations, neither was night manifest nor day . . . neither male nor female. Beings were reckoned just as beings only. And to those beings, Vasettha, sooner or later after a long time, earth with its savour was spread out in the waters. Even as a scum forms on the surface of boiled milky rice that is cooling, so did the earth appear. It became endowed with colour, with odour, and with taste. Even as well-made ghee or pure butter, so was its colour; even as the flawless honey of the bee, so sweet was it.[12]

The Victorian scriptural tone of the translation captures, I think, some of the actual resonances which the Indologist Richard Gombrich has found in the text. For he has shown that much of the imagery, and indeed some of the actual wording, echoes origin myths found in the older Brahmanical texts.[13] These speak of a primeval chaos, of darkness, of undifferentiated existence, and of a film like a scum on boiled milk forming on the waters. So here again is quotation, just as the Brahmanical myth of the cosmic man was quoted earlier in the discourse.

And here, too, is satirical intent. Some greedy being then tasted the earth, and he or she began to crave it. Others followed, and from those gluttonous impulses the self-luminance of the beings disappeared, and the sun, moon, and stars came into being. The beings continued feeding on the earth for a long time. Then:

As those beings carried on eating that nourishment . . . their bodies grew coarse, and *vanna*-ness and un-*vanna*-ness appeared. Some beings were *vaṇṇa*-full, some were *vaṇṇa*-less. The *vaṇṇa*-full beings scorned the *vaṇṇa*-less, saying, 'we are more *vaṇṇa*-full than they, they are more *vaṇṇa*-less than we'. And through the pride and arrogance arising in that *vaṇṇa*-conceit the sweet earth disappeared. With the disappearance of the sweet earth the beings gathered together and wailed, 'Oh, the taste! Oh, the taste!' And so now whenever someone tastes something good, they say, 'Oh, the taste! Oh, the taste!' They are only following an ancient, primeval saying, whose meaning they do not know.[14]

Consider the possibilities for performance here. The beginnings of the origin myth, for example, could be intoned in a solemn Brahmanical style, as could the puns on *vaṇṇa*—meaning 'beauty' and 'colour' as well as 'estate' or 'rank'. Moreover the tone could carry easily through the punch-line, for the words 'Oh, the taste!' mean no more and no less than 'Mmmm, good!' It is like being told from the pulpit that, on the eighth day, God made . . . Kentucky fried chicken. Here the thrill of recognition is all the greater for juxtaposing a lofty, solemn theme and a silly one. And there is satire as well in the very fact that a phoney etymology caps the episode. For one of the characteristics of Brahmanical thought is the ceaseless production of etymologies, often false etymologies, purporting to explain the significance of one thing or another.

This is one of the passages where the *Aggañña* comes closest to broad comedy. But it bears too the mark of reflection and commentary. The division of beings into the beautiful and ugly, and through the pun on *vaṇṇa* into higher and lower estates, is presented as a mere happenstance of the process of decline. But it is a happenstance which, through folly and greed, has serious consequences. It echoes the reflection of Pasenadi, that he possesses un-*vaṇṇa*-ness. And here too there comes to the surface, I think, a more intimate reminder, an implicit reference to the spirit of the Order of monks itself, the listeners to the story. They are, by comparison, undifferentiated. They are all 'gone forth from homes into the homeless life from various peoples, various names, various clans, and various families'. So the folly of the beings was typical of the world, the opposite of the unworldliness which brings the monks together into the single estate of homelessness. This theme, begun earlier, is echoed again more powerfully later.

The story then follows the decay of the beings through two more phoney etymologies, one of which concerns an expression meaning something like 'alas, all is lost'. By this time the beings are reduced to working for a living, farming rice. They have gone so far as to divide land up into private property, and you would think they could sink no further. But they do, for one greedy being takes another's plot of land. The others then catch him, scold him, and throw clods of dirt at him. But someone else follows his example, and then another, and soon they all fall to stealing, scolding, and blaming each other. This is what they did about it:

The beings gathered together and complained. 'Now stealing and blame and lying and punishment have come into existence. Let us agree on one being. He can become properly peeved when there's something to be peeved about, he can criticize properly what is to be criticized, he can expel properly when expelling is necessary. We'll give him a share of our rice.'

So they went to the handsomest, the most attractive, the most pleasing, the most influential being, and said to him, 'you, Mr. Being, become properly peeved when there's something to be peeved about, properly criticize what is to be criticized, expel properly when expelling is necessary.'

'Alright,' he said.[15]

There then follows a rash of etymologies:

Agreed by the people, Vasettha, thus 'the great agreed-on' was the first expression to appear. [*mahājana-sammato → mahāsammato*]

Lord of the fields, Vasettha, thus 'Khattiya' was the second expression to appear. [*khettānaṃ pati → khattiyo*]

He pleases others by truth, Vasettha, hence 'king' was the third expression to appear. [*dhammena pare rañjeti → rājā*]

Thus, Vasettha, originated the circle of Khattiyas, according to these ancient, primeval expressions. They were of those beings, not of any others. They were the same kind as those beings, not different. It was done according to form, not unjustly.

The words for 'king' and for 'warrior' are well known in the rest of Pali literature and are well understood today. These etymological puns, and the thrill of recognition of everyday words in a new setting, are quite straightforward. The term 'great agreed-on', however, is problematic, because it does not appear in this form in the early Pali literature. So what did it mean? What was recognized in a new light when the monks heard this etymology?

I think I can make a beginning by returning to the circumstances of the *Aggañña*'s speaking. The monastic speaker and audience, as I have stressed, shared certain values and—I now want to say—a certain social experience. That social experience included, first, the reduction upon entering the Order of all estates, all ranks, and all walks of life to one condition, that of monkhood. Second, the Order was consequently organized according to roughly egalitarian and consensual principles—or at least according to principles far more egalitarian and consensual than the society around them. The principles were expressed in a strong emphasis, woven throughout the Buddhist texts, on harmony, mutual support, and mutual regard.

The institutional counterpart of these values was a careful, even meticulous, concern for unanimity and concord. Official acts of the Order, such as the ordination of a new monk, the appointment of a monk to some special task, or the settlement of a dispute, were to be done by unanimous consent of an assembly of monks. If we speak of the Buddhist Order as having a constitution, then the earliest form of that constitution was one which insisted on such unanimous consent as the chief tool of collective government (along with a practical gerontocracy in the conduct of everyday affairs). Hence, as Steven Collins has pointed out, the most lively candidate for the original of the term 'the great agreed-on' lies in the Order's organization: *sammata* and related words were used to designate appointments and practices which had been certified by unanimous consent.[16] The 'great agreed-on' was just a monk appointed as such for some, usually temporary, purpose. This echo is carried through to the end of the passage, where the agreement on Mr Being and the origin of Khattiyas is done 'according to form' among people 'of the same kind'. So on Collins's account, which is the most plausible one available, this fanciful first king and first Khattiya pops into the narrative, and into Buddhist history, wearing a monastic legal term and reminding listeners of their monastic constitution.

But there is a further dimension as well. The Order's constitution is explained in another famous Buddhist text as being modelled on the constitution of a Khattiya people very like the Sakyas. These people, the Vajjis, conducted their republic according to unanimity and harmony, 'meeting in concord, rising in concord, and doing their business in concord'.[17] And like the Sakyas, they were threatened and eventually engulfed by a neighbouring king. This specific event is not adduced in the *Aggañña*. Yet as the text took form this conquest must have contributed, like the conquest of the Sakyas, to the wider social and historical consciousness evoked by the *Aggañña*. The *Aggañña*'s Khattiyas and 'the great agreed-on' were altogether more 'attractive, pleasing, and influential' than the ugly and 'little heeded' Pasenadi. Pasenadi's power was far from 'agreed on'. But the present and future belonged to him and his kind. So pathos lingers near the humour of this passage, a pathos arising from a remembered but rapidly disappearing or already vanished political order.

Could 'the great agreed-on' have had some currency in that political setting as well? Could *mahāsammata* have been an appellation for a leader chosen by Sakyas, for example, from among the equals of an oligarchic republic? Perhaps. It would add a further depth to the discourse if this were so, but we simply do not know.

Yet the origin story is by no means a merely political commentary, for once the origin of Khattiyas has been explained the speaker turns to the Brahmans. They, it seems, began among some of the beings who observed that 'now stealing and blame and lying and punishment and expelling have come into existence'. The expelling, of course, was new, being done by the attractive and influential Mr Being. These beings decided to 'put away from them evil and unskilful customs' by going to the forest to meditate in leaf huts. There is a distant but explicitly marked pun on 'putting away' and Brahmans (*bāhenti* → *brāhmaṇā*), and the passage also uses Buddhist terminology, now echoing clearly the Order's practices and point of view. Moreover the description of the beings going to the forest, of their leaving behind the domestic and ritual appurtenances of the Brahmanical household, and of going into villages to beg for alms, comprises the longest and most explicit quotation of a Brahmanical text. This mixture of Buddhist terminology and Brahmanical quotation continues the sense of humorous whimsy which surfaces so frequently in the origin myth.

Thus originated the Strivers and meditators. Some of those beings, however, found that they could not stand up to the ascetic life, so they settled down around villages and started compiling Brahmanical texts. These failed Strivers, who were not 'meditators' (*jhāyakā*) became 'reciters' or 'non-meditators' (*ajjhāyakā*): 'reciters' of the Brahmanical literature, the Brahmans as we know them. 'They were agreed to be the lowest at that time, Vasettha, but now they are thought to be the best.'[18] Thus the Brahmans are dismissed. Nor do Husbandmen and Menials fare very well. Husbandmen were beings who took up sexual intercourse and various trades, while Menials took up hunting—none of these activities were approved of in Buddhist teaching. As a whole the other estates come off very badly in this section, while the Strivers and Khattiyas come off rather well.

There the story ends, and the Buddha returns to earlier themes in a sermonizing, categorizing, paradigmatic style. One of any estate may become a monk, and so the 'circle of monks' is made of the 'four circles' of the estates. One of any estate can live morally, or evilly. One of any estate can become a monk and achieve liberation, and so forth. In these final passages the perspective draws away again, and grows more distant from the earlier warmth or at least nostalgia for the

Khattiya estate and the Sakyas' vanished way of life. In this light the implicit 'merely' in the concluding verse should be further emphasized:

> Khattiyas are supreme among this folk
> who believe (merely, and pointlessly) in lineage
> But supreme among gods and men
> Is the one replete with wisdom and virtue.

And thus ends the *Aggañña-suttanta*. 'Thus spoke the Buddha. Vasettha and Bharadvaja were deeply pleased by what he had said.'

The world in a mirror

If we think for a moment of the *Aggañña* as evidence, as a historical document, as simply reflecting its world passively as a mirror on the wall reflects the passing scene, then that world was clearly metamorphic, a world in continual transformation. One of those transformations was the long, slow decline of an older political and social order and the rise of monarchical states leading to empire. The people of the Gangetic plain were thus linked by what Wolf calls the 'tributary mode of production', in which rulers extract a surplus from their subjects by the threat or exercise of military force. Such a mode of production transcends any one society, culture, or people: the Sakyas and Vajjis could attest to that. These new relations are not the overt topic of the *Aggañña*, but they are in effect the warp of its fabric.

The other transformation, which is not mentioned explicitly at all, but is none the less the weft of the *Aggañña*, is the rise and establishment of the Buddhist Order. Before the arrival of the Buddha there was, to be sure, the loose group, really more a social category, of the Strivers, and they were no doubt contentious enough. But after his death he had left a new landmark on the scene, a new institution, and new kinds of relationship. Some of those relationships were within the Order, but others were with other Strivers and with the circumambient society.

Let me take this a step further. The metamorphic nature of

the world refracted through the *Aggañña* is but the obverse of the coin. The reverse is the plural character of that world. Though the text is composed from a relatively coherent viewpoint and from within what Erving Goffman might call a 'total institution', it nevertheless depicts the Order and the monks in relation to other institutions which embody different and mutually contradictory practices and values. It is true that the Buddhist monks presented, on the evidence of the *Aggañña*, a unified opinion of others in that world. Indeed they sought what might be called 'conquest by generality', intellectual victory by explaining or explaining away everyone else's opinions and attitudes: conquest, in short, by devising one's own form of paradigmatic thought and putting it forward in arguments. But that does not mean that Brahmans in general joined the Order or that they were in fact vanquished. On the contrary, the firmer the Buddhists became, the more entrenched grew the opposition of Brahmans and Jains and all the other sects and cults of that inventive civilization. There were many centres in that world, but no one centre, no one authority, that spoke for and to everyone.

Moreover, if we look closely at the *Aggañña*, we can see that it is, in an important sense, composed of that plurality. Or, more precisely, it is composed of the relations of the Order and monks with contradicting and hostile others. Consider, for a moment, the final verse: it is a statement of superiority, and were there nothing or no one to whom the implicit comparison could be made, there would be no sense in it. Similarly, the statement of the nature of the Order, that it is one circle of people who originate in the four circles of the estates, can only be made through the comparison. If we could perform a brutal thought experiment and remove from the *Aggañña* all traces of consciousness of self-and-other, then there would be nothing left.

This is the interactive character of the *Aggañña*. To be sure, the interaction here is quite different from the interaction between Mr S the story-teller and myself. That interaction was of a primary sort, a direct, face-to-face meeting and exchange.

The interactions of the *Aggañña*, on the other hand, are what might be called 'exploded interactions'. The image I have in mind is one of those mechanical drawings of a machine, say a child's bicycle, which are used by fumbling parents as a guide to assembly. The machine is shown as though caught in a moment of explosion, flying apart, separated, but with its nuts and bolts still properly related to each other in their right order and position.

The central exploded interaction of the *Aggañña* is that between the hearers of the discourse and the Buddha. True, the hearers do not actually meet and hear the Buddha, but only the monk who delivers the discourse. Yet in an extended and vividly imagined sense, they are brought face to face with their great predecessor: they are oriented towards him, just as monks today are instructed to orient themselves to him as teacher and preceptor when they do obeisance to his image. I think here of Benedict Anderson's notion that modern nation-states are 'imagined communities'. He suggests that through various media the citizens of a nation-state come to imagine themselves as though the whole nation were a face-to-face community. And that imagining of self-and-other, even though the others are not and never will be present, helps to create a real and effective sense of nationhood. By the same token the exploded interactions of the *Aggañña* and its setting create a complicit sense of the Order and its Teacher beyond any present assembly and in the face of the wider world.

I think it sensible, too, to extend the notion of an exploded interaction further. The audience engages with the Buddha, but then through his (narrated) agency they either witness, or confront, a series of further characters as well: the Brahman relatives, Pasenadi, the Sakyas, the beings. The reported interactions are indirect, taking place between people never met by the listeners, some of whom do not even exist. From a purely literary point of view the way in which these characters and their relations are depicted is artful and complex. The mixture of truth and irony, of direct statement and indirect implication, is intricate. Yet in one way or another the char-

acters and their relationships achieve vividness and verisimili-
tude, as though the audience were looking directly and plainly
into a world and recognizing its reality.

In this sense, of course, it is important to realize that the
interaction between Siddhasagar and the bull's owner was also
an exploded interaction. True, Siddhasagar's story as told to
me by Mr S and the *Aggañña* as told by generations of monks
are poles apart. One is short, spontaneous, and apparently
artless, the other long, cultivated and, artful. Yet both hold
up a mirror to a world far away from the situation of the
interlocutors. And both force upon the listener a relevance
between that distant world and the present one.

Holding up the mirror

In this respect the *Aggañña* is far from being a document, a
passive, fixed mirror. It is an instrument, as a mirror is an
instrument when someone holds it up for you to see whether
you approve your haircut or to show you a lipstick smudge on
your nose. It is created and used by people on other people for
a purpose. In this case the purpose was to edify and inform, to
set out an interpretation of spiritual truth within an interpretation of the Gangetic world, with its characters, its typical
plots, and its flow of action. The *Aggañña* promulgated a
social understanding.

What was the nature of that understanding? On the one
hand, part of it was specific, attaching to particular persons
and places: Savatthi, the Buddha, Pasenadi. But part of the
artfulness of the *Aggañña* consists in the way it leads from
such particular persons to more generic types. Vasettha and
Bharadvaja, for example, are named, but are in effect a type,
the type of good Brahmans from the Buddhist point of view,
Brahmans willing to support or join the Order. Their relatives,
on the other hand, are the type of bad Brahmans. Pasenadi is
quite specific, and his relationship to the Sakyas is quite
specific. But he is important for his generic relationships as
well, as a king to the generic ideal of Khattiyas, and to the
ideal of the realized Striver. The understanding thus promulgated was not, as I have stressed earlier, the understanding

of a god or of distant historical hindsight. It was rather just enough to orient a monk to the flow of action and to let him move accountably, with relevant social awareness, in the person of a monk. (That awareness is not the same as my interpretation of it, for monks had to be monks, not historians or anthropologists.) In this light the reciting of the *Aggañña* was part of the flow of action of the Gangetic world, one of a number of things that people did to other people to make things happen.

It is easy to see the founding of the Order and the collective composition of the *Aggañña* and related texts as creative acts, and as contributing to metamorphosis. Yet this raises another question. The *Aggañña* has a life now, as well as a life then. How should we regard something which, though it must at first have had a freshness, came to be preserved for more than two thousand years? Would we not then regard the *Aggañña* as being associated, not with metamorphosis and creativity, but with tradition and stasis? Of course anything can become hackneyed, taken for granted, tired and repetitious. Anything can come to be regarded as traditional, as a fixed landmark in the social flow. But the fate of the *Aggañña* itself is instructive, for it gave rise to a long series of further permutations and creative acts.

On the one hand, there is no trace in subsequent history of the ideal of the republican Khattiyas or of the social contract which, in the origin myth, gave rise to the first king. Though the myth stands out for us as the sort of thing that might have become the founding story of an egalitarian political order, nothing of the sort happened. The oligarchic republics disappeared from the Indian scene, perhaps shortly after the Buddha's death. In this respect the *Aggañña* as a whole became buried among the mass of transmitted Buddhist literature: it must have enjoyed some currency early in its life, but its force was lost and it is little quoted as a whole.

But that was by no means the end. Though the text as such apparently fell into desuetude, one character was rescued from it, a character who gloried in the name of 'The Great Agreed-on', Mahasammata. It is impossible to trace his origin, but we can say something of his setting: he arose in a Buddhist literature that took form in Buddhist kingdoms. For, as Indian civilization continued to metamorphose, there grew up Buddhist monarchs, among them the great Emperor Asoka, who flourished in the third century BC. The Buddhist Order adapted well to this change, and stories fit to tell an approved and approving Buddhist monarch gained currency. Among those stories was a slightly new one with a slightly new character, a story of the first emperor of the Sakyas, Mahasammata, ancestor of the Buddha and of the 'Solar Dynasty' of kings. Here Mahasammata had undergone a notable promotion, both in trappings and in importance. The Indian history of such stories is obscure, but Asoka sent a Buddhist mission to Sri Lanka, and in the fullness of time it, too, became a Buddhist kingdom, one with kings who traced their lineage to none other than the emperor Mahasammata himself.

Mahasammata continued to flourish and to seed new stories in new settings. The Buddhism of Sri Lanka was transplanted to Burma. There, as Robert Lingat observes, the Burmese Buddhist monks of Pagan in the eleventh century AD became, as they had become in Sri Lanka, the scribes and intelligentsia supporting a monarchical political order. They were in charge, for example, of codifying local law, and had to cast about for some original precedent to which their codification could be attached. Mahasammata came to mind. In Lingat's words,

Mahasammata, the world's first king, chosen by his people to put an end to discord, alone offered elements of a solution. It must have been tempting to attribute the precepts of the [local law] to Mahasammata. . . . But Mahasammata had to remain above all the model of the just king and could only be the interpreter of the law. Thus our authors, seizing upon the legend, completed it conveniently. They gave Mahasammata a counsellor, the [otherwise Brahmanical] hermit Manu. . . . They imagined that that Sage was raised into the celestial regions and reached the *cakkavala*, the wall which surrounds the world and which bears, carved in letters high as a bull, the law which rules it. It is this very text of the law which, rehearsed from memory by the hermit Manu, is set down in the [codified local law].[19]

And so on right down to the recent past in Sri Lanka, where, as the anthropologist S. J. Tambiah notes, Sinhalese villagers regarded Mahasammata 'as the institutor of the caste system and referred the degraded status of certain groups within the [local high] caste to a decree of this first king'.[20]

I have used the *Aggañña* to illustrate metamorphosis and creativity in human life, and to show how people use stories to create new social forms. But the *Aggañña* has also been used for a contradictory purpose, to argue for what I have here called a 'sea-shell' view of culture and society. On this view, espoused by S. J. Tambiah himself, the *Aggañña* is the deadly serious founding myth of Buddhist kingship. Its meaning in contemporary Sri Lanka is, on this view, essentially, beyond the accidents of history, and beyond its admitted differences, the same as it was in ancient India. It is, on his account, a story about the sacred origin of kings and the sanctioning of kingship by the Buddha. In that perspective, argues Tambiah, things have not changed.

But this cannot be right, for it falsifies even the plainest interpretation of the *Aggañña*'s words, and it misses the extraordinary transformations that the term *mahāsammato* has undergone. As a close reading of the *Aggañña* shows, it stands as evidence, not for some immutable cultural pattern echoing down the ages, but for the irreducibly plural and unstoppably metamorphic character of common social life.

8

The Bugbear, Science

LET me recapitulate the argument so far. I began by pointing out that human variability is rather more difficult to explain than had been thought. We are not just animals who are passively moulded by our respective societies and cultures, for we actively make and remake societies into new ways of life as well, and that calls for altogether more impressive abilities. I then argued that we have evolved those abilities, which I summarized as sociality. These capacities, which include social intelligence, an intense awareness of self-and-other, creativity, and narrative thought, are the common human nature which underlie social and cultural variability.

In the last three chapters I have explored these capacities and their implications. I gave precedence to narrative thought because it has been little explored as such, but also because it summarizes human sociality, allowing people to act with an awareness of the flow of action in which they are immersed. I have shown how thoroughly interactive is our social world and our knowledge of the social world. And I have shown how the metamorphic character of human experience—or, to put it another way, our remarkable fecundity of social forms—is intimately related to that interactive property.

So I have covered, however sketchily, a large arc of the circle of questions which compose anthropology's problem, human unity-in-diversity. I now turn to the remaining arc, the question of anthropology itself.

Perhaps the best way to phrase the difficulty is this: anthropology, too, has been invented, like other ways of life and thought that I have discussed here. It too lives within a created, mutable, specific form of life; it too is part of the metamorphic flow of human social experience. On the scale of things it is a recent and a parochial set of institutions and ideas which took root in the late nineteenth century in Britain, the United States, France, and Germany, and flourished in the twentieth century. It is, in other words, very much a product of a particular setting in a particular time, the late colonial and neo-colonial societies of the North Atlantic rim, just as Buddhism and Jainism were products of a different setting.

Now to make such a comparison undermines a great deal of the confidence which many anthropologists have felt or expressed in their writings. Indeed, if taken to its limit, it would undermine much of what I have said here. If anthropologists are to see themselves as only one form of life among others, only one human possibility among many, then how— other than by sheer unfounded arrogance—can such a limited perspective speak to and for our diverse species as a whole? What could justify a trust that anthropologists have something special and authoritative to say, when they themselves often insist that knowledge is relative to its historical and cultural setting? It is a question which has frequently been raised. Indeed it is endemic to the discipline, and quite properly so, because anthropologists must professionally doubt their own presuppositions. How else could they learn to see others' presuppositions clearly? But in the last decade or so the problem has given rise to a more encompassing, more corrosive doubt concerning the value and nature of the anthropological enterprise.

This doubt has centered on that substantial collective effort which constitutes most of anthropology, namely ethnography. Ethnography is the mapping, so to speak, of the diversity of human social life. It is the archive of human possibilities which provides the knowledge of actual diversity with which this book began. Most of the archive comes in large packages, i.e. monographs comprising book-length studies of one people or another. Here the notion has been that any way of life is so complex, and its facets so complexly mingled with one another and so subtle, that extensive treatment at length is best. Moreover these monographs in turn arise from relatively lengthy fieldwork, the intensive study of a fairly small group

through more or less face-to-face relations for a period measured in years rather than months. As George Stocking
remarks, 'this style of inquiry is much more than a mode of
data-gathering', for it places all value 'on fieldwork itself as
the basic constituting experience not only of anthropological
knowledge but of anthropologists'.[1]

In this perspective, uncertainty attaches to two facets of the
ethnographer's work. On the one hand, she must not only
enumerate or list this or that facet of peoples' lives—their
landholding, their family size, their diet—but she must also
learn how they relate to each other. And the best way, indeed
the only way, to do that is to engage personally with them, as
an accountable member of the social setting. This is often
called 'participant observation', but I would rather call it
'engaged learning' in order to capture the inescapably sticky
and involving nature of the process. Anthropologists learn
how people judge each other by being judged themselves, or
by being so closely a part of the scene that they react directly,
intimately and inwardly, often with discomfort and perplexity,
to people's judgements of each other. So anthropologists are
forced to learn about aesthetic standards in much the same
way that children do, using the same equipment.

Consequently anthropological knowledge begins as personal
knowledge about particular people in a particular place at a
particular time. This might be regarded as a strength, but it is
also subject to the objection that, if the knowledge is only
personal, then it is only your knowledge, and therefore is
not necessarily valid knowledge for others. This reflects in
miniature the larger uncertainty, that anthropology is your
society's knowledge, not a valid knowledge for everyone at all
times.

This uncertainty also attaches to the products of fieldwork,
the monographs of the ethnographic archive. Here the point
has been that these monographs are written in a particular
genre, one which stresses, directly or indirectly, that the
anthropologist has actually experienced what she writes about.
But this opens ethnography to the objection that its plausibility
is not factual, but merely literary. This objection has been

rendered the more believable by the prominence elsewhere in contemporary North Atlantic intellectual life of styles predicated on deconstruction and postmodernism. On this line, the authority of ethnographic writing is achieved by the authors' persuading the readers, as Clifford Geertz says, of 'their having actually penetrated . . . another form of life, of having . . . truly "been there".'[2] In this light, ethnography begins to seem more the fruit of (mere) imagination, and of interaction between pen and paper or keyboard and phosphor, than of real experience. Thus Geertz writes 'like quantum mechanics or the Italian opera, [ethnography] is a work of the imagination, less extravagant than the first, less methodical than the second. The responsibility for ethnography, or the credit, can be placed at no other door than that of the romancers [great anthropologists of the past] who have dreamt it up.'[3] In the last two chapters I will take these objections seriously, as objections that go to the heart of the anthropological enterprise and of anthropologists' understanding of human diversity.

My general argument will be as follows. Yes, anthropological research is based on personal experience, and indeed on personal capacities. Those capacities are the same ones which allow people to engage in social life, to learn aesthetic standards in the first place as children, or to learn, or create, new aesthetic standards or forms of life in adulthood. Just as immigrants can learn their way around their host society, and just as converts can take part in the institutions of a new religion, so can anthropologists learn to understand a new way of life. In this perspective anthropological fieldwork is a minor variant of a great theme in human life. It represents the continuing encounter, in the flow of events, with new and unprecedented social circumstances. Anthropologists face the same difficulties as Ramon, if with more privileges. I have argued that people are richly constituted to cope with that enduring contingency, so we should not be so surprised that anthropologists can do so as well.

The question then arises, what is the nature of the knowledge anthropologists produce from the encounter? I suggest that it is in fact a very complex sort of thing, made up partly of knowledge of an everyday sort, such as mind-reading and narrative. Upon that basis is then erected a superstructure of paradigmatic knowledge. This knowledge is a collective product, one made and certified within a particular institution by particular criteria at a particular time. This does, indeed, make anthropological knowledge relative, not absolute. But we must look to other sorts of knowledge to see how best to weigh that relativity.

I have argued, for example, that Buddhist monks have a collective product, their sacred literature, which has been made and certified within a particular institution by particular criteria. Is anthropology like that? Or is it more like other human products, such as the scientific knowledge which, collectively made and collectively applied, delivers that computer to your desk? I will suggest that, however we regard it on that scale, we can speak of anthropological knowledge as having reliability, so we can repose enough confidence in (good) ethnography to justify anthropologists' spending money and health on fieldwork and time and anguish on writing.

Art or science?

In this chapter I will concentrate on the fieldwork side of the question, and discuss the reliability of what ethnographers learn in the field. One writer who has already made some headway in this enterprise is Dan Sperber, and I will begin with the same sample of anthropological evidence that he began with, drawn from E. E. Evans-Pritchard's *Nuer Religion*:

I was present when a Nuer was defending himself against silent disapproval on the part of his family and kinsmen of his frequent sacrifices. He had been given to understand that it was felt that he was destroying the herd from inordinate love of meat. He said that this was not true. . . . It was all very well for his family to say that he had destroyed the herd, but he had killed the cattle for their sakes. It was 'kokene yiekien ke yang', 'the ransom of their lives with cattle'. He repeated this phrase many times as one by one he recounted cases of serious sickness in his family and described the ox he had sacrificed on each occasion to placate the spirit *deng*.[4]

Sperber goes on to explain that

this is about as raw a factual account as you will ever find in most ethnographic works. Yet not a single statement in it expresses a plain observation. 'Silent disapproval' cannot be observed but only surmised. Similarly, that a man 'had been given to understand that it was felt that . . .' is an inference from a variety of often ambivalent and complex behaviors. These inferences are likely to have been made not directly by the ethnographer, but by his informants. The resulting description is actually what the ethnographer selected from what he understood of what his informants told him of what they understood.[5]

It is difficult to do justice in a short space to Sperber's subtle argument, but his basic attitude is as follows. We can realistically hope for a 'factual account', a 'plain observation', or a 'description' from anthropology, but not from an anthropology which conceives itself as based in ethnography and ethnographic fieldwork as now practised. The real anthropology would be rather like cognitive psychology, and for Sperber cognitive psychology falls unambiguously into the category of 'science'. Ethnography on the other hand is an interpretive discipline which aims at the understanding and translation of culture, that is, the rendering of the unintelligible intelligible. Anthropology, on the contrary, would aim at scientific explanation, particularly of certain mental characteristics. The interpretations of ethnography could become the scientific material for anthropology only if accompanied by 'an appropriate descriptive comment that clarifies their empirical import'. In the light of the example from *Nuer Religion*, that comment would include an explicit statement of what was actually stated by whom and what was inferred by the ethnographer. In the present practice of ethnography, however, ethnographic evidence as presented is not factual, is not plain observation, is not description. It is interpretation and its empirical import is undetermined: we cannot tell unambiguously what the object of what statements is nor who their author might be. Nor could the bulk of ethnography ever aspire to truly scientific status.

Sperber is therefore quite crisp and clear, and I will disagree with him crisply and clearly. I will argue to the contrary that the notion of scientific knowledge underlying these remarks is erroneous, that the implied opposition between 'plain observation' and Evans-Pritchard's interpretation is a false one, that we can therefore take him to have 'observed' something like 'silent disapproval', that the 'inference' could have been made directly by the ethnographer, and that such evidently interpretive statements can easily be given useful empirical import.

The bugbear, science

Much of this chapter is a large but necessary detour. The problem lies in a received and abbreviated version of science which so deeply influences many social science writers. It may seem peculiar to deal with the question of anthropology by thinking first about physics or botany. It may seem pointless even to think of anthropology in such a frame. But in fact, just as the Buddha and his followers had no recourse but to speak of society in terms of the estate theory, however much they rejected the assumptions underlying it, so we must speak of knowledge in terms of scientific knowledge. Thus we find Geertz, for example, remarking on 'the oddness of constructing ostensibly scientific knowledge out of experiences broadly biographical': his point is to explain his notion of ethnographic evidence, but he finds he can only do so by comparing it with science. We in contemporary North Atlantic societies regard the natural sciences as the very type of knowledge, the very type of certainty and clarity, and we refer other sorts of knowledge to science as a benchmark.

So to make a virtue of necessity, I will begin by dealing with scientific knowledge. I will suggest that the notion of scientific knowledge as an absolute benchmark is an unrealistic and misguided conception of science. A more realistic grasp of science would inoculate anthropologists against the need to caricature their own activity by way of contrast. Once liberated from the anxiety of deciding whether what anthropologists do is scientific or not, we can then discern the actual character of their enterprise more decisively.

For a view of scientific practice I rely chiefly on what might be called the 'modified sociological realism' of Michael Polanyi, John Ziman, and Ian Hacking.[6] The central intuition of these writers is that science is a human activity, and as such is not so alienated from the world of human practice as to produce an absolute truth, absolute facts, or an absolute confidence in itself. Their theory of truth is not one of correspondence—facts simply match the way the world is—but rather a pragmatic one which considers the measure of truth to be in its use.

It is in fact a false dichotomy between knowledge and activity which has created the spectre of an unconditional and disembodied knowledge which now passes for science. As Hacking puts it, 'The harm comes from a single-minded obsession with representation and thinking and theory, at the expense of intervention and action and experiment.'[7] Or in other words, if we delved more deeply into the actual conduct of scientific work (as I suggest we delve into the conduct of anthropological work) we would find a more nuanced and less absolute image. Indeed Hacking regards activities such as calculating, modelling, structuring, theorizing, speculating, and approximating as only part of what scientists do. They also measure, scrutinize, notice, manipulate, mix, build, calibrate, make machines work—and, I may add, they also consult, argue, lecture, publish and do many other constitutively social things as well. Scientists do of course make representations—as for example, a table, a graph, a diagram, a set of equations, a verbal description, a model—but we are not to think of these as being true, but only as being more or less useful. 'When there is a final truth of the matter, then what we say is brief, and it is either true or false. It is not a matter of representation. When, as in physics, we provide representations of the world, there is no final truth of the matter.'[8] This contrasts with our usual, inaccurate view of science, which Hacking characterizes thus: 'When science became the orthodoxy of the modern world we were able, for a while, to have the fantasy that there is one truth at which we aim. That is [what we took to be] the correct representation of the world.'

A necessary part of modified sociological realism is that there be different representations of some subject, representations which may compete but which may also be just alternatives, each offering some advantages in manipulating the matter at hand. It is moreover a conception of science which is comfortable with a broader and historically informed view of scientific change and mutability. For my purposes the effect of Hacking's argument is to remove the sense of metaphysical absoluteness which we unthinkingly attach to science through the attribution of 'truth' to scientific judgements.

Finally, modified realism is sociological in that it recognizes that the sorts of knowledge thus produced are produced by people configured in relation to each other and flowing within a much larger stream of human events. As Ziman puts it, 'the cognitive contents of science depend for their form and integrity on the manner by which this social institution shapes and governs its members'.[9] Science has a social as well as an intellectual history, for new notions of evidence and argumentation may arise, old ones may perish, and the explanation for such events cannot be limited to the impersonal success of their results. No knowledge is knowledge *simpliciter*, but rather all knowledge is relative to a community of knowers. We need not think of science as transcending the human world, but rather as being embedded within the human world as one of the sorts of things that we do—or have done, for a little while, in some places.

Now if this general view of science is accepted, then I think its implications for the writings of Sperber, for others who have less explicitly compared anthropology and natural science, and for the absolute realist view which they implicitly espouse, are very great. On the absolutist view, scientific evidence and argument transcend the sociality and historicity of our merely human world, and measured against that standard ethnography cannot but seem insecure and trifling. Yet we see that scientific practices do not transcend our human world: they are human activities as well, part of human history and part of what humans do to, and with, each other as well as to the natural world. In that perspective science is more provincial, less universal, and less powerful than we might have thought. So one pole in the opposition between interpretive and scientific knowledge would be removed. We would be liberated from the powerful underlying compulsion to compare anthropological knowledge with an impossibly rigorous standard. We would be spared the lash driving us to absolute truth. Only such a compulsion could have called forth the reaction that ethnography is the product of 'romancers who dreamt it up'.

Liberation can be carried further as well. As Hacking and others have argued, this modified realism also entails that there are distinct modes of reasoning and different forms of evidence appropriate to different disciplines, to different kinds of representations, interventions, and manipulations. Such differences support the rejection of a unitary scientific touchstone of truth, but some particular rigour and some particular canon of evidence is still appropriate to each discipline. Indeed we can broaden our perspective, for on this account there is no reason to dwell solely upon the natural sciences. Even in the social sciences we may still be concerned with, as Paul Roth put it, 'how properly to warrant claims from within a chosen perspective'.[10]

Intersubjective pattern recognition

Since we are embarked on this detour into science, we can bring back some further ideas as well. I want now to introduce some notions used by Ziman to characterize many forms of natural science as what he calls 'reliable knowledge'. I recognize that there is a danger in this, since when I then apply the ideas to ethnography I might be thought to be asserting that ethnography is like, say, botany, full stop. It is not. What I mean to say is that there is a general design in the practices developed by North Atlantic societies for the collective creation of knowledge, and there are shared human capacities underlying that creation. It so happens that the general design and one set of capacities have so far been best understood in regard to the natural sciences.

Ziman's understanding of scientific knowledge comprises

three elements: a community of knowers, that which is perceptually consensible to them, and that on which they reach consensus. For the present I will be concerned with two elements, the community and consensibility.

The community is constituted of all those who can in principle perceive and report the same natural phenomena, such as a change in the colour of litmus paper. In this sense all observers are interchangeable and, as Ziman stresses, interchangeability or equivalence of observers is 'the foundation stone of all science'.[11] To discern the sense of this we have only to ask ourselves how science would differ if only members of the Church of England could observe a change in litmus paper, or only registered Democrats could detect neutrinos, or only Bantu speakers could measure crystal growth. Entry into the community of scientific observers is in principle universal, even though in practice access is limited by many contingencies. This 'in principle' universality guides the self-understanding and routine procedures of science. By the same token, the 'in principle' face-to-face community of members of a nation-state, though it is largely fictional, is nevertheless real in that it guides citizens' sense of self-and-other.

The universality of scientific observation is prominent in our received understanding of science while its collective character is less so. But of course the principle of interchangeability would mean little if the observations so made were idiosyncratic or hermetically private. In that sense the whole edifice of science rests upon perceptual consensibility, the ability of people to perceive things in common, to agree upon and to share perceptions.

Moreover, Ziman continues, the 'very possibility of perceptual consensibility depends upon a very ordinary faculty, shared by all human beings and by many animals. Without conscious effort, we all have remarkable skill at recognizing patterns.'[12] This 'intersubjective pattern recognition', he says, 'strikes deeper at the roots of "logicality" in science than the positivists seem to realize.' To illustrate his point Ziman presents the following, which he calls a 'message', designed to convey the results of a visual inspection to other scientists:

'Deciduous shrub, glabrous or nearly so, with weak, trailing sub-glaucous, often purple-tinted stems, either decumbent or forming low bushes 50–100 cm high, or climbing over other shrubs, rarely more erect and reaching 2 m. Prickles hooked, all more or less equal. L'flets 2–3 pairs, 1–3.5 cm, ovate or ovate-elliptic, simply, rarely doubly serrate . . .'[13] 'What is this strange plant?' he asks. Nothing other than a species of rose, the common field rose of Britain. 'It does indeed have the characteristics listed above; in the picture, however, we perceive a pattern which the botanist learns to distinguish like the face of a friend.'[14] And in fact even an American anthropologist can recognize it, if, that is, he lives in Britain and breaks out of a habitual daze from time to time.

In Ziman's account, the picture and its message—what Sperber would call its descriptive comment—are not simply a verbal and a pictorial representation of the same thing, and they are certainly not two versions of a single propositional truth. Rather, the pattern is just the pattern, which is not in that sense propositional at all. It cannot be true or false, though it might be faithful or less faithful, well drawn or badly drawn. On the other hand, the description, the message, is used to 'refer to other remembered visual patterns. How would one define the adjective "serrate", except to say that it was "like a saw"?'[15] The message helps to place the image in an 'archive' of images.

The message performs other functions as well: it may, for example, place in the archive other information about dates or locations or time of day or persons present or other identifying tags. Indeed the whole archive consists in a lacework of images with their messages. Some of the archive might be propositional, but to think of the lacework or any of its individual constituents merely as bearing a truth-value can hardly do justice to the complexity of its construction and use. This is the sense in which a logical positivist view of science is plainly inadequate. The point here is analogous to one I have made about narrative and paradigmatic thought: paradigmatic thought, or at least the cases I have so far mentioned, is made of propositions which can be simply, straightforwardly, true or false. That is the power of paradigmatic thought, but also its limitation, because it cannot comprehend what is perceived in a pattern or in a story.

Moreover the messages are intersubjective in that they make the patterns available to those who use them. The messages are used by persons to create the consensibility, the shared perception, which allows the image to be used as evidence among a collectivity—perhaps better, a lacework—of other persons: in this case, of botanists. (It is important to bear in mind here that the creation and registering of such patterns is only a small part of the process. Thereafter, even though consensibility is the basis of the enterprise, the conversion of consensible evidence into consensual bodies of reliable knowledge still depends upon a complex and by no means infallible social process.)

Finally, it is important to note that the ability to perceive the pattern and the ability to produce the pattern are not the same thing. A line-drawing of a field rose, for example, could only have been produced by someone with the requisite training and skills, while anyone with reasonable eyesight can perceive the pattern once it has been produced. At the other end of the process experience intervenes as well, for one can perceive the finally elicited pattern, read the message, and still not be able to do much with it, as I suppose most readers of this book could do little with a micrograph of the cells of the stem of a field rose. The trained biochemist, however, could place the pattern in a useful setting and use it to, say, manipulate cellulose into another configuration. A consensible pattern is only one, but an essential, part of the laborious weaving of scientific knowledge.

Ziman's is an intricate argument, but for my purposes I want to take from it just one question: is there anything in ethnographic practice which corresponds to intersubjective pattern recognition? Note that this question involves the following analogy. Just like a physicist or botanist, the anthropologist might be provided with certain equipment, an ability to recognize certain kinds of patterns, just by virtue of being human. Anthropologists study humans, so are there human patterns which anthropologists can recognize using the original equipment they came with, plus, perhaps, a little experience?

Human patterns

In making a point very similar to the one I wish to make here, Raymond Firth presents what can be regarded as just such pattern recognition. During his fieldwork among the Tikopia in Polynesia he received word that his friend, Pa Rangifuri, son of the local chief, was *teke*, which means 'unwilling (to do something)' or 'angry', or 'objecting (even violently)':

This message [that Pa Rangifuri was *teke*] left the degree of objection open, but when it was also reported that this much respected senior man had been seen striding to his house in a greatly disturbed state people inferred that he was angry, though they were as yet ignorant of the cause. The whole village was concerned. When we got to his house we found him highly agitated. He and I greeted each other with the usual pressing of noses, as publicly recognized friends, but for him this was an unusually perfunctory gesture, and he paid me little attention. He was uttering brief incoherent statements: 'I'm going off to sea' . . . 'They said their axe should cut first . . .' 'But was it for a dirge, no! It was for a dance!' Men were trying to sooth him down by respectful gestures, and to enquire the reason for his agitation. Tears were streaming down his cheeks, his voice was high and broken, his body quivering from time to time.[16]

Now the simplest answer here, and in the following examples, is that this is intelligible as a story, and we are richly provided with the tools of narrative thought. But now I want to delve more closely into some of the reasons that narratives might be understood across cultures.

Let me first note that anthropologists have an informal but widely influential code of practice which would prevent any very easy interpretation of these events. They are to cultivate a thorough scepticism that one understands directly and easily the experience and thought of people with very different socio-cultural backgrounds from oneself. Differences of values and attitudes between societies can often be profound, and we are too likely to project our own ideas and values on to others;

for after all part of the point of acquiring one's own aesthetic standard is to see, in Michelle Rosaldo's words, 'emotionally oriented themes and images' which 'maintain for [a particular people] a sense of consistency in things that people do, thereby permitting them to see over time that people act in more or less familiar ways for more or less well-known reasons'.[17] So we might be importing our own judgements, our own aesthetic standards, inappropriately.

Hence an anthropologist would ask first for what is culturally specific in the affair of Pa Rangifuri. It is likely, for example, that some of Pa Rangifuri's display of emotion was specific to the style and emotional registers of the Tikopia. The high, broken voice and the tears do not for example sound very British, or at least not very British for a 'much respected senior man'. It is also likely—and Firth later makes this clear—that the occasion for the emotion was strongly determined by local conceptions of rights and obligations and by the particular circumstances of Pa Rangifuri's life in relation to others. Indeed something of this dimension is already inherent in the actions and judgements of those surrounding him. Perhaps the events accompanying Pa Rangifuri's distress followed the cultural grain of Tikopia life in what Edward Schieffelin has called a 'cultural scenario', a particular sense of how narratives of real life should move. And it should also be stressed that some literary skill has gone into presenting the pattern, which is set out in lucid, well-written prose.

But however Firth achieves his result, the pattern in itself is 'intelligible'—the word used by Firth—and Anglophone readers do not need the translation of the word *teke* or the whole social and cultural setting to get the basic idea. Just as Ziman did not require a theory of perception to make his point that visual patterns are consensible, so Pa Rangifuri's demeanour is consensible without us having to embrace any particular view of how this comes about. We need not subscribe, for example, to a theory of 'hard-wired', innate perception of particular emotions to realize that Pa Rangifuri is upset. We do not need to know the details of Tikopia aesthetic standards or folk psychology or of Pa Rangifuri's place in social relations to grasp the fundamentals of the pattern. Indeed there is something peculiarly pure about our apprehension of Pa Rangifuri's state: we, like the other Tikopia then present, are mystified about the causes of Pa Rangifuri's condition. Yet we, like them, can perceive that something has happened and we can place very roughly the character of that something. For us now it would be a matter of leisurely curiosity, though for the Tikopia then it was a matter of pressing urgency, to connect this consensibly recognized pattern with some larger explanation.

Let me look more closely at the reasons for the intelligibility of Pa Rangifuri's behaviour. In this book I have stressed certain universal traits of humans, but I have left out many others. I am prepared to accept, for example, following Gananath Obeyesekere, that there is a capacious sheaf of attitudes and relationships that centre upon desire and domination in human families[18]—the Oedipus complex, but the Oedipus complex quite stretched and reconfigured into different forms in different societies with different forms of households and kinship practices. But in this case the universal pattern is hardly as contentious or as elaborate. It is one we have all experienced intimately: the exhibition of distress by human infants and children, and occasionally, as here, by human adults. We can see the distress in Pa Rangifuri's behaviour, and that impression is bolstered by the reaction of others around him, who tried to sooth him. I grant that there must be a great deal that goes into the production and recognition of distress, but that is not my concern here. Firth, the other Tikopia, you, and I recognize what is happening to Pa Rangifuri because we have all, in Geertz's words, 'been there'.

I have begun with this example of Firth and Pa Rangifuri not because it is absolutely simple—it is not—but because it is simple relative to the sorts of consensible patterns which ethnographers usually use. Often the reader is asked to compass at a glance a pattern comprehending several individuals at once. Here is a passage from Gilbert Lewis's book *Day of Shining Red*, in which the ethnographer is explaining how the

Gnau of Papua New Guinea pass on their ritual knowledge:

When I questioned people about how they had learned or failed to
learn about something, for example, a myth, or genealogies, or the
meaning of some ritual action, they sometimes mentioned individuals
who told them . . . or they said it was the sort of thing men used to
talk about in the evening in the [men's house] when they were lying
on their beds before going off to sleep, or on rainy days when they
hung around by the fireside. In similar circumstances, although
rarely, I have heard men by some chance get round to a myth and tell
it, or go into some explanatory point about the meaning of a rite.[19]

In other words, the point of Lewis's exposition is that the
Gnau do not systematically and purposefully go about passing
on such knowledge and they have no institutions devoted to
that end. The evidence for this argument consists in the un-
planned and purposeless occasions on which the Gnau do pass
on such knowledge. These occasions form a consensible
pattern. The relevant part of the message that goes with the
pattern might be something like 'sociable purposelessness', or
better, 'hanging around'. It is true that a rainy afternoon in,
say, a college dormitory in Connecticut is in many ways very
different from a 'similar occasion' in a men's house up the
Sepik, but the sense of similarity which gathers these and the
other nameless occasions Lewis mentions into one set would
be difficult to miss. I suppose that part of the consensibility lies
in the contrast with that 'social activity' or 'doing something
together' which is so characteristic of us as a species. But
however that may be, the image which bears Lewis's argument
is socially complex, comprehended as a number of individuals
taken together. Yet it is immediately graspable—again partly
through Lewis's art, but largely because we recognize immediately what he is describing.

Some of the most compelling, and yet complex, consensible
patterns used by ethnographers are those that add a further
level of complexity, namely temporal change and movement,
to a situation shared by a number of people. In the following
passage Godfrey Lienhardt describes such a movement in

order to reveal what counts for the Dinka as the most significant part of a sacrifice. He begins by pointing out that during a sacrifice the Dinka invoke divinities over and over again:

This rhythmical repetition of particular sets of words and ideas, spoken first singly then in unison, gradually has an effect which may be observed by anyone attending a sacrifice and, moreover, comes to be felt by the foreign observer himself. At the beginning of such a ceremony there is usually a lot of chatter and disorder. People come and go, greet each other. . . . It is common for those officiating to try to call people to some order. . . . As the invocations increase in tempo, however, the little bursts of incisive speech by the invoker and his chorus draw the congregation more and more towards the central action. . . . As the invocations proceed, the repeaters of the invocations work together more smoothly in rhythmical speech, and a collective concentration upon the main theme and purpose of the gathering becomes apparent. This concentration of attention on a single action ends when the sacrificial victim is thrown and killed.[20]

The assertion towards which Lienhardt leads us is that the killing of the victim is the central act of sacrifice and is so considered by the Dinka. The evidence he adduces for this consists in a pattern which can be grasped hardly less immediately than Lewis's 'hanging around', though it is a pattern which moves and develops over a considerable time. Lienhardt does not spell out how he knows that 'collective concentration' becomes apparent, but we can easily see that this is a fairly straightforward example of self-and-other consciousness. We can follow people's gaze, we can compare what they were doing earlier to what they are doing now, we can see people orient their bodies collectively to one point and grow quiet. Part of the accompanying message might indeed be 'collective concentration', which suggests a family resemblance to many other such occasions throughout the world. Lienhardt conveys a slightly less abstract message with more art by using such words as 'congregation', so evocative of assemblies with a quite specific cultural provenance in North Atlantic societies. Other comparisons could usefully be made, and indeed one such comparison appears in the chief identifying tag, 'sacrifice'. Yet there is no reason to believe either that these messages or any other, either singly or together, should exhaust the possibilities for comparison. The pattern itself is consensible apart from any particular messages that might be associated with it.

The Dinka sacrifice raises a number of issues which were not so easily distinguishable in the earlier examples. In the first place, as Robert Layton has reminded me and as I can richly attest, fieldwork usually begins for the ethnographer in a welter of confusion and incomprehension. Even the most elementary matters, such as when a ceremony begins or even if it is going on, are far from obvious. It therefore seems quite conceivable that Lienhardt would not have been able at first to appreciate fully the pattern in what he was watching. Indeed he admits as much when he writes that the effect 'comes to be felt by the foreign observer himself'. The idea of consensibility does not, however, require that patterns be immediately and easily elicited. The only requisite is that once patterns are elicited they be mutually intelligible.

It might also be suggested that Lienhardt's very artfulness militates against reliable consensibility. But once again the notion of consensibility does not preclude care and workmanship going into the representation of patterns. A line-drawing of a field rose is artfully made, but such craftsmanship, far from being superfluous or deceitful, is an absolute requirement for the archive of botany.

Moreover from this it follows that intersubjective patterns need not be conceived as having one correct, canonical form. Though there might be other and very different ways of representing some matter—a rose, a sacrifice—this does not invalidate the consensibility or the evidential character of a pattern as represented. A new dimension of the matter at hand can be explored by devising a new representation without rendering a former representation erroneous. Indeed for the same reason the message accompanying the pattern need not be regarded as single, simple, or closed: as we learn more about Dinka or about other ways of life we might want to draw out other entailments of the Dinka sacrifice by using new messages.

Finally, there is no reason to believe that the consensibility of patterns exhibited by ethnographers comprise a lexicon of patterns. Here once again the analogy with natural scientific pattern recognition is useful: we do not suppose that we would fail to learn and recognize the form of even an indefinitely large spectrum of rose species, even if each were only slightly different from the field rose. Whatever it is that allows us to see patterns, it is not a foreordained dictionary of images to which the world conforms. And so, analogously, we need not assume that there is only a limited or specifiable number of patterns to be found in human life. The point of Richard Hofstadter's argument concerning humans' ability to recognize themes or patterns and variations is just that it is—for practical purposes anyway—infinitely extensible.

Narrative patterns

I make this point about the infinite extensibility of pattern recognition because I now turn to a familiar theme: narrative. The most complex patterns of all are narrative ones, made of people with intentions, attitudes, and notions set in a flow of action. Firth's story about Pa Rangifuri develops into just such a pattern. Those gathered around Pa Rangifuri gradually pieced together what had happened. He had burst out of his father the chief's house without taking formal leave, that is, without the decorum proper to his station as son and commoner. The men present then instructed Firth, as a relatively neutral party, how to take Pa Rangifuri's wrist and lead him back to apologize. When this was done

the background to his [Pa Rangifuri's] outburst then became clear to us [all those present before the chief]. My friend's son had been lost at sea some months before (as I knew) and he had wanted to make preparations for a celebratory mortuary rite. . . . But when he had gone to ask his father for an axe to begin to cut down trees to make barkcloth for the graveclothes the old chief had temporized, and he had thought his father was refusing him, so threw himself out of the house. (As it emerged later, in private, he had put this down to manipulations by his brothers whom he had suspected of wanting a dance festival to precede the mourning ritual, so making their drain on family resources take priority.) His father now explained that he had not refused the request for the axe, that he had had something else on his mind, and that if his son had only waited, permission to go ahead with the funeral preparations would have been given to him. After this, the axe was handed over, and the way to the funeral rites was now open.[21]

Let me first separate the workmanship of representation in this passage from the pattern itself. There are some terms— 'celebratory mortuary rite', 'barkcloth', 'graveclothes', 'mourning ritual', 'dance festival', 'funeral rites'—which must be supposed to indicate Tikopia words, practices, and articles which are not further specified. The craft lies partly in the elegant variation so prized in English expository prose, partly in what is suggested in English by 'funeral', 'mortuary', and 'mourning', but also in a suggested contrast between a 'dance festival' and 'funeral rites'. By this contrast Firth hints that the strong opposition between such activities conveyed in the English words is likewise felt among the Tikopia and was important to Pa Rangifuri. So in that sense we need not know the actual contents of a 'dance festival' or 'funeral rites', for their significance is provided by the flow of events. An analogous argument could be made for 'chief'. In the course of the passage we learn that the son 'requested' the axe of him, that he had not 'refused', and that his 'permission' was required. So even if we don't know very much about Tikopia chiefs, we do understand their relevant characteristic in this series of actions and reactions, and that is the ability to give or withhold permission.

Still it is not perhaps immediately clear wherein the pattern consists. But I think we can do better than that. We can begin by unpacking the passage on different scales of time. In the foreground, in the immediate past and present of Firth's narrative, are the events of the quarrel and reconciliation, taking place on a scale of minutes or hours. This flow is intelligible on an understanding of self-and-other consciousness, of action and reaction, centring on the perception of Pa Rangifuri's state of distress and the immediate cause for it, his father's refusal of the axe. Moreover we are shown by Firth that the Tikopia have a method of reconciliation, a method that is their own (taking Pa Rangifuri by the wrist to lead him back, a particular form of apology). And we can discern a more widely available intelligibility in this, for just as distress often arises because of what A does to B, so reconciliation restores harmony to A and B.

But this action in the foreground itself became a problem to those present. They simply did not know what accounted for these events, and for an explanation they had to look to a larger flow, one measured on a scale of months and years. That flow consists in an explanation that was finally forthcoming: the loss of Pa Rangifuri's son at sea, Pa Rangifuri's consequent grief, and his further disappointment at his father's refusal of the axe. Once again there is something generic here, but something is also revealed about Pa Rangifuri himself, his predicament and his character within that predicament. It is his character amidst events that renders the foreground understandable.

Moreover there is a larger setting yet, one measured in decades and generations, in which the old chief took office, had sons who rivalled each other, and so forth, in the characteristic ways of the Tikopia at that time. This larger frame is usually presented by anthropologists in a disassembled form, in the form of norms or the schemes of social organization, and in an explanatory passage Firth summarizes this background in just such terms. But this material, too, is based on narrative material such as legends, myths, or reported events which connect an understood, intelligible past with occurrences of the recent past and present. I have already made this point at great length. The people involved in the action need the narrative understanding, for that is what enables them to act accountably and intelligently. Anthropologists, too, need such a narrative understanding. But from that understanding they go on to construct something else, a view of a society or culture framed in anthropology's characteristic paradigmatic thought.

I think it important to stress that the apprehension of others which is predicated in narrative thinking is not an absolute, impersonal, and unqualified Cartesian knowledge, as though an X-ray of someone's grey cells. It is rather an understanding that arises only within the give and take of common life, and so is qualified by time, place, persons present, and the actual flow of events and relations within which those persons are immersed. It was not Pa Rangifuri's state of being *teke*, its psychological description and its physiological manifestations, which concerned the Tikopia or which constituted their explanation, but the significance of that state for what was going on. He was not *teke* in some abstract or absolute sense, but relative to the persons involved—his father, his brothers, his dead son—and to the swiftly changing situation in which he and the others present found themselves. In that intersubjective sense the designation *teke* was a seed, bearing the potential to grow into an elaborated narrative of persons, relations, and events—a plot with characters which would satisfy initial puzzlement.

Indeed the only thing that could satisfy that puzzlement was a story which set Pa Rangifuri's distress in a narrative flow of people acting in respect of each other. Moreover this story, as Firth presents it, was not one he or anyone else devised in private, but arose rather out of events and utterances occurring before a body of concerned persons. Not just the events themselves, but also their unfolding explication and commentary were widely known. There might, of course, have been various interpretations of events at various times during the action and especially afterwards; but in order to act relevantly the participants had to fasten on some minimal shared understanding, an understanding which grew more explicit as the affair moved towards resolution.

Against the scepticism and doubt with which this chapter began, it is important to emphasize that narrative as used by anthropologists presupposes a thoroughly intersubjective account of emotions, intentions, attitudes, and motives. Anthropologists 'read minds', but only in the limited, fallible, everyday, and universally human way in which everyone reads minds by attributing attitudes, intentions, understandings, and emotions to each other. I make this point because so many, including an illustrious company of social anthropologists and social theorists, have treated intentions, emotions, attitudes, and motives as essentially hidden, private, unaccountable, or irrelevant. They have perhaps done so in reaction to our academic folk psychology (based on our philosophical folk psychology), which has deemed it reasonable to consider people quite apart from their social setting. But in the light of the more radically, fundamentally social and interactive view of human nature which I have set out here, states of mind are not so much personal as interpersonal.

In fact the yardstick against which mind-reading is to be judged is not omniscience but relative success. By the same token, the attributions of motive and attitude which appear in narration need only be adequate to account usefully for the stream of action and reaction. Indeed it is difficult to see how such attributions could go beyond what is revealed in the stream of action. We cannot seek an absolutely correct, unequivocal, 'scientific' understanding of such mental states apart from interaction, for it is only interaction which gives them sense and makes them available to consensible representation.

A sceptic of anthropological evidence might still ask about the accuracy of Firth's account. Do I mean to say that it is just a plain, straightforward and true account, or is it something else? Well, it must be something else, for it is not simply and straightforwardly accurate. Rather, the pattern is a synthesis, an artefact, but one produced under a particular constraint: it had to set out in a perspicuous order those events and attributions adequate to produce an account of what made participants act, and what the consequences of those acts were. The criterion for including any detail was just that it contribute to showing how one thing led to another. As a synthesis it is no less 'created' than Lienhardt's account of Dinka sacrifice or the drawing of the field rose.

The negative side of such a synthesis is that there is absolutely no guarantee whatsoever that all possible relevant details were included or that all relevant viewpoints were considered. Perhaps the old chief had a much deeper plan than anyone realized, or there was conflict over another, unmentioned matter which had been simmering. Perhaps Firth himself was unwittingly the vessel of a pervasive and disruptive colonial influence. There are myriad possibilities and no account of human events can be wholly proof against such rude surprises.

On the other hand the synthesis does possess five characteristics which inspire confidence:

1) It does account for the flow of events;
2) The attributions of attitude and motive are closely and intelligibly tied to people's interactions;
3) The attributions are those disclosed by the participants in the course of events;
4) The action is unequivocally and vividly related to the particular circumstances of life among the Tikopia; and
5) The episode as told has robustness and independence from its use by Firth.

The first four characteristics are most closely relevant to the fidelity of the story. Firth was himself closely implicated and was therefore in a position to follow events closely: you could hardly hope to have a more intimate view. But it is the last which has the most interesting implications. Because the story is in principle independent of its use by Firth, it becomes a sort of common property. It could be used by someone else, and indeed could be used to illustrate very different things: fraternal rivalry, generational conflict, an anxiety to pacify chiefs, or the very peculiar position of axes among the Tikopia at the time. In that sense the episode has a distinct character as evidence rather than argument, as an item in the archive rather than the reasoning made from such items, as a foundation rather than the edifice rising above the foundation. For all these reasons, then, we would be justified in accepting and using Firth's account, until, that is, some startling new datum is revealed.

Evans-Pritchard vs. *Sperber*

The little story of the Nuer justifying his frequent sacrifices has much the same character as Firth's tale of Pa Rangifuri. It is elliptically told and it refers to a flow of events understandable in both a larger and a more immediate frame. It does not suggest a theoretical use in itself but would be amenable to many such uses. Let me take Sperber's comments on it one by one.

Sperber says that 'this is about as raw a factual account as you will ever find in most ethnographic works. Yet not a single statement in it expresses a plain observation.' But, first, the ideas of 'plain observation' and 'raw factual account' are, as I have argued, inappropriate. Representing the patterns used as evidence in either case takes a good deal of art and energy. Second, if it be thought that 'observation' could be direct, immediate, and achieved without skill or application, then that too is false. Evans-Pritchard had not just parachuted in, but had already spent time among the Nuer, time which was absolutely vital to his perceiving and reporting patterns in Nuer life. So, for good or ill, a good deal of artifice and experience have already gone into what is reported, and would do so in any discipline.

Sperber's next observation concerns the following statement by Evans-Pritchard: 'I was present when a Nuer was defending himself against silent disapproval on the part of his family and kinsmen of his frequent sacrifices.' Sperber remarks: ' "Silent disapproval" cannot be observed but only surmised.' But to the contrary I suggest that 'silent disapproval' is just the sort of thing that people grasp pretty directly.

Let us look at this more closely. In the first place, Evans-Pritchard's remark is set in an elliptical but quite unambiguous narrative frame. That narrative frame is revealed in the next sentences: 'He [the Nuer in question] had been given to understand that it was felt that he was destroying the herd from inordinate love of meat. He said that this was not true. . . . It was all very well for his family to say that he had destroyed the herd, but he had killed the cattle for their sakes.' Sperber could complain that the who, when, and where of this story are obscure, but the basic narrative flow is not. For some time the Nuer had been killing cattle from his herd in frequent sacrifices. This had depleted the herd, indeed severely so in the eyes of his 'family and kinsmen'. They conveyed their objections to him and—now the action switches to the immediate scene witnessed by Evans-Pritchard—they met his prolonged protestations with silent disapproval. So in this setting the 'silent disapproval' is understood as part of a flow of actions and reactions among a group of people, the Nuer and his kinsmen. 'Silent disapproval' gains its sense and meaning as a consequence of earlier events—the frequent sacrifices and the kinsmen's reaction to them—and it leads on to further action, the protestations of the man against unspoken but implicit accusation. There is no question here of some mystical understanding of brain waves or of information beyond what any competent participant could acquire.

So provided that Evans-Pritchard was privy to the stream of events in which the silent disapproval was set, he could have used the phrase with confidence. Was Evans-Pritchard privy to the stream of events? Sperber is sceptical. He writes that the preceding part of the narrative, unravelled from the phrase 'he had been given to understand that it was felt that', is 'an inference from a variety of often ambivalent and complex behaviors. These inferences are likely to have been made not directly by the ethnographer, but by his informants.'

The material does not permit an unequivocal response to this. Sperber may be right. But there is evidence to the contrary. One circumstance which would make us incline strongly to Evans-Pritchard's account would arise if he had actually witnessed an earlier argument between the Nuer and his relatives over sacrifice. There is no way of knowing whether this is so, but Evans-Pritchard has noted more than once that his Nuer research was carried out mostly without the advantage of informants, simply by living among the Nuer. So he might have had that sort of confidence in his own judgement.

But what if he had merely been told of antecedent disagreements? Is it likely that the disagreements were merely surmised by the informant? Perhaps, but if the informant had local knowledge then we would not think it mere 'inference' or a 'surmise' if he or she told Evans-Pritchard that the Nuer and his family quarrelled over frequent sacrifice. It just is the sort of thing that neighbours know as a matter of course. One hears raised voices. One hears what the quarrel is about. We would not think such knowledge ambivalent, even though it would certainly be complex, based as it is on the powerful intellectual abilities inherent in human sociality.

The most plausible reading is that the antecedents were revealed by the Nuer himself in the course of expostulation. Perhaps he said something like 'you always say I sacrifice too much, but I don't!' And Evans-Pritchard's statements support that view. The following indirect speech, 'it was all very well for his family to say that he had destroyed the herd', suggests that the clue to the continuing quarrel appeared right before Evans-Pritchard when the Nuer spoke. To expand whatever the Nuer said to 'he had been given to understand that . . .' is perhaps inference, but it is hard to see it as invalid or misleading. Evans-Pritchard came in during an argument, and there were enough clues available for him to pick up the threads.

The implication is, I think, that we must attribute to Evans-Pritchard a kind of practical knowledge of events. Such knowledge is of course neither omniscient nor abstract, but it has at least one desirable characteristic: it arises out of the stream of events which alone can make the details intelligible. This does not amount to treating Evans-Pritchard as a Nuer, or to saying that he understands all dimensions of Nuer life, or even to saying that he could hold his own in argument with a Nuer. Rather it is to accept that, in the setting of this particular case, he possessed enough competence to make his way sensibly.

I suggest therefore that the measure of such knowledge is not abstract, but pragmatic: could you act appropriately in its light? Or—since the knowledge is sometimes discovered in retrospect or in a failure to act properly—could you have acted appropriately had you only known? In the case of Evans-Pritchard and the protesting Nuer we take that limited competence already to have been achieved. Elsewhere, for example when Lienhardt remarks that the effect of Dinka invocation 'comes to be felt by the foreign observer himself', a process of achieving the knowledge by oneself is fleetingly revealed. In other cases, as when Firth was shown just how to lead Pa Rangifuri by the wrist to apologize, the knowledge is explicitly taught. And in some very marked and painful cases, the evidence arises not from a finished competence but from a very protracted course of learning. It might be thought that anthropologists' inexperience invalidates their evidence, but on the contrary, it is often from their very lack of expertise, and its correction, that the most persuasive testimony originates.

From consensibility to consensus

I began with an apparent paradox, namely the problem of constructing public and reliable knowledge out of material that seems irreducibly personal and autobiographical. But once we understand ethnography as an activity the paradox resolves itself.

Let me put it this way: there are, in effect, two kinds of knowledge. One kind of knowledge is a practical one used in social life. It is the knowledge used by, for example, the Nuer themselves as accountable agents in a flow of action in their society. To an extent such knowledge is personal, for it is a knowledge of persons exercised by persons in respect of each other. It is the knowledge that, for example, Jains have of their local gastro-politics and gastro-religious relations. But it also has a generic side, or at least generic potential: it can be extended to new people in new circumstances. In this respect the knowledge concerns an aesthetic standard, a sense of what is more or less appropriate or expected in one circumstance or another. The only test of such knowledge, the only way in which anyone can know whether someone has it or not, is the test of daily life. Each person's understanding is thereby verified or corrected in public, though the public is not a college of scholars but the school of hard knocks.

In the first instance, an ethnographer such as Evans-Pritchard engages with this expertise as he meets it in those around him. He does not necessarily do so perfectly, but to get along at all he must make some headway in learning it himself, for he must live as an accountable person among those studied. And from the experience of so living he begins to learn consensible patterns. This the anthropologist does in much the same way, and with much the same equipment, as anyone might: a traveller, a trader, an immigrant, a child.

But, unlike these characters, the anthropologist has an extra use for that knowledge. He records it—and of course by 'recording' I mean something more than just writing down various incidents and scenes. For the anthropologist reflects on such events, brings them to consciousness, compares them with other events and rehearses them in his mind. The object of such rehearsal is the creation of a second sort of knowledge, one founded upon the Nuer knowledge of persons by persons, but validated among a much wider and more diffuse community, including not only the world of anthropology but also often the informants themselves. For this community the knowledge is transformed from knowing how to knowing that, from a performer's to a critic's consciousness, from narrative to paradigmatic thought. Indeed it is just the taking of an intimate social knowledge and transforming it into paradigmatic knowledge that stamps ethnography with its own distinctive values and character as a discipline.

Now it is a very very long way from participating in a quarrel between a son and his father the chief to the use of that incident in an ethnographic text. It is, in other words, a long way from one form of knowledge to the other. The way is marked by a great deal of further effort on the part of the ethnographer. For example, many other things must be recorded, such as a census of the local population, a survey of methods of gaining a living, oral texts, and so forth. Again, these latter forms of, so to speak, countable or enumerable forms of information must be set beside the practical knowledge of social life in a mutually illuminating way, and that requires a great deal of hard thought as well. And beyond these labours, the anthropologist has to phrase his judgements in such a way as to attract the credence of his readers. He has, in other words, to create consensus among a loose or even very disparate group of people, a group which may now include those anthropologized as well as his peers and perhaps a broader readership in his native society. But whatever consensus is achieved, it is based upon the consensibility of the narrative and other patterns he sets before them.

So there is much more that goes into making anthropological knowledge. It is by no means a matter merely of stringing together a few tales about things that happened in the field. For the present, suffice it to say that we place requirements upon the new knowledge which are quite foreign to its original matrix: it must fit into a more abstracted view of human societies and it must be corrigible or falsifiable. Some anthropologists mix this knowledge with a literary skill whose effect is not to mystify but to clarify. Yet if the anthropological knowledge thus created did not retain its animating spirit in the Nuers' personal knowledge of each other, it would not be knowledge but mere fancy.

9

An Untidy Box of Sweets

IN the previous chapter I asked this question: if anthropology itself is created out of the flow of human life and human relations—created, in other words, out of something so mutable and metamorphic—how can we repose confidence in it? And to that I gave the answer (as far as it goes) that we might repose roughly as much confidence in anthropology as in any other collective activity. On one hand, this required a measured decrease in our confidence in the natural sciences. On the other, it suggests an increase in our reliance on personal—which is to say, on *interpersonal and intersubjective*—judgement.

Let me recapitulate the longer journey that brought us to this answer. At the very beginning I began by asking three closely related questions. First, what unity underlies the cultural diversity of humanity? To that question I gave the reply that we, as a species, possess a particular set of traits and capacities, our sociality. That sociality culminates in the ability to track a complex flow of social action. This is not a full and comprehensive reply, for I left out many promising candidates, many attributes that might be included in the 'psychic unity of humankind'. But the abilities which I included in sociality were those which, I judged, had been most prominent in creating the social and cultural diversity of our species. In other words, I stressed those things we all share which have allowed us to differ so greatly.

These considerations led directly to the second question: how does the diversity come about? I did not cover all relevant senses of the question, but took it only to mean, how could the diversity come about? In reply I argued that people are not only capable of tracking a complex flow of action, but also of responding appropriately within such a flow. I stressed that, when we conceive our human plight in these terms, the sense of 'appropriately' must be flexible and approximate rather than unbending and absolute. We need not, indeed must not, conceive ourselves as automatons or puppets, since the social circumstances we meet are, in Nicholas Humphrey's words, 'ephemeral, ambiguous and liable to change, not least as a consequence of our own actions'. And I also suggested that our sense of a social flow, and of what to do within the flow, are subject to negotiation by those involved. And so, I concluded, we are able individually to grasp, and collectively to create, new situations, understandings, and forms of life.

This answer brought us to the third question: how can we come reliably to understand that diversity? And in Chapter 6 on Siddhasagar's story, as well as in Chapter 8, I argued that the basis of anthropological knowledge is no different than the basis of anyone's knowledge of the social world. It is a useful, if limited, understanding, tailored to the flexible, adaptable conduct of human relationships. But I said, too, that anthropologists make that social knowledge into another kind of knowledge, known as ethnography. Ethnography is a style of paradigmatic learning which is closely tied to particular people in particular places at particular times. In this chapter I say something of the nature of, and the value and use of, that learning.

Is it bigger than a bread-box?

From time to time in this book, and especially in the previous chapter, I have written of the 'archive' of ethnography. The notion that there is such an archive, attesting decisively to human socio-cultural diversity, is something I have laid down as a basic assumption. Now, however, I want to call that idea gently into question. I do so because the idea does not quite capture, or does not wholly capture, the character of what anthropologists do.

Let me begin by exploring the idea of the ethnographic archive and some of its ramifications. The archive represents the accumulated work of ethnographers as a collectivity. I have a small part of that archive on the shelves in my room here, and a much larger part of it lies on the shelves in the university's main library. The whole archive is collected in no one place but is enshrined in the various library cataloguing schemes which have a category for 'Anthropology'. And beyond that, the archive idea is also enshrined in various practices, such as the practice prevalent in British universities of giving final examinations: three hours per subject to see how much of the archive you can pour out in that time.

I do not think the notion of 'pouring out' knowledge is entirely fanciful. In an important respect the archive idea is very close to that of knowledge as substantial, as the contents of a vessel, contents which can be poured from one place to another, from teacher to pupil or from book to brain. And here the difficulty begins to surface: for whereas it is easy to see knowledge as the contents of a repository or vessel when we think of libraries and examinations, it is harder to see it in that light when we ask after the use of such knowledge. What do you do with it? Does anthropological knowledge have any significance beyond its being poured endlessly from mind to book and back to mind? It is a nightmare vision, or at least a vision of futility, which haunts the academic world. Perhaps Murray Gell-Mann was right when he said somewhere that twentieth-century education is like going into the greatest restaurant in the world . . . and being given the menu to eat.

These considerations may seem even more pressing if we look at the social process of making the ethnographic archive. In the twentieth century anthropology has become a profession, a way to earn a living. This is a valuable resource in itself, and so is subject to close control by the professionals. An anthropologist requires a doctorate, which is awarded for contributing some further ethnographic knowledge to the collective storehouse. Such work is supervised by other anthropologists and then examined by yet further anthropologists. Jobs in the profession are controlled by anthropologists, largely on the basis of publications, and those publications are reviewed and accepted or rejected by anthropologists. Later in a career, promotion depends on further publications, which are reviewed by anthropologists, and so it goes. In this perspective, ethnographic knowledge, like a commodity, may appear to have a value in and of itself.

A further corollary of this commodity-like character of the archive is that its entries should indeed be like objects: they should be objective. They should not be the product of individual whimsy. They should not mean one thing to one person and quite another to someone else. They should have the same value for anyone who encounters them, beyond the limitations of their social and historical origins. And this view is often reflected in what anthropologists say about ethnography. Here, for example, is Robert Borofsky considering the matter at the end of his ethnographic study on the people of the Polynesian island of Pukapuka: 'Though not objective in an absolute sense, anthropology does possess a degree of objectivity that makes it more than simply another folk model or "local" form of knowledge. At its core, anthropology involves comparison, the analysis of cultural differences and similarities.'[1] So far Borofsky's words might be an echo of Radcliffe-Brown, or of Benedict, with their museum-like imagery of ethnography and their notion of the gradual accumulation of more and more knowledge for comparison. And so far, too, we see that the archive has some implications that are unappealing and, to a degree, discouraging. If doing ethnography merely aims to produce items of this sort, items which may sometime be compared, it may hardly be worth the sweat and tears.

But in the sentences which immediately follow, Borofsky takes a different tack. He steps decisively beyond the notion of an ethnographic storehouse and throws an altogether more intriguing and realistic light on the matter.

By the nature of its research, anthropology opens itself to a dialogue with other people possessing different insights and perspectives on the same situation. Anthropological accounts make ideas considered self-evident in one culture subject to doubt, subject to comparison with alternative styles common in the other. Anthropology is still embedded in contexts, but it is relatively freer of these contexts because it continually opens itself to a diversity of perspectives that challenge its own.

This, with its key words 'dialogue', 'doubt', and 'challenge', is, I think, more faithful to the practice, to the aspirations, and to the actually achieved value of anthropology. For many purposes there does exist an ethnographic archive, but, in its creation and use, ethnographic knowledge is actually very far from being a storable commodity. If we wished to characterize such knowledge from this perspective, it would seem both more mutable and more powerful, part of a fluid process of interaction and mutual engagement.

Borofsky's statement comes at the end of a book which has demonstrated repeatedly the questioning and sometimes combative nature of ethnographic fieldwork. So in the first instance, the dialogue, doubt, and challenge are those of fieldwork itself and its experience of engaged learning. But Borofsky's words also reflect a dawning realization among anthropologists that what they write is likely to be read by those whom they study. In earlier generations it was possible for anthropologists to ignore the demands that such a knowledgeable and sensitive readership would put on them. It was then possible to be objective partly by objectifying those studied. But nowadays the ethics of the maturing profession, the sophistication of those studied, and the end of any straightforwardly colonial relationship between North Atlantic societies and others has made those anthropologized—in Douglas Caulkins's usage, an anthropologist's consultants—into readers and critics as well. For them, ethnographic knowledge can only seem one voice in the continuing conversation of their society.

So Borofsky's argument runs beyond the face-to-face relations of the field to the exploded interactions of the writing desk and the reading chair. Much of the challenge of anthropological knowledge occurs, not between ethnographer and consultant, but between writer and reader. Margaret Mead and Ruth Benedict knew this when they addressed American society and made knowledge of other societies into a powerful criticism of their own. Most anthropologists have more modest ambitions and a more modest and academic readership. But those shadowy presences, the readers, are no less important, no less a part of the social setting of the completed ethnography than the ethnographer and the society of the consultants.

So what we have here is some sense of anthropology in use: in use, it is knowledge as an argument or knowledge as a challenge. This makes it at once less fixed and more interesting. What I want to do now is work more or less to these same conclusions, but from a different direction, from the direction of anthropological writing itself.

Plaster of Paris

I will start again from the beginning, and regard ethnographic knowledge for the moment out of context—or at least only in such context as you, the reader, and I provide tacitly. I begin with some passages from Edward Schieffelin's *The Sorrow of the Lonely and the Burning of the Dancers*, concerning the Kaluli, who live near Mount Bosavi in Papua New Guinea. The passages are taken from a section that begins with the general remark that among the Kaluli 'interest in food is not due to a lack of it. . . . Rather, food is important because it is a vehicle of social relationship.' He goes on:

I became aware of this as soon as I entered a longhouse on the plateau for the first time. I sat down wearily on the edge of the men's sleeping platforms and was pulling the leeches out of my socks when a man approached with a blackened, loaf-shaped packet in his hand. He broke off a piece and handed me a chalky-looking substance covered with grayish, rubbery skin. There was a pause while the people of the longhouse watched to see what I would do. Reluctantly, I took a bite. The flavor was strongly reminiscent of plaster of paris. "Nafa?" ("Good?") asked one of my hosts hopefully . . . "Nafa," I answered when I could get some saliva back in my mouth. "Ah," said my host, looking around to the others. They relaxed. Having eaten sago, I was established as a fellow creature.[2]

Let me note first that this is a passage very much like that concerning Pa Rangifuri. It is a minimal narrative passage, written to make clear the motives and states of mind of the participants: the initial tension when the risk was taken to offer food, followed by the general relaxation when Schieffelin responded amicably. The detail of the leeches in the socks may seem extraneous, but in fact it sets the tempo of the encounter, and shows how the Kaluli man drew Schieffelin's attention away from what he was doing to the offer of food. A good deal of art has gone into the passage, and indeed some of that art is in the nature of Deborah Tannen's 'involvement strategies', only here the involvement is between the reader and writer. For example, the leeches also serve to identify a common focus in the scene, a focus that would assuredly be of shared interest both to Schieffelin and to any reader unused to leeches.

The feature that I want to stress, though, is just the relationship between the initial generalization—'food is important because it is a vehicle of social relationship'—and the story. For what we are going to see in this brief analysis is a constant weaving back and forth between the broad, generic statement about Kaluli in general, and the specific, vivid incident which illustrates it. It would be wrong to treat the specific details, the stories and similar material, merely as proof or evidence for an abstract argument, or to suggest that the abstract argument is the real point of the discourse. There is, on the one hand, no attempt to show a precise relationship between the stories and the abstraction; on the other, the stories themselves advance the understanding, just as the story of Siddhasagar did. Here, for example, we learn through the story just what scale of importance attaches to food offering: it is the sort of event that would make a roomful of people stop to see what happens. This is not made explicit by Schieffelin, but is nevertheless integral to what he is saying. It becomes part of our understanding, though it is not marked explicitly. And so our understanding swings forward, from generic statement to particular incident, and forward again to another generic statement.

I now skip a paragraph and pick up Schieffelin's argument here:

The giving and sharing of food among the Kaluli communicates sentiment; it conveys affection, familiarity, and good will. A toddler who burst into tears on seeing me for the first time was reproached by his father, who said, 'don't cry, he gives salt.' The man then explained to me that one should give food to little children 'so that they will know you and like you and not be afraid of you.'[3]

This passage parallels the earlier one: a generic statement followed by a very short story. But it also advances Schieffelin's argument in three distinct ways. First, it offers a generic statement which is clearly related to the earlier one ('food is the vehicle of social relationship'), but this generic statement shows a different side of matters. It stresses sentiment and affection, not just the sheer fact of relating through food. Second, Schieffelin now shows Kaluli relating to each other, rather than to him. So if anyone had thought that Kaluli had a special behaviour reserved for strangers, it will now be clear that it is not so. And third, the passage demonstrates how Kaluli themselves talk about, and reflect upon, their basic orientation to food and social relations. In other words, here Schieffelin lets a Kaluli offer a generic statement on his own account.

I will set out just one more passage, one which takes up where the last left off ('one should give food to little children "so that they will know you and like you and not be afraid of you." '):

The advice would apply equally to the whole range of Kaluli social relationships. Kaluli exercise it as soon as a child comes into the world.

A day or so after a child is born, his parents and a few relatives take him on an expedition to a forest camp where they spend a few days catching crayfish and sago grubs to feed him. The common concern is to 'make the child strong' and to please him and make him feel welcome so that he will not 'go back' to where he came from and die. It provides others beside the mother, who feeds the baby at her breast, with the opportunity to relate to him by giving him food.

Thereafter, the giving and sharing of food continues to be the social idiom in which close relationships and affectionate sentiment are given form. A young man smitten by a girl may try to slip her a small packet of salt or meat to let her know how he feels. A man expressing his grief over a friend's death will say, 'He gave me pork!'[4]

In this passage the development of generic statements about Kaluli life continue, now sketching a broad sweep from birth to courtship to death. But the detailed statements now take a different form. They are no longer specific incidents which happened at specific times, but are rather more generic themselves. They reflect what is typical in Kaluli life. We may, indeed we must, assume that Schieffelin himself witnessed such incidents as the bringing of food to a newborn baby or the lamenting over death. But we are also invited to see that any one such incident is more or less routine, more or less expected and conventional, the sort of thing that Kaluli would naturally do, given their experience and their society. And indeed it is just this conventionality of things which had motivated the use of the more specific incidents recounted earlier. It would, of course, be wrong to think of these acts as automatic or as being done without thought. Their very mark is that they are, as we would say, thoughtful. But they represent the Kaluli's common aesthetic standard and aesthetic sense of what is the right thing to do, to whom, on what occasion.

Though these passages comprise only a small part of *The Sorrow of the Lonely and the Burning of the Dancers*, they are a good demonstration of the whole. They are, in effect, a sample of fabric, a piece which shows its basic colours and texture. Some of the fabric is distinctively Schieffelin's, but the fundamental weave is not, for it represents fairly the character of anthropological knowledge at its most fundamental level. That knowledge is composed precisely of the progressively developing generic statements, of the particular incidents, and of their relationship to each other in a developing whole. This whole is the basic stuff of paradigmatic knowledge in anthropology: it is the fundamental understanding which a learner must begin to visualize in its connectedness, to review inwardly, and to explore in the imagination when she first comes to read ethnography. If the individual incidents are each a pattern, then the ethnography is a pattern of patterns, and the work of ethnographic thinking lies in playing with these meta-patterns. Ethnographic knowledge is indeed an encounter, but it is an encounter which begins in this particular kind of expansive thought. It is a way of thinking which weaves into a single intelligibility such varied occasions as a death lament and a gift to a visiting stranger.

There are larger scales of organization, larger patterns, in Schieffelin's book as well. The passages I have reproduced above appear at the beginning of a chapter called 'I Don't Eat That, Brother!', and in it Schieffelin goes on to explore just how the sharing of food creates this or that relationship—between siblings, between in-laws, between exchange partners, between husband and wife, between mother and child. Then—and this is the point of the chapter's title—he changes tack, and shows how certain restrictions on eating certain kinds of food, and therefore on sharing them, have a different effect. Whereas sharing creates bonds, such food taboos create barriers between people, as between unmarried and married men, or between women and men. In this perspective the sharing of food with which the chapter began is seen as one example of how Kaluli manipulate their relations to each other: they do so by many means, but prominent among those means are the giving or withholding, the eating or avoiding, of various foodstuffs. So the generic statement that 'food is important because it is a vehicle of social relationship' leads eventually to a more or less comprehensive coverage of the nature and style of Kaluli relationships as a whole.

This larger patterning in Schieffelin's ethnography opens on to patterns beyond the Kaluli and beyond the book itself. In fact the chapter 'I Don't Eat That, Brother!' fulfils a function that might, in a more conventional or older ethnography, have been titled 'Kinship'. And kinship, when anthropology considered itself the study of primitive, small-scale societies, was the entire entrée section on anthropology's menu. Indeed even now it still figures prominently, as say the meat vs. the pasta section. Schieffelin does not explicitly compare Kaluli forms and styles of relationship with those of other peoples, but the detail with which he presents the topic, here and elsewhere in the book, makes clear that some eventual, possible, comparison with those other forms are very much on his mind.

In a similar vein, this chapter of Schieffelin's book blends with others in the book to examine another great theme in ethnography as a whole, that of reciprocity and exchange. It was anthropologist Marcel Mauss who set the matter of *The Gift* firmly on anthropology's agenda. His basic observation, illustrated from widely scattered ethnographic examples, was more or less that material goods are not just commodities, but are, in Schieffelin's words, 'vehicles of social relationship'. If we consider just the Kaluli and their neighbours, then there is a special sense in which the constant give and take of gifts, not only of food but of other items, is a theme which distinguishes Papua New Guinea and the larger Melanesian area of which it is part. But beyond that the use of material objects as one of the chief idioms of human sociality is universal. In the terms I have set out in this book, it is not surprising that anthropologists have discovered this—for anthropology, in one guise or another, has always been about diversity in the forms of human relationships. But then I have the benefit of 70 years of ethnography which has cultivated Mauss's ideas.

These are certainly comparative perspectives, and they must count as some of what Borofsky referred to when he spoke of anthropology as comparative. Yet so far as I have explicated them here, these comparisons are only a peculiarly rarified kind of challenge. To treat kinship as Schieffelin does, for example, as a realm of activity that is partly dissolved within another, the giving and taking of food, is provocative. But it is provocative only within a very narrow range, a range limited to some specialists on kinship within anthropology as a whole. That is not to say that Schieffelin's work is not, or could not be regarded as, knowledge as challenge to North Atlantic societies in general. Most of it could be so regarded. But I turn instead to another ethnography to explore how a more general challenge might be issued.

The ultra-natural

The following quotation constitutes the beginning of the main section of Godfrey Lienhardt's *Divinity and Experience: The Religion of the Dinka*. The Dinka are pastoralists of the southern Sudan.

Within the single world known to them (for they dwell little upon fancies of any 'other world' of different constitution) the Dinka claim that they encounter 'spirits' of various kinds, which they call generically *jok*. In this account I call them 'Powers'. These Powers are regarded as higher in the scale of being than men and other merely terrestrial creatures, and operate beyond the categories of space and time which limit human actions; but they are not imagined to form a separate 'spirit-world' of their own, and their interest for the Dinka is as ultra-human forces participating in human life and often affecting men for good or ill. They emerge in the interpretation of events, and hence the broad Dinka division of the world into 'that which is of men' and 'that which is of Powers' is in part a classification of events into two kinds. Man and that which shares his terrestrial nature may be contrasted in thought to Powers, considered collectively as exhibiting a different nature. Dinka religious notion and practice define and regulate the relations between beings of these two different natures in the single world of human experience which is their common home.

I have not found it useful to adopt the distinction between 'natural' and 'supernatural' beings or events in order to describe the difference between men and Powers, for this distinction implies a conception of the course or laws of Nature quite foreign to Dinka thought. When, for example, the Dinka attribute lightning to a particular ultra-human Power, it would falsify their understanding, and indeed exaggerate its difference from our own, to refer to a *supernatural* Power. The force of lightning is equally ultra-human for ourselves as for the Dinka, though the interpretation we place upon that fact is very different from theirs. It is part of my later task to demonstrate how many features of Dinka religious thought and action are connected with their experience of what we call 'Nature', and of the scope and limits of human control within their particular environment.[5]

Now by comparison with the passages of Schieffelin that I set out above, this by Lienhardt lies entirely on the generic side. These are the prefatory general remarks which introduce the characteristic ethnographer's rhythm (particular alternating with generic) which is to follow.

Moreover, the argument set out is one which resonates with ideas set out by other anthropologists. For example, it echoes, and rejects, Tylor's definition of religion as a 'belief in supernatural beings', a definition which itself had already been fought over extensively, beginning with Émile Durkheim. It rejects a general tendency among anthropologists and sociologists to speak of a 'spirit world' or to use the Victorian coinage 'otherworldly' to describe ideas and practices like those of the Dinka. It is a characteristic of Lienhardt's style to leave these resonances more or less implicit, but the effective force of his argument runs beyond the words themselves. He says in effect the following: it might be thought by anthropologists that such-and-such is the case in general, but for the Dinka something rather different, and rather subtler, is in fact the case. If those ideas do not apply to the Dinka, they are by that very fact not universally applicable, and may be inappropriate in other cases as well.

So Lienhardt's ethnography, like the part of Schieffelin's discussed above, makes a challenge within anthropology itself. But the notion of a challenge set out by Borofsky is a broader one, for it asserts that 'anthropological accounts make ideas considered self-evident in one culture subject to doubt, subject to comparison with alternative styles common in the other'. And it is here, in its challenge not narrowly to anthropological but to more general North Atlantic ideas of religion, that Lienhardt's Dinka ethnography has its greatest impact.

Consider his treatment of the division between natural and supernatural. It is a distinction which was not devised by anthropologists, and their use of it mirrors wider North Atlantic usage. It is a division of things which goes back at least to the encounter of Christian theology with Greek, and particularly Aristotelian, ideas of the natural world. Moreover, the tremendous growth of natural science in the nineteenth century did nothing to contradict the distinction itself, but only reinforced it, even while calling into question the reality and importance of one side of the division, the supernatural, spiritual realm. So the use of the distinction implicitly or explicitly by anthropologists cannot be regarded as the application of a plain and unambiguous technical term. On the contrary, we have here a knot of ideas regarded as 'self-evident in one culture [made] subject to doubt, subject to comparison' by ideas from another.

Now Lienhardt's, and through him the Dinka's, challenge is not to deny that there is some distinction. Indeed the chapter in which this passage appears is entitled 'Division in the World'. Lienhardt recognizes this division by writing of 'Powers' as opposed to humans. No, the challenge is far subtler: it shows the Powers and the humans inhabiting one world, 'the single world of human experience which is their common home'. Moreover, Lienhardt stresses that this 'single world' is effectively the same world of human experience, in Borofsky's words 'the same situation', that people of the North Atlantic inhabit as well. Lienhardt makes this point vividly by the example of lightning, which is just as 'ultra-human' for us as for the Dinka.

So the invitation to North Atlantic readers is an explicit and powerful one: to regard the world of their ordinary experience through Dinka eyes. In my experience of teaching in North Atlantic societies, I have found that ideas such as those put forward—or transmitted—by Lienhardt can be extraordinarily hard to grasp. This is not because of their intrinsic difficulty but because of the thoroughness with which they contradict received notions. One received notion lies in the tendency of North Atlantic people to foist on to the Dinka a degree of detail and elaboration which is alien to their ideas. Lienhardt makes it plain that the Powers 'emerge in the interpretation of events'. The point here is that the Dinka do not engage in elaborate speculation. They do not therefore endow the Powers with attributes beyond those relevant to their immediate effect on people. As Lienhardt puts it a little later in the chapter:

Dinka religion, then, is a relationship between men and ultra-human Powers encountered by men, between the two parts of a radically divided world. As will be seen, it is rather phenomenological than theological, an interpretation of signs of ultra-human activity rather than a doctrine of the intrinsic nature of the Powers behind those signs.[6]

The key contrast here is between 'interpretation of signs' as opposed to a 'doctrine of intrinsic nature'. Lightning, for example, is thought of as a 'direct intervention of Divinity in human affairs, and in thunderstorms it is customary to sit quietly and respectfully, for people are in the immediate presence of Divinity'.[7] To act in this way reveals an interpretation of what is going on, a sense that the Dinka have of Divinity appearing directly. But such behaviour does not imply an elaborate doctrine about Divinity. It does not require that the Dinka should entertain an idea of the substance, location, size, colour, number, origin, or movements of Divinity. On the contrary, Dinka are more likely to regard much about that Divinity as being plainly unknown: it is, after all, ultra-human. Similarly a lay Christian might consider, or might have considered in the past, that angels are the agents responsible for an odd or uncontrollable event. But that lay Christian would not need to know, as a theologian might, how many angels can dance on the head of a pin. The point Lienhardt makes here is related to one I have already made, that the addition of a theology and philosophy to a religion is not inherently necessary, but is the product of specific historical developments. Christians have had theologians to elaborate an unseen other world, but the Dinka have had none. They have dwelt 'little upon fancies of any "other world"'.

Lienhardt's fidelity to this immediacy in Dinka religion is attested by something which he does not do. He does not rely on or, so far as I can see, even use the words 'believe' or 'belief' at all. And the reason is that these are words which bear with them particular, and particularly Christian, notions and practices. When one believes, one believes in propositions or statements, and one believes in those statements even when they are not directly experienced. One believes, say, that God is triune, constituted of three Persons. It is, on one hand, a statement highly cultivated and elaborated by theologians, a statement not about the 'natural' but about the 'supernatural' world. But on the other hand, it also constitutes an act of faith, a credo, an explicit assent to the truth of the statement, and the particular practice of assenting to such statements has been installed quite explicitly (and at great cost to the heretics who did not assent) in Christian ritual. Among Dinka, as

Lienhardt makes clear, there is nothing corresponding to these ideas and practices. The Powers 'emerge' from events, and are connected with Dinka 'experience of what we call "Nature"'. No Dinka is ever asked to 'believe' in such Powers, and it is correspondingly pointless to attribute 'belief' to Dinka.

So *Divinity and Experience* constitutes a challenge to received ideas among North Atlantic peoples. It is true that the challenge is issued most explicitly to Christianity. Lienhardt frequently reveals an awareness of that readership by addressing it explicitly. But the fundamental notion that, for example, religion is constituted by 'belief', is one which reaches well beyond any community of practicing Christians. It is one of the features attributed to 'religion' as such, even by secular or avowedly atheistic people. It calls up, as Lienhardt puts it, 'undefined, yet for everyone fairly definite, conceptions of our own,'[8] and these are conceptions which—in my experience—are very difficult for us of the North Atlantic to overleap. It is difficult even to see that there is an alternative to them.

So a painstaking and adventurous reading of *Divinity and Experience* yields more than acquisitions for a personal archive of knowledge. It also calls into doubt dimensions of thought otherwise implicit and unquestioned. It suggests another perspective on common human situations, a perspective which, I am convinced, we could not easily have imagined or dreamed had the Dinka not already done so, and had Lienhardt not taken such care to learn and translate their way of life. I have referred throughout this book to Hofstadter's notion of 'slippability', the ability to imagine alternatives to what is presented directly to us. Lienhardt's book shows how ethnography, considered as something over and above archival knowledge, can amplify that slippability. It is a form of knowledge that can amplify our imagination and our readiness to entertain novel and potentially more powerful notions of human characters in typically human situations.

An untidy box of sweets

I have devoted much of this book to the thesis that anthropology must go beyond the notion of its task as the translation of cultures to cultivate a more historical style and a keener consciousness of metamorphosis in human life. Yet I have taken a conservative—or perhaps better, a preservative—view of ethnographies which are largely translations of culture. And Lienhardt's and Schieffelin's ethnographies make it plain that I have done so with good reason. For they lend to the notions of comparison and translation in anthropology a specially rich and innovative colouring. I nevertheless want to insist that reassembly, the act of putting the disassembled specificity of one way of life back into its actual historical and larger social setting, still adds value, and would add value even to such excellent disassembled accounts. To make that final point, I turn to another ethnography, Juliet du Boulay's *Portrait of a Greek Mountain Village*.

On the face of it, du Boulay's ethnography fits not the mould of reassembly but of disassembly and cultural translation. It is almost wholly given over to rendering intelligible a way of life not immediately understood, or easily understandable, by its proposed readership. And in that respect it belongs precisely within the tradition of Lienhardt and Schieffelin. Yet from the very outset du Boulay takes a slightly different tack. She begins:

This book is a study of a phenomenon which is becoming all too frequent in the present day—a dying village community. However, since it is concerned mainly with the values and attitudes which are derived from a long tradition and which even in the present times sustain the villagers in a sense of purpose and destiny, it is concerned more with life than with death.[9]

Now from a strictly historicist, reassembling point of view, the very notion of 'a long tradition' which du Boulay sets out here, and which she uses throughout, might be thought exaggerated. It might be possible to show that the tradition had been more mutable, less fixed, than du Boulay assumes. But on the other hand, du Boulay is largely concerned, and justifiably so, only with the scale of changes which touch the living memory of present inhabitants. Indeed she reveals a keen sense of mutability on a smaller, more immediate scale as well. For example, she observes that between her departure in 1968 and a second visit in 1970, five houses had been abandoned, largely because of emigration. The emigrants left the land and went to cities or abroad to find work. In that respect they were caught up in larger processes, not precisely the processes most closely chronicled by Wolf but rather present-day developments out of those processes. On this scale of change, 'traditional', and for that matter 'modern', have clear meanings which then corresponded to attitudes of the Greek villagers themselves.

Let me begin with du Boulay's translation of the sense of community in the village, Ambéli. I take up her argument in the middle, where she is contrasting the sense of community in Ambéli with a corresponding sense elsewhere. She writes of the moment when 'the We of the community leans towards the They of the outside world', and the process of change makes itself vividly felt.

In this event, the villagers remain united in so far as the whole community lives in the same place and is bound by the same values . . . but the community has begun to lose confidence in itself in so far as its identification with its traditional and inherited . . . way of life has begun to be discredited, and that of the modern world to draw its loyalties. This is the situation in which the villagers of Ambéli now find themselves. But it is a stage which is more integrated than that which is found in the less remote villages, where a deep fragmentation of values is seen to have occurred within each village itself. In these villages there are immediately apparent various strata of respectability—a word coincident in this context with modernity— and where the old women, for instance, will dress one way and refer their way of dressing to a particular set of values, while the young women, with their refined way of speaking and their smart sleeveless dresses, will say to me, 'You don't want to pay any attention to backward old women.'

This situation does not obtain in Ambéli where, in spite of the degree of depopulation, the culture to be found in the village is still relatively homogeneous. The villagers' ambition, in the sense of their desire for an easier life for themselves, for the glamour of the towns, and for education for their children, is focused on the outside world.

In that respect—their failure to translate their traditional values into an acceptable twentieth-century good—they may be heard referring to themselves as backward people, living like animals. Yet, although shaken, the central core of their self-respect has not yet been mortally wounded.[10]

For the moment let me pause just to remark how—and how well—du Boulay here evinces the character of ethnographic translation. There is, first, the reference to a greater comparative theme in anthropology and indeed in sociology, that of the nature of community. Second, du Boulay offers us generic statements about the people of Ambéli, whose culture is 'still relatively homogeneous'. In the quoted passage she illustrates this in a particularly subtle way, by contrasting Ambéli with other, nearby villages which are nevertheless closer to the cosmopolis. And third, she offers a very compressed, but very vivid vignette which she manages to make at once generic and specific—'the young women, with their refined way of speaking and their smart sleeveless dresses, will say to me, "You don't want to pay any attention to backward old women."' Here one can see that—bearing in mind the duty of fidelity that du Boulay discharges to people actually met—the ethnographic sensibility merges with a novelistic one.

She carries on to certify the villagers' still strong and implicit sense of community.

All this is not to say that there are no secondary or other standards of behaviour to which people may appeal. . . . But it is to emphasize the moral solidarity of such a community where a central self-confidence in the main body of its own traditional values system still survives. . . . The individual who is speaking or acting does so in his capacity not as a solitary individual but as a member of the total community. In illustration of this I quote an incident at which a young woman was preparing to lay out the *loukoúmia* (sweets known in England as Turkish delight) for a name-day, and put the whole box on the tray. It was an untidy box with ragged bits of paper hanging out, and I said I thought she ought to take out the bits of *loukoúmi* and put them on a dish.

'No,' she said, 'that's not as it should be.'

'I don't agree,' said I.

'It's not that you don't agree, it's that you don't know,' she replied, with finality.[11]

I think that, though they represent a modest domestic matter, these words are as effective as any that ethnographers have set on the page. What could du Boulay say next? What could anyone say? The woman's retort in its setting is a powerful translation of culture. But it is more, for it opens compellingly on to a reassembled understanding, to a sense of this encounter in its larger social, interactive, and metamorphic setting.

In the first place, the encounter with the 'young woman' embodies just that sense of engaged learning and of creative interaction which, I have stressed, is characteristic of ethnography. But this trait has another side as well, for the encounter is at the same time a good example of how everyone learns what is going on around them in practical terms. It has, in other words, a comparative suggestiveness, just as the example of the the Kaluli giving Schieffelin a piece of sago was suggestive. It shows 'different insights and perspectives on the same situation', the situation of learning an aesthetic standard. It can be appreciated by anyone who can recall the experience, in childhood, of learning the proper way of doing things. Indeed, the encounter is the sort of abrupt experience which, I think we must assume, the young woman's relatives might have had when they emigrated to, say, England or Germany. It typifies the surprise and creativity of the way that things happen between people, not within them.

But, finally, the incident, and its interpretation by du Boulay, have an extra poignancy because it reflects another version of the plight of Ramon. Ramon, you will recall, was Benedict's informant, a chief, 'a Christian and a leader among his people in the planting of peaches and apricots on irrigated land'. He had taken an active hand in transforming his world. The young woman, on the other hand, takes a different part in the process of change and metamorphosis. She represents, for the moment at least, the voice of those resisting transformation. It is as if the anthropologists had momentarily interposed themselves into a conversation: in Benedict's case, she faces the voice of change, in du Boulay's case, the voice of resistance to change.

But on closer inspection neither case quite fits that simple dichotomy. Ramon, so far as I know, had no direct personal effect on later events. But he represented both adaptation and nostalgia, and this combination, mingled with anger and a sense of injustice, was later to make a visibly effective intervention in the social life of the United States, the Native American movement. Benedict's own prognosis, of the eventual extinction of Ramon's past in a new present, did not come to pass. What did come to pass was a metamorphosis, made partly of elements of the past but, in its combination, a real innovation. It was an innovation created by no one person, but by people working jointly, sometimes in opposition to one another and sometimes in co-operation.

This helps us to see the young woman more clearly. Rural Greece, too, is in the throes of change, change which is after all a stable and enduring feature of human life. Du Boulay is keenly aware of that metamorphosis and, in her writing, places the woman decisively in that larger flow of events. For the moment the woman could confront du Boulay unselfconsciously, secure in her well-supported traditional knowledge. But she is framed by du Boulay in a larger tragedy, or at least a story with an unhappy ending. In this du Boulay takes the same stance that Benedict did, looking towards an extinction, an ending which she regards as sad and irreparable. Yet, as the case of Ramon and Benedict should teach us, the voice and attitude of the young women will not be wholly lost, but transmogrified in a new setting with a new significance. Indeed, as Paul Sant Cassia has pointed out to me, much of the sense of Greek nationalism at home, and of ethnicity abroad, is founded in nostalgia for this rural Greece, which thus does not disappear but is carried forward transformed.

The beginning

The young woman also represents the voice of transformation in another sense. She did, after all, alter du Boulay's understanding as surely as those nameless figures who inducted Ramon into the world of commercial agriculture altered his understanding. And through du Boulay and the exploded interactions of print, she can alter others' understanding too.

So the doing of anthropology can at least achieve an alteration and a deepening of people's mutual comprehension. This is one clear use for the toils of fieldwork and of writing. But how are we to weigh this? We commonly think of some transformations—the learning of new customs by immigrants, the learning of commercial agriculture by the colonized—as being the real stuff of history. They are the weighty transformations that make our world. Other transformations, such as the subtler ones worked upon us by Lienhardt or Schieffelin, or worked by the woman upon du Boulay, we think of as immaterial, insubstantial, or ineffective. They seem to be the transformations merely of empathy, changing one person's understanding of another's aesthetic standard or situation. They seem altogether lighter. Are they nevertheless worth the trouble?

With this question I reach the end of this prologue to anthropology. This is, so to speak, the threshold at which anthropology proper—the doing of it rather than the thinking about the doing of it—actually begins. I will give two brief answers to the question, and will hope that you, if you have come only recently to anthropology, will go on to give your own answers.

The first is simple and direct. Yes, anthropology is worth it, just to the extent that it comes to bear upon the world of practical affairs. Governments and international agencies have, here and there, begun to discover the benefits for recipients of public policy of the intimate, social knowledge created by anthropologists. This form of ethnography, generally called applied anthropology, has a ready argument for itself in the form of already achieved results. It does work and it does make a difference. Its case, however, still needs to be made again and again, for those exercising power are not always aware of how much they need the challenge of anthropological knowledge.

The second answer is more general and more uncertain. In this book I have painted a picture of people as inextricably involved with each other in a world in continual metamorphosis. In this world there are some landmarks, some aesthetic standards and recalled traditions, which people use to guide their relationships and their institutions. And I have also stressed that people have the creativity and social intelligence to make use of these resources to remake their cultures. To this extent my picture may have seemed a positive one. But this changing world is moved not only by our need for one another, but also by narrow construals of our own interests, and by domination, destructiveness, and misrepresentation, sometimes wilful, sometimes accidental. These seem often to rule human affairs, excluding any gentler counsels of dialogue.

Yet I think that there is still place for a measured faith in anthropology. We might hope, for example, that the habit of ethnographic thinking, and the subtle skills of opening ourselves to others' viewpoints and experiences, could at least partly alter the climate of a society. On this view, we would regard anthropology as a desirable part of general education, of what people need to know to live successfully. Ethnographic knowledge would be deemed necessary to a world in which people are routinely dependent on relations between themselves and others of different aesthetic standards, and with different interests. Anthropology would challenge people and encourage them to consider new possibilities in the conduct of such relations. Anthropology would make a difference because relationships make a difference.

I cannot be absolutely certain of this answer, and I will have to leave it with you. The question may only be answerable in the doing of it, and in seeing what kind of world follows from the doing.

Notes

Further details of the works referred to briefly here may be found in the Bibliography which follows.

Chapter 1: The question

1. Godelier, *The Mental and the Material*, 1.
2. Harrison, 'Letters'.
3. Bullock, 'Socializing the Theory of Intellectual Development', 187.

Chapter 2: The great arc

1. Benedict, *Patterns of Culture*, 15.
2. Ibid. 16.
3. Ibid. 15.
4. Ibid. 16.
5. Mead, quoted in Fox, *Lions of the Punjab*, 192.
6. Benedict, *Patterns of Culture*, 17.
7. Radcliffe-Brown, quoted in Kuper, *Anthropology and Anthropologists*, 53.
8. Radcliffe-Brown, 'Preface', p. xii.
9. Benedict, *Patterns of Culture*, 16.
10. Radcliffe-Brown, 'Preface', p. xi.
11. Benedict, *Patterns of Culture*, 12.
12. Turnbull, *The Mbuti Pygmies*, 5.
13. Wolf, *Europe and the People without History*, pp. ix–x.
14. Ibid. 4.
15. Benedict, *Patterns of Culture*, 12.
16. Wolf, *Europe and the People without History*, 4.
17. Ibid. 76.
18. Ibid. 6.
19. Ibid. 5.
20. Ibid. 3.
21. Ibid. 387.
22. Lesser, quoted in Wolf, *Europe and the People without History*, 19.
23. Wolf, *Europe and the People without History*, 386.

24. Carrithers, 'Jainism and Buddhism as Enduring Historical Streams', 161.
25. Peel, 'History, Culture, and the Comparative Method: A West African Puzzle', 108–9.
26. Godelier, *The Mental and the Material*, 1.
27. Hannerz, quoted in Clifford, *The Predicament of Culture*, 17.

Chapter 3: Beginning to make history

(A fuller list of references for the arguments in this chapter can be found in Carrithers, 'Why Humans Have Cultures', published in *Man* NS, 25: 189–206.)

1. Obeyesekere, *The Work of Culture*, 92.
2. Geertz, *The Interpretation of Cultures*, 73.
3. Mauss, *Sociology and Psychology*, 9.
4. White, quoted in Sahlins, *Culture and Practical Reason*, 105.
5. Wilson, *Sociobiology: The New Synthesis*, 16–18.
6. Sober, *The Nature of Selection*.
7. Humphrey, 'The Social Function of Intellect', 309.
8. Ibid. 310.
9. Wynn, 'Tools and the Evolution of Human Intelligence'.
10. Dennett, *The Intentional Stance*.
11. Levinson, 'Interactional Biases in Human Thinking'.
12. Byrne and Whiten (eds.), *Machiavellian Intelligence*, 9.
13. Axelrod, *The Evolution of Cooperation*.
14. Godelier, *The Mental and the Material*, 1.
15. Landau, *Narratives of Human Evolution*.
16. Tobias, quoted in Landau, *Narratives of Human Evolution*, 164–5.
17. Wilberforce, quoted in Rachels, *Created from Animals*.
18. Tobias, quoted in Landau, *Narratives of Human Evolution*, 166.
19. Darwin, quoted in Rachels, *Created from Animals*, 1.
20. Rachels, *Created from Animals*.

Chapter 4: The anatomy of sociality

1. Trevarthen and Logotheti, 'Child in Society, and Society in Children', 167.
2. Bruner, *Child's Talk*, 26.
3. Vygotsky, quoted in Butterworth and Grover, 'The Origins of Referential Communication in Human Infancy', 9.

4. Trevarthen and Logotheti, 'Child in Society, and Society in Children', 166–7.

5. Dennett, *The Intentional Stance*.

6. Whiten (ed.) *Natural Theories of Mind*.

7. Byrne and Whiten (eds.), *Machiavellian Intelligence*.

8. Grice, 'Utterer's Meaning and Intention'; Bennett, *Linguistic Behaviour*.

9. Strecker, *The Social Practice of Symbolization*, 73–4.

10. Brown and Levinson, *Politeness: Some Universals in Language Usage*.

11. Premack, 'Pedagogy and Aesthetics as Sources of Culture', 18.

12. Maynard Smith, 'Game Theory and the Evolution of Cooperation', 452.

13. Rosaldo, *Knowledge and Passion*, 27.

14. Schieffelin, *The Sorrow of the Lonely*, 2.

15. Scribner, 'Thinking in Action: Some Characteristics of Practical Thought', 28.

16. Rosaldo, 'Toward an Anthropology of Self and Feeling', 140.

17. Bakhtin, quoted in Holquist, *Dialogism*, 62–3.

18. Hofstadter, *Metamagical Themas*, 238.

19. See Smith and Wilson, *Modern Linguistics: The Results of Chomsky's Revolution*.

20. Bruner, *Child's Talk*, 18–19.

21. Tomasello, 'The Social Bases of Language Acquisition, 83.

22. Austin, *How to Do Things with Words*; Searle, *Speech Acts*.

Chapter 5: Reading minds and reading life

1. Bruner, *Actual Minds, Possible Worlds*, 14.

2. Astington, 'Narrative and the Child's Theory of Mind'.

3. Trevarthen and Logotheti, 'Child in Society, and Society in Children', 173.

4. Schutz, *Reflections on the Problem of Relevance*.

5. Bruner, *Actual Minds, Possible Worlds*, 13.

6. Latimore and Grene (eds.), *Sophocles I*.

Chapter 6: The bull and the saint

1. Dumont, *Homo Hierarchicus*.

2. Gergen and Gergen, 'The Social Construction of Narrative Accounts'.

3. Shaha, *Śrī 108 Siddhasāgar Muni Mahārāj*, 1.

4. Haviland, quoted in Keesing, 'Models, "Folk" or "Cultural": Paradigms Regained?', 382.
5. Appadurai, 'Gastro-politics in Hindu South Asia'.
6. Hutchins, *Culture and Inference: A Trobriand Case Study*.
7. Fernandez, *Persuasions and Performances*.

Chapter 7: Metamorphosis

1. Gellner, *Spectacles and Predicaments*, 41.
2. Wolf, *Europe and the People without History*, 76.
3. An expanded version of this argument is found in my book, *The Buddha*.
4. Rhys-Davids, *Dialogues of the Buddha*, 105–6.
5. Ibid. 107.
6. Norman, *Pali Literature*.
7. *Dīgha Nikāya* III. 81.
8. Ibid.
9. Tannen, *Talking Voices*.
10. *Dīgha Nikāya* III. 83–4.
11. Ibid. 84.
12. Rhys-Davids, *Dialogues of the Buddha* III. 82.
13. Gombrich, 'The Buddha's Allusions to Vedic Literature'.
14. *Dīgha Nikāya* III. 86.
15. Ibid. 92–3.
16. Collins, 'Notes on the Word *mahāsammata* and the Idea of a Social Contract in Buddhism'.
17. Rhys-Davids and Carpenter (eds.), *Dīgha Nikāya* II. 73–6.
18. *Dīgha Nikāya* III. 94.
19. Lingat, quoted in Tambiah, 'King Mahāsammata', 116.
20. Tambiah, 'King Mahāsammata', 119.

Chapter 8: The bugbear, science

1. Stocking (ed.) *Observers Observed*, 7.
2. Geertz, *Works and Lives*, 4.
3. Ibid. 140.
4. Evans-Pritchard, *Nuer Religion*, 222.
5. Sperber, *On Anthropological Knowledge*, 14–15.
6. See Polanyi, *Personal Knowledge*; Ziman, *Reliable Knowledge*; and Hacking, *Representing and Intervening*.
7. Hacking, *Representing and Intervening*, 131.
8. Ibid. 144.
9. Ziman, *Reliable Knowledge*, 125–6.

10. Roth, 'Ethnography without Tears', 561.
11. Ziman, *Reliable Knowledge*, 43.
12. Ibid. 43–4.
13. Ibid. 44.
14. Ibid. 44–5.
15. Ibid. 45.
16. Firth, 'Degrees of Intelligibility', 39.
17. Rosaldo, *Knowledge and Passion*, 27.
18. Obeyesekere, *The Work of Culture*.
19. Lewis, *Day of Shining Red*, 50.
20. Lienhardt, *Divinity and Experience*, 233.
21. Firth, 'Degrees of Intelligibility', 40.

Chapter 9: An untidy box of sweets

1. Borofsky, *Making History*, 154.
2. Schieffelin, *The Sorrow of the Lonely*, 47.
3. Ibid. 47–8.
4. Ibid. 48.
5. Lienhardt, *Divinity and Experience*, 29.
6. Ibid. 32.
7. Ibid. 54.
8. Ibid. 30.
9. du Boulay, *Portrait of a Greek Mountain Village*, 3.
10. Ibid. 48–9.
11. Ibid. 49–50.

Bibliography

Appadurai, A., 'Gastro-Politics in Hindu South Asia', *American Ethnologist* 8 (1981), 494–511.

Astington, J., 'Narrative and the Child's Theory of Mind', in B. Britton and A. Pellegrini (eds.), *Narrative Thought and Narrative Language* (Hillsdale, NJ: Lawrence Erlbaum Associates, 1991).

Austin, J., *How to Do Things with Words* (Oxford: Oxford University Press, 1962).

Axelrod, R., *The Evolution of Cooperation* (New York: Basic Books, 1984).

Benedict, R., *Patterns of Culture* (London: Routledge and Kegan Paul, 1935).

Bennett, J., *Linguistic Behaviour* (Cambridge: Cambridge University Press, 1976).

Borofsky, R., *Making History: Pukapukan and Anthropological Constructions of Knowledge* (Cambridge: Cambridge University Press, 1987).

Brown, P. and Levinson, S., *Politeness: Some Universals in Language Usage* (Cambridge: Cambridge University Press, 1987).

Bruner, J., *Actual Minds, Possible Worlds* (Cambridge, Mass.: Harvard University Press, 1986).

—— *Child's Talk: Learning to Use Language* (Oxford: Oxford University Press, 1983).

Bullock, D., 'Socializing the Theory of Intellectual Development', in M. Chapman and R. A. Dixon (eds.), *Meaning and the Growth of Understanding: Wittgenstein's Significance for Developmental Psychology* (Berlin: Springer Verlag, 1987).

Butterworth, G. and Grover, L., 'The Origins of Referential Communication in Human Infancy', in L. Weiskrantz (ed.), *Thought without Language* (Oxford: Clarendon Press, 1988).

Byrne, R. and Whiten, A. (eds.), *Machiavellian Intelligence: Social Expertise and the Evolution of Intellect in Monkeys, Apes and Humans* (Oxford: Clarendon Press, 1988).

Carpenter, J. E. (ed.), *The Dīgha Nikāya*, vol. III (London: Pali Text Society, 1960).

Carrithers, M., 'Buddhism and Jainism as Enduring Historical

Streams', *Journal of the Anthropological Society of Oxford* 21/2 (1990), 141–61.

Carrithers, M., 'Is Anthropology Art or Science?', *Current Anthropology* 31/3 (1990), 263–82.

—— *The Buddha* (Oxford: Oxford University Press, 1983).

—— *The Forest Monks of Sri Lanka* (Delhi: Oxford University Press, 1983).

Clifford, J., *The Predicament of Culture: Twentieth-Century Ethnography, Literature and Art* (Cambridge, Mass.: Harvard University Press, 1988).

Collins, S., 'Notes on the Word *mahāsammata* and the Idea of a Social Contract in Buddhism', typescript.

Dennett, D., *The Intentional Stance* (Cambridge, Mass.: MIT Press, 1987).

du Boulay, J., *Portrait of a Greek Mountain Village* (Oxford: Oxford University Press, 1974).

Dumont, L., *Homo Hierarchicus: The Caste System and its Implications* (London: Weidenfeld and Nicolson, 1970).

Evans-Pritchard, E. E., *Nuer Religion* (Oxford: Clarendon Press, 1956).

Fernandez, J. W., *Persuasions and Performances: The Play of Tropes in Culture* (Bloomington, Ind.: Indiana University Press, 1986).

Firth, R., 'Degrees of Intelligibility', in J. Overing (ed.), *Reason and Morality* (London: Tavistock, 1985).

Fox, R., *Lions of the Punjab: Culture in the Making* (London: University of California Press, 1985).

Geertz, C., *The Interpretation of Cultures* (New York: Basic Books, 1973).

—— *Works & Lives: The Anthropologist as Author* (Stanford, Calif.: Stanford University Press, 1988).

Gellner, E., *Spectacles and Predicaments: Essays in Social Theory* (Cambridge: Cambridge University Press, 1979).

Gergen, M. and Gergen, K., 'The Social Construction of Narrative Accounts', in K. Gergen and M. Gergen (eds.), *Historical Social Psychology* (Hillsdale, NJ: Lawrence Erlbaum Associates, 1984).

Godelier, M., *The Mental and the Material* (London: Verso, 1986).

Gombrich, R., 'The Buddha's Allusions to Vedic Literature: The Aggañña Sutta', in L. S. Cousins (ed.), *Festschrift for K. R. Norman*, special issue of *Indo-Iranian Journal*, forthcoming.

Grice, H. P., 'Utterer's Meaning and Intention', *Philosophical Review* 78 (1969), 147–77.

Hacking, I., *Representing and Intervening: Introductory Topics in the Philosophy of Natural Science* (Cambridge: Cambridge University Press, 1983).

Harrison, G., 'Letters', *Current Anthropology* 32/1 (1991).

Hofstader, D., *Metamagical Themas: Questing for the Essence of Mind and Pattern* (New York: Basic Books, 1985).

Holquist, M., *Dialogism: Bakhtin and His World* (London: Routledge, 1990).

Humphrey, N. K., 'The Social Function of Intellect', in P. Bateson and R. Hinde (eds.), *Growing Points in Ethology* (Cambridge: Cambridge University Press, 1976).

Hutchins, E., *Culture and Inference: A Trobriand Case Study* (Cambridge, Mass.: Harvard University Press, 1980).

Keesing, R., 'Models, "Folk" or "Cultural": Paradigms Regained?', in D. Holland and N. Quinn (eds.), *Cultural Models in Language and Thought* (Cambridge: Cambridge University Press, 1987).

Kuper, A., *Anthropology and Anthropologists: The Modern British School* (London: Routledge and Kegan Paul, 1983).

Landau, M., *Narratives of Human Evolution* (New Haven, Conn.: Yale University Press, 1991).

Latimore, O. and Grene, D., *Sophocles I* (Chicago: University of Chicago Press, 1954).

Levinson, S., 'Interactional Biases in Human Thinking' (paper prepared for the Workshop on Social Intelligence, Wissenschaftskolleg zu Berlin, May 1990).

Lewis, G., *Day of Shining Red: An Essay on Understanding Ritual* (Cambridge: Cambridge University Press, 1980).

Lienhardt, G., *Divinity and Experience: The Religion of the Dinka* (Oxford: Clarendon Press, 1961).

Loizos, P., *The Heart Grown Bitter: A Chronicle of Cypriot War Refugees* (Cambridge: Cambridge University Press, 1981).

Mauss, M., *The Gift: Forms and Functions of Exchange in Archaic Societies*, trans. I Cunnison (London: Routledge, 1970).

—— *Sociology and Psychology* (London: Routledge and Kegan Paul, 1979).

Maynard Smith, J., 'Game Theory and the Evolution of Cooperation', in D. S. Bendall (ed.), *Evolution from Molecules to Man* (Cambridge: Cambridge University Press, 1983).

Norman, K. R., *Pali Literature*, vol. VII, fasc. 2, *A History of Indian Literature* (Wiesbaden: Otto Harrassowitz, 1983).

Obeyesekere, G., *The Work of Culture: Symbolic Transformation in*

Psychoanalysis and Anthropology (Chicago: University of Chicago Press, 1990).

Peel, J., 'History, Culture, and the Comparative Method', in L. Holy (ed.), *Comparative Anthropology* (Oxford: Basil Blackwell, 1987).

Polanyi, M., *Personal Knowledge* (London: Routledge and Kegan Paul, 1958).

Premack, D., 'Pedagogy and Aesthetics as Sources of Culture', in M. Gazzaniga (ed.), *Handbook of Cognitive Neuroscience* (London: Plenum Press, 1984).

Rachels, J., *Created from Animals: The Moral Implications of Darwinism* (Oxford: Oxford University Press, 1991).

Radcliffe-Brown, A. R., 'Preface', in M. Fortes and E. E. Evans-Pritchard (eds.), *African Political Systems* (London: Oxford University Press, 1940).

Rhys-Davids, T. W., *Dialogues of the Buddha*, part I (London: Oxford University Press, 1899).

—— and Carpenter, J. E. (eds.), *The Dīgha Nikāya*, vol. II (London: Pali Text Society, 1966).

Rosaldo, M., *Knowledge and Passion: Ilongot Notions of Self and Social Life* (Cambridge: Cambridge University Press, 1980).

—— 'Toward an Anthropology of Self and Feeling', in R. Shweder and R. LeVine (eds.), *Culture Theory: Essays on Mind, Self and Emotion* (Cambridge: Cambridge University Press, 1984).

Roth, P., 'Ethnography without Tears', *Current Anthropology* 39 (1990), 555–69.

Sahlins, M., *Culture and Practical Reason* (Chicago: University of Chicago Press, 1976).

Schieffelin, E., *The Sorrow of the Lonely and the Burning of the Dancers* (New York: St. Martin's Press, 1976).

Schutz, A., *Reflections on the Problem of Relevance* (New Haven, Conn.: Yale University Press, 1970).

Scribner, S., 'Thinking in Action: Some Characteristics of Practical Thought', in R. Sternberg and R. Wagner (eds.), *Practical Intelligence: Nature and Origins of Competence in the Everyday World* (Cambridge: Cambridge University Press, 1986).

Searle, J., *Speech Acts: An Essay in the Philosophy of Language* (Cambridge: Cambridge University Press, 1969).

Shaha, S., *Śrī 108 Siddhasāgar Muni Mahārāj* (Kolhapur: Sanmati Prakashan, 1983).

Smith, N. and Wilson, D., *Modern Linguistics: The Results of*

Chomsky's Revolution (London: Penguin Books, 1979).

Sober, E., *The Nature of Selection: Evolutionary Theory in Philosophical Focus* (Cambridge, Mass.: MIT Press, 1984).

Sperber, D., *On Anthropological Knowledge: Three Essays* (Cambridge: Cambridge University Press, 1985).

Stocking, G. W., Jr. (ed.), *Observers Observed: Essays on Ethnographic Fieldwork* (Madison, Wis.: University of Wisconsin Press, 1983).

Strecker, I., *The Social Practice of Symbolization: An Anthropological Analysis* (London: Athlone Press, 1988).

Tambiah, S., 'King Mahāsammata: The First King in the Buddhist Story of Creation, and his Persisting Relevance', *Journal of the Anthropological Society of Oxford* 20/2 (1989), 101–22.

Tannen, D., *Talking Voices: Repetition, Dialogue, and Imagery in Conversational Discourse* (Cambridge: Cambridge University Press, 1989).

Tomasello, M., 'The Social Bases of Language Acquisition', *Social Development* 1/1 (1992), 67–87.

Trevarthen, C. and Logotheti, K., 'Child in Society, and Society in Children: The Nature of Basic Trust', in S. Howell and R. Willis (eds.), *Societies at Peace: Anthropological Perspectives* (London: Routledge, 1989).

Turnbull, C., *The Forest People* (London: Jonathan Cape, 1961).

—— *The Mbuti Pygmies: Change and Adaptation* (New York: Holt, Rinehart and Winston, 1983).

Whiten, A. (ed.), *Natural Theories of Mind: Evolution, Development and Simulation of Everyday Mindreading* (Oxford: Basil Blackwell, 1991).

Wilson, E. O., *Sociobiology: The New Synthesis* (Cambridge, Mass.: Harvard University Press, 1975).

Wolf, E., *Europe and the People without History* (London: University of California Press, 1982).

Wynn, T., 'Tools and the Evolution of Human Intelligence', in Byrne and Whiten (eds.), *Machiavellian Intelligence*.

Ziman, J., *Reliable Knowledge: An Exploration of the Grounds for Belief in Science* (Cambridge: Cambridge University Press, 1978).

Index

OXFORD

MORE OXFORD PAPERBACKS

This book is just one of nearly 1000 Oxford Paperbacks currently in print. If you would like details of other Oxford Paperbacks, including titles in the World's Classics, Oxford Reference, Oxford Books, OPUS, Past Masters, Oxford Authors, and Oxford Shakespeare series, please write to:

UK and Europe: Oxford Paperbacks Publicity Manager, Arts and Reference Publicity Department, Oxford University Press, Walton Street, Oxford OX2 6DP.

Customers in UK and Europe will find Oxford Paperbacks available in all good bookshops. But in case of difficulty please send orders to the Cash-with-Order Department, Oxford University Press Distribution Services, Saxon Way West, Corby, Northants NN18 9ES. Tel: 0536 741519; Fax: 0536 746337. Please send a cheque for the total cost of the books, plus £1.75 postage and packing for orders under £20; £2.75 for orders over £20. Customers outside the UK should add 10% of the cost of the books for postage and packing.

USA: Oxford Paperbacks Marketing Manager, Oxford University Press, Inc., 200 Madison Avenue, New York, N.Y. 10016.

Canada: Trade Department, Oxford University Press, 70 Wynford Drive, Don Mills, Ontario M3C 1J9.

Australia: Trade Marketing Manager, Oxford University Press, G.P.O. Box 2784Y, Melbourne 3001, Victoria.

South Africa: Oxford University Press, P.O. Box 1141, Cape Town 8000.

OPUS

General Editors: Walter Bodmer, Christopher Butler, Robert Evans, John Skorupski

OPUS is a series of accessible introductions to a wide range of studies in the sciences and humanities.

METROPOLIS

Emrys Jones

Past civilizations have always expressed themselves in great cities, immense in size, wealth, and in their contribution to human progress. We are still enthralled by ancient cities like Babylon, Rome, and Constantinople. Today, giant cities abound, but some are pre-eminent. As always, they represent the greatest achievements of different cultures. But increasingly, they have also been drawn into a world economic system as communications have improved.

Metropolis explores the idea of a class of supercities in the past and in the present, and in the western and developing worlds. It analyses the characteristics they share as well as those that make them unique; the effect of technology on their form and function; and the problems that come with size—congestion, poverty and inequality, squalor—that are sobering contrasts to the inherent glamour and attraction of great cities throughout time.

Also available in OPUS:

The Medieval Expansion of Europe   J. R. S. Phillips
Metaphysics: The Logical Approach   José A. Benardete
The Voice of the Past 2/e   Paul Thompson
Thinking About Peace and War   Martin Ceadel

HISTORY IN OXFORD PAPERBACKS

As the Oxford Paperbacks' history list grows, so does the range of periods it covers, from the Pharaohs to Anglo-Saxon England, and from Early Modern France to the Second World War.

EGYPT AFTER THE PHARAOHS

Alan K. Bowman

The thousand years between Alexander the Great's invasion in 332 BC and the Arab conquest in AD 642 was a period of enormous change and vitality in the history of Egypt. The Hellenistic era under the powerful Ptolemies ended with the defeat of Antony and Cleopatra in 30 BC, and Egypt became a province of Rome.

Throughout the millenium, however, many of the customs and belief of old Egypt survived, adapting themselves to the new rulers, who were in turn influenced by Egyptian culture. The heritage of the Egypt of the Pharaohs remained a vital force in the history of the land until the coming of Islam.

A vast collection of papyrus texts has survived from this period recording not only the great events but the everyday letters, lawsuits, accounts, and appeals of ordinary Egyptians. From these texts and from the evidence of archaeology, Dr Bowman draws together the Egyptian, Greek, and Roman strands of the story, presenting a masterly survey of the history, economy, and social life of Egypt in this thousand year span.

'eminently readable . . . should be studied by anyone who is seeking details of everyday life in the Roman period' *British Archaeological News*

Also in Oxford Paperbacks:

A History of the Vikings   Gwyn Jones
A Turbulent, Seditious, and Factious People   Christopher Hill
The Duel in European History   V. G. Kiernan

OXFORD LETTERS AND MEMOIRS

Letters, memoirs, and journals offer a special insight into the private lives of public figures and vividly recreate the times in which they lived. This popular series makes available the best and most entertaining of these documents, bringing the past to life in a fresh and personal way.

RICHARD HOGGART

A Local Habitation
Life and Times: 1918–1940

With characteristic candour and compassion, Richard Hoggart evokes the Leeds of his boyhood, where as an orphan, he grew up with his grandmother, two aunts, an uncle, and a cousin in a small terraced back-to-back.

'brilliant . . . a joy as well as an education' Roy Hattersley

'a model of scrupulous autobiography' Edward Blishen, *Listener*

A Sort of Clowning
Life and Times: 1940–1950

Opening with his wartime exploits in North Africa and Italy, this sequel to *A Local Habitation* recalls his teaching career in North-East England, and charts his rise in the literary world following the publication of *The Uses of Literacy*.

'one of the classic autobiographies of our time' Anthony Howard, *Independent on Sunday*

'Hoggart [is] the ideal autobiographer' Beryl Bainbridge, *New Statesman and Society*

Also in Oxford Letters and Memoirs:

My Sister and Myself: The Diaries of J. R. Ackerley
The Letters of T. E. Lawrence
A London Family 1870–1900   Molly Hughes

OXFORD LIVES

Biography at its best—this acclaimed series offers authoritative accounts of the lives of men and women from the arts, sciences, politics, and many other walks of life.

STANLEY

Volume I: The Making of an African Explorer
Volume II: Sorceror's Apprentice

Frank McLynn

Sir Henry Morton Stanley was one of the most fascinating late-Victorian adventurers. His historic meeting with Livingstone at Ujiji in 1871 was the journalistic scoop of the century. Yet behind the public man lay the complex and deeply disturbed personality who is the subject of Frank McLynn's masterly study.

In his later years, Stanley's achievements exacted a high human cost, both for the man himself and for those who came into contact with him. His foundation of the Congo Free State on behalf of Leopold II of Belgium, and the Emin Pasha Relief Expedition were both dubious enterprises which tarnished his reputation. They also revealed the complex—and often troubling—relationship that Stanley has with Africa.

'excellent . . . entertaining, well researched and scrupulously annotated' *Spectator*

'another biography of Stanley will not only be unnecessary, but almost impossible, for years to come' *Sunday Telegraph*

Also available:

A Prince of Our Disorder: The Life of T. E. Lawrence
John Mack
Carpet Sahib: A Life of Jim Corbett   Martin Booth
Bonnie Prince Charlie: Charles Edward Stuart   Frank McLynn

PAST MASTERS

General Editor: Keith Thomas

The *Past Masters* series offers students and general readers alike concise introductions to the lives and works of the world's greatest literary figures, composers, philosophers, religious leaders, scientists, and social and political thinkers.

'Put end to end, this series will constitute a noble encyclopaedia of the history of ideas.' Mary Warnock

HOBBES

Richard Tuck

Thomas Hobbes (1588–1679) was the first great English political philosopher, and his book *Leviathan* was one of the first truly modern works of philosophy. He has long had the reputation of being a pessimistic atheist, who saw human nature as inevitably evil, and who proposed a totalitarian state to subdue human failings. In this new study, Richard Tuck shows that while Hobbes may indeed have been an atheist, he was far from pessimistic about human nature, nor did he advocate totalitarianism. By locating him against the context of his age, Dr Tuck reveals Hobbs to have been passionately concerned with the refutation of scepticism in both science and ethics, and to have developed a theory of knowledge which rivalled that of Descartes in its importance for the formation of modern philosophy.

Also available in Past Masters:

PAST MASTERS

General Editor: Keith Thomas

Past Masters is a series of concise, lucid, and authoritative introductions to the thought of leading intellectual figures of the past whose ideas still affect the way we think today.

'One begins to wonder whether any intelligent person can afford not to possess the whole series.' *Expository Times*

FREUD

Anthony Storr

Sigmund Freud (1865–1939) revolutionized the way in which we think about ourselves. From its beginnings as a theory of neurosis, Freud developed psycho-analysis into a general psychology which became widely accepted as the predominant mode of discussing personality and interpersonal relationships.

From its inception, the psycho-analytic movement has always aroused controversy. Some have accepted Freud's views uncritically: others have dismissed psycho-analysis as unscientific without appreciating its positive contributions. Fifty years have passed since Freud's death, so it is now possible to assess his ideas objectively. Anthony Storr, psychotherapist and writer, takes a new, critical look at Freud's major theories and at Freud himself in a book which both specialists and newcomers to Freud's work will find refreshing.

Also available in Past Masters:

Homer   Jasper Griffin
Thomas More   Anthony Kenny
Galileo   Stillman Drake
Marx   Peter Singer

PHILOSOPHY IN OXFORD PAPERBACKS

Ranging from authoritative introductions in the Past Masters and OPUS series to in-depth studies of classical and modern thought, the Oxford Paperbacks' philosophy list is one of the most provocative and challenging available.

THE GREAT PHILOSOPHERS
Bryan Magee

Beginning with the death of Socrates in 399, and following the story through the centuries to recent figures such as Bertrand Russell and Wittgenstein, Bryan Magee and fifteen contemporary writers and philosophers provide an accessible and exciting introduction to Western philosophy and its greatest thinkers.

Bryan Magee in conversation with:

A. J. Ayer	John Passmore
Michael Ayers	Anthony Quinton
Miles Burnyeat	John Searle
Frederick Copleston	Peter Singer
Hubert Dreyfus	J. P. Stern
Anthony Kenny	Geoffrey Warnock
Sidney Morgenbesser	Bernard Williams
Martha Nussbaum	

'Magee is to be congratulated . . . anyone who sees the programmes or reads the book will be left in no danger of believing philosophical thinking is unpractical and uninteresting.' Ronald Hayman, *Times Educational Supplement*

'one of the liveliest, fast-paced introductions to philosophy, ancient and modern that one could wish for' *Universe*

Also by Bryan Magee in Oxford Paperbacks:

Men of Ideas
Aspects of Wagner 2/e

RELIGION AND THEOLOGY
IN OXFORD PAPERBACKS

Oxford Paperbacks offers incisive studies of the philosophies and ceremonies of the world's major religions, including Christianity, Judaism, Islam, Buddhism, and Hinduism.

A HISTORY OF HERESY

David Christie-Murray

'Heresy, a cynic might say, is the opinion held by a minority of men which the majority declares unacceptable and is strong enough to punish.'

What is heresy? Who were the great heretics and what did they believe? Why might those originally condemned as heretics come to be regarded as martyrs and cherished as saints?

Heretics, those who dissent from orthodox Christian belief, have existed at all times since the Christian Church was founded and the first Christians became themselves heretics within Judaism. From earliest times too, politics, orthodoxy, and heresy have been inextricably entwined—to be a heretic was often to be a traitor and punishable by death at the stake—and heresy deserves to be placed against the background of political and social developments which shaped it.

This book is a vivid combination of narrative and comment which succeeds in both re-creating historical events and elucidating the most important—and most disputed—doctrines and philosophies.

Also in Oxford Paperbacks:

Christianity in the West 1400–1700   John Bossy
John Henry Newman: A Biography   Ian Ker
Islam: The Straight Path   John L. Esposito

LAW FROM OXFORD PAPERBACKS

Oxford Paperbacks's law list ranges from introductions to the English legal system to reference books and in-depth studies of contemporary legal issues.

INTRODUCTION TO ENGLISH LAW
Tenth Edition .

William Geldart
Edited by D. C. M. Yardley

'Geldart' has over the years established itself as a standard account of English law, expounding the body of modern law as set in its historical context. Regularly updated since its first publication, it remains indispensable to student and layman alike as a concise, reliable guide.

Since publication of the ninth edition in 1984 there have been important court decisions and a great deal of relevant new legislation. D. C. M. Yardley, Chairman of the Commission for Local Administration in England, has taken account of all these developments and the result has been a considerable rewriting of several parts of the book. These include the sections dealing with the contractual liability of minors, the abolition of the concept of illegitimacy, the liability of a trade union in tort for inducing a person to break his/her contract of employment, the new public order offences, and the intent necessary for a conviction of murder.

Other law titles:

Freedom Under Thatcher: Civil Liberties in Modern Britain
Keith Ewing and Conor Gearty
Doing the Business Dick Hobbs
Judges David Pannick
Law and Modern Society P. S. Atiyah